IMAGES
of America

CHAMBERSBURG

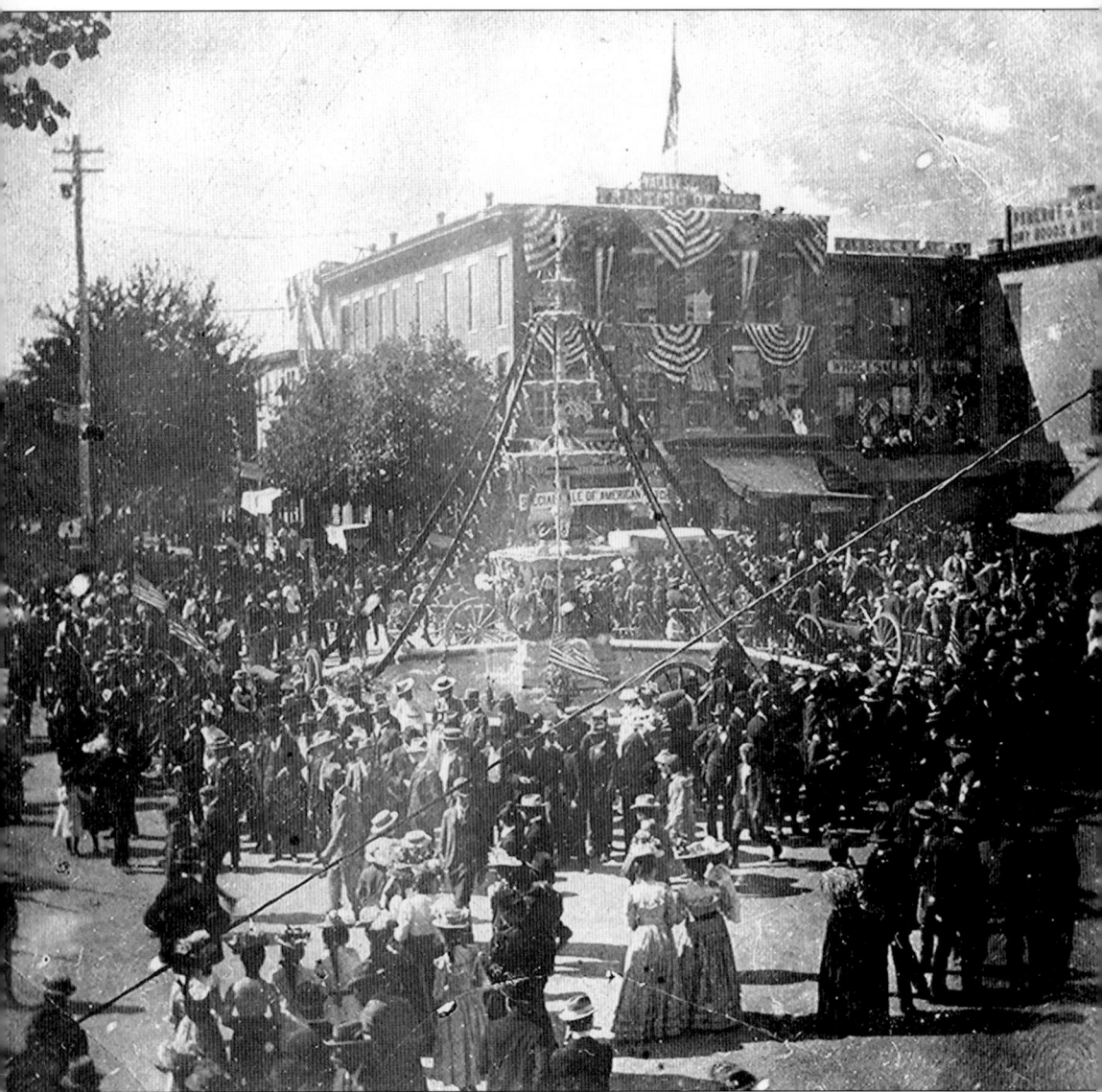

Memorial Fountain and the Diamond are decorated for the 1896 dedication of the four Civil War cannons, one placed at each of the four cardinal points. Residents throughout Franklin County came for the dedication.

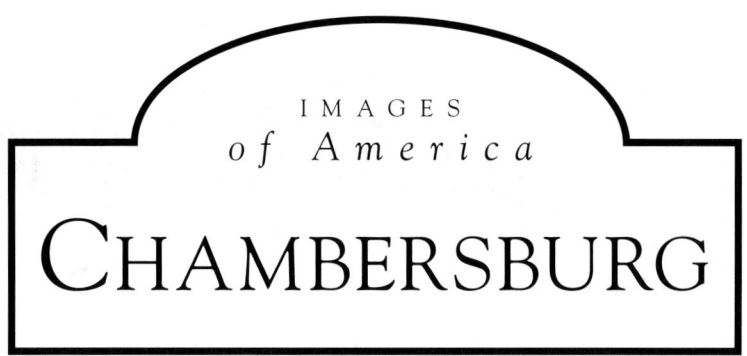

IMAGES of America
CHAMBERSBURG

Maurice Leonard Marotte III
and Janet Kay Pollard
with the Chambersburg Heritage Center

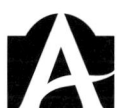

Copyright © 2005 by Maurice Leonard Marotte III and Janet Kay Pollard with the Chambersburg Heritage Center
ISBN 0-7385-3909-0

Published by Arcadia Publishing
Charleston SC, Chicago IL, Portsmouth NH, San Francisco CA

Printed in Great Britain

Library of Congress Catalog Card Number: 2005930289

For all general information contact Arcadia Publishing at:
Telephone 843-853-2070
Fax 843-853-0044
E-mail sales@arcadiapublishing.com
For customer service and orders:
Toll-Free 1-888-313-2665

Visit us on the internet at http://www.arcadiapublishing.com

I would like to dedicate this book in honor of my dad, M. L. "Mike" Marotte Jr., who loved history and antiques and took the time to teach me the value and importance of the history in Franklin County. Additionally, I would like to dedicate this to the rich historic past and bright future of our town and the Chambersburg Heritage Center, in which thousands of people from all over the world have entered, enjoyed, and learned many interesting historical events of the past.

—Mike Marotte III

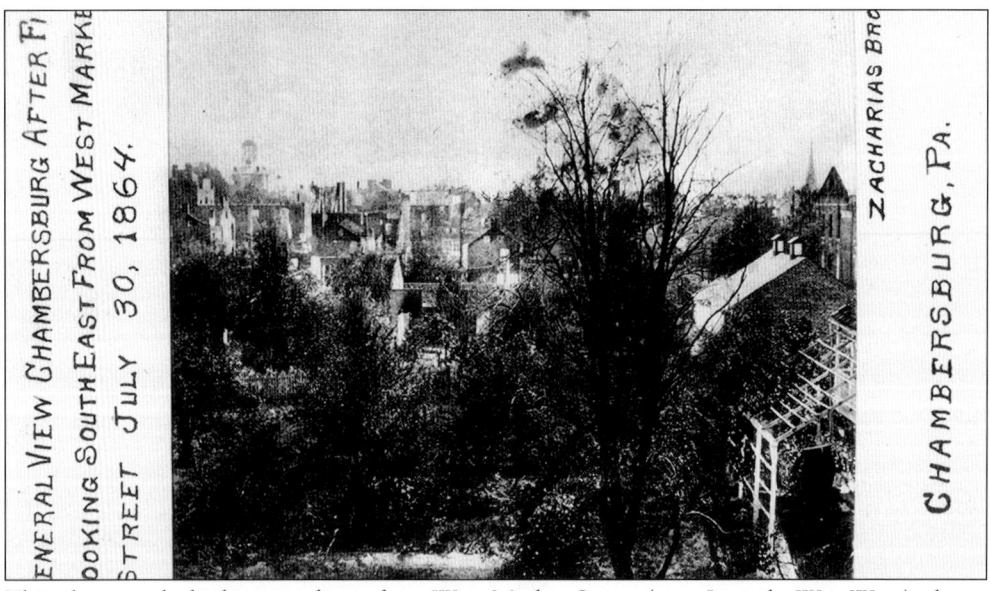

This photograph, looking southeast from West Market Street (now Lincoln Way West), shows the town after the Great Fire of July 30, 1864.

Contents

Acknowledgments		6
Introduction		7
1.	Views of History	9
2.	Life on the Diamond	23
3.	Trains, Trolleys, and Airplanes	31
4.	Circuses, Parades, and Amusements	45
5.	Snowstorms, Floods, and Fires	59
6.	Answering the Alarm	77
7.	Business and Industry	87
8.	Advertisements of the Old Queen City	103
9.	Streetscapes	111

Acknowledgments

Shortly after the Chambersburg Heritage Center opened on July 16, 2004, a representative of Arcadia Publishing visited the Greater Chambersburg Chamber of Commerce to explain Arcadia Publishing's Images of America series and to show the volumes that existed for Franklin County. Surprisingly, Chambersburg was not represented, but thanks to the persistence of Arcadia, it is now part of Images of America.

Special recognition is extended to the Greater Chambersburg Chamber of Commerce and the Chambersburg Area Development Corporation, the organizations that worked to preserve the 1915 marble building that houses the Chambersburg Heritage Center, which tells the history of Chambersburg and Franklin County.

About 99 percent of the photographs included in *Chambersburg* are from the unique and extensive collection of Mike Marotte III. It was a pleasure to write text about such a wonderful collection of photographs, postcards, and memorabilia. Special appreciation is also extended to Harmon's Furniture, Ludwig's Jewelers, and Olympia Candy Kitchen for the use of their photographs.

Over the past 20 years, Ted Alexander has researched and written about Chambersburg and its role in the Civil War. Alexander's efforts have helped Civil War enthusiasts to recognize Chambersburg and provided local residents with a better understanding of their community's place in history.

On a personal note, special gratitude is given to Christina, Jonathan, Sarah, and Matthew Pollard for freely giving their support and for understanding that what is worth doing entails sacrifice, and to Will Pananes for sharing his knowledge of local history, maintaining an unwavering commitment to his community, and patiently nudging us in the right direction. Finally a special thank you is offered to the leaders and staff of the Greater Chambersburg Chamber of Commerce—David Sciamanna, Paul Cullinane, Sandy Chambers, Anita Coy, Athena Defreest, Cindy Haden, Melissa Knepper, Rosie Lidard, Pat Massa, Jeff Otto, and Shelby Wagner—for their efforts to ensure Chambersburg is as strong in the 21st century as it was in the preceding ones.

—Janet Pollard

Introduction

From 1715 to 1776, some 250,000 Scots-Irish immigrated to America, with a concentration of immigrants settling along the east coast, particularly in Pennsylvania and regions southward. Among those whom America beckoned was Benjamin Chambers. After settling for a few years along the Susquehanna River, Chambers traveled into the Cumberland Valley and selected the waterpower of the Conococheague Creek and the Falling Spring to run his mill operations. He acquired the land rights to 400 acres from the family of William Penn and turned his vision of a settlement into Chamberstown.

With the Northwest Ordinance, westward expansion established Chambersburg as a major transportation and commercial crossroads. Throughout the 19th century, stagecoaches, freight wagons, and Conestoga wagons filled the roads. Travelers needed an array of services: wagon repair, lodging, livery stables, dining, and the services of a blacksmith. As travel increased, the need for better roads brought the construction of a series of turnpikes and toll roads that led to Chambersburg from Baltimore, Pittsburgh, and Harrisburg. Chambersburg's streets were lined with shops and customers, and the town experienced an era of economic and social vitality.

Each era moves to another, and as the Age of Steam progressed, steam power replaced horsepower. In 1837, the Cumberland Valley Railroad came to Chambersburg, and the town continued to prosper as a transportation center. In fact, it was Chambersburg's central location and accessibility to transportation that were key factors in bringing 20,000 Union troops to Chambersburg in 1861 to be trained and dispersed into the Shenandoah Valley.

At the outset of the Civil War, two-thirds of the nation's rail miles were in Union territory. Early in the war, the Confederacy recognized the need to neutralize the railroad's ability to transport soldiers and supplies. In 1862, the Cumberland Valley Railroad drew Confederate general J. E. B. Stuart and his cavalry to Chambersburg, where the Southern troops foraged the town, burned the railroad shops, and cut the telegraph wires. Chambersburg's strategic location and role as a transportation and supply center attracted Southern attention throughout the Civil War.

The most unforgettable event in Chambersburg's Civil War history is the burning of the town by Confederate troops on July 30, 1864. The eyewitness account of Jacob Hoke, a merchant on Chambersburg's square, describes that day:

> At an early hour in the morning—Saturday, July 30th—General McCausland placed about two thousand of his command in line upon a hill near the western suburb of the town, and about one mile from its center. Six pieces of artillery were also placed in

position, and three shells were fired into the place without any notice to the citizens. The remaining nine hundred of the force were sent into the town, and the Court House bell was rung as a sign for the citizens to assemble to hear his requisition. No response being made, a guard under Maj. Harry Gilmore, of Baltimore, was sent around, who captured some six or eight of our leading men and conducted them to front of the Court House. Captain Fitzhugh, McCausland's chief of staff then read to them General Early's requisition, demanding the immediate payment of one hundred thousand dollars in gold, or five hundred thousand dollars in United States currency, and in default of payment ordering the destruction of the town.

The money demanded was not, and could not be paid, for the reason that there was nothing like the amount demanded remaining in the town. Besides the citizens did not feel like contributing aid in the overthrow of their government.

Detachments were sent to different parts of the town. Houses were opened, furniture was broken and piled upon heaps in rooms and fired. In some cases fire was kindled in closets, bureaus, and other depositories of, clothing. Many of the Confederate soldiers entered into this work with evident delight, and to the entreaties and tears of the aged, the infirm, of women and children, they turned a deaf ear. Others, to their credit be it said, entirely disapproved of the work, and only entered upon it because compelled to do so.

The conflagration at its height was a scene of surpassing grandeur and terror. As building after building was fired, or caught from others, column after column of smoke rose black, straight, and single; first one, then another, and another. Each of these then, like huge serpents, writhed and twisted into a thousand fantastic shapes, until all finally blended and commingled, and formed one vast and livid column of smoke and flame which rose perpendicularly to the sky, and then spread out into a huge crown of sackcloth. It was heaven's shield mercifully drawn over the scene to shelter from the blazing sun the homeless and unsheltered ones that had fled to the fields and cemeteries around the town, where they in silence and sadness sat and looked upon the destruction of their homes and the accumulations of a lifetime.

The images of Chambersburg taken immediately after the burning show the devastation; Hoke's words convey the feelings.

In the years following the Civil War, Chambersburg was rebuilt. It remained the county seat and again became a leader in industry, transportation, agriculture, and medicine. Early-20th-century Chambersburg thrived. The streets bustled with people, trolleys, cars, and all sorts of events. Life was good. *Chambersburg* tells the story of an American town—its settlement, its growth, its challenges, and its survival.

One

VIEWS OF HISTORY

On July 30, 1864, nearly 100 years after founder Benjamin Chambers laid out Chambersburg, Confederate general John McCausland, under order of Gen. Jubal Early, set the core of Chambersburg ablaze when residents failed to pay a ransom of $100,000 in gold or $500,000 in Yankee currency. The Great Fire destroyed over 550 structures—including homes, businesses, and out buildings—left 2,000 people homeless, and caused property damage of $783,000.

The rebuilding after the burning bridged the old Chambersburg to the new. Unscathed buildings included the Masonic temple, which, tradition holds, was saved by a Masonic officer of the Confederacy; the home of Chambersburg physician Dr. Jacob Suesserott, at the corner of South Main and Washington Streets; and the 1782 home of Dr. John Colhoun, the present-day location of Seller's Funeral Home. A variety of carpenters crafted new three-story buildings in the downtown. The courthouse, churches, homes, and businesses were rebuilt. Chambersburg healed.

In 1878, the community honored the valor of those who fought and died during the Civil War by placing a magnificent, 26-foot, cast iron and bronze fountain in the center of Chambersburg. A seven-foot sentry is posted at the southern point of the fountain to guard the town from future invasion. For more than 125 years, this stoic gentleman has watched history continue its path through Chambersburg. And although the world around him has changed, he remains steady, constant, and prepared, much like the community he safeguards.

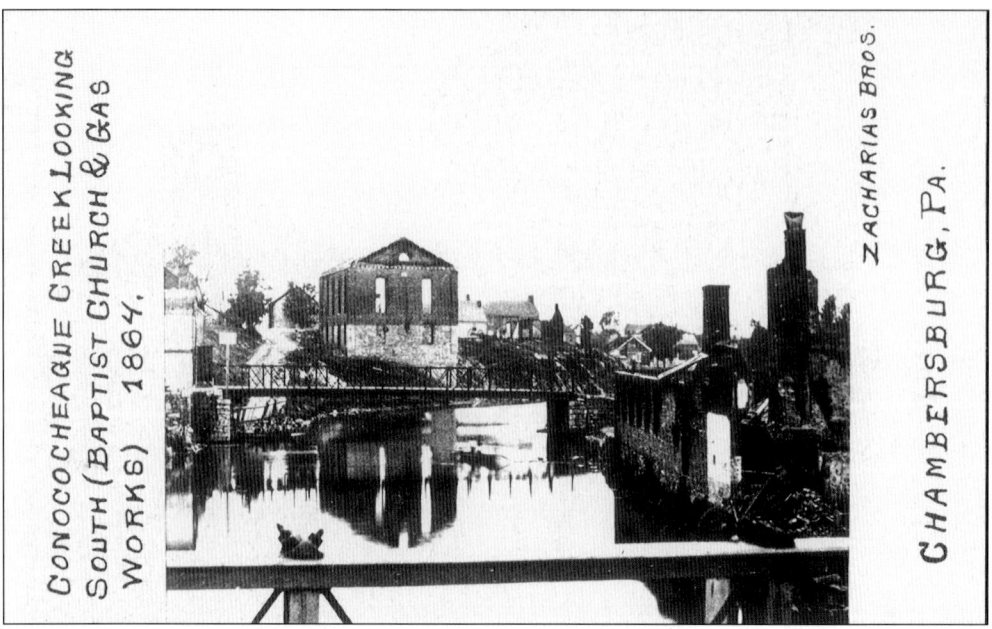

This 1864 view looks along the Conococheague Creek and south to the Baptist church and Chambersburg Gas Works. The ruins of the Baptist church were rebuilt to serve as the Housum Post #309 Grand Army of the Republic (GAR). The photographer was standing on the bridge at Lincoln Way West. The next bridge is Burkhart Avenue. In the 1880s, the Western Maryland Railroad built a line through town that ran to the left of the GAR building.

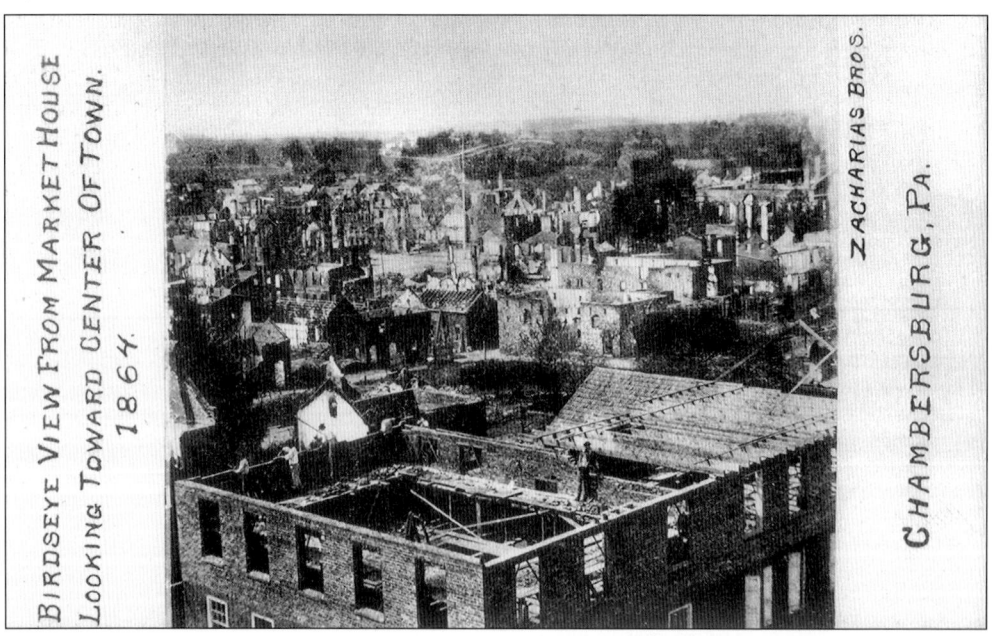

A post-burning photograph depicts a bird's-eye view from the Market House toward the center of town. Today the Market House is used as Chambersburg Borough Hall, housing the administrative offices of the borough, town council's chambers, and adjoining police headquarters.

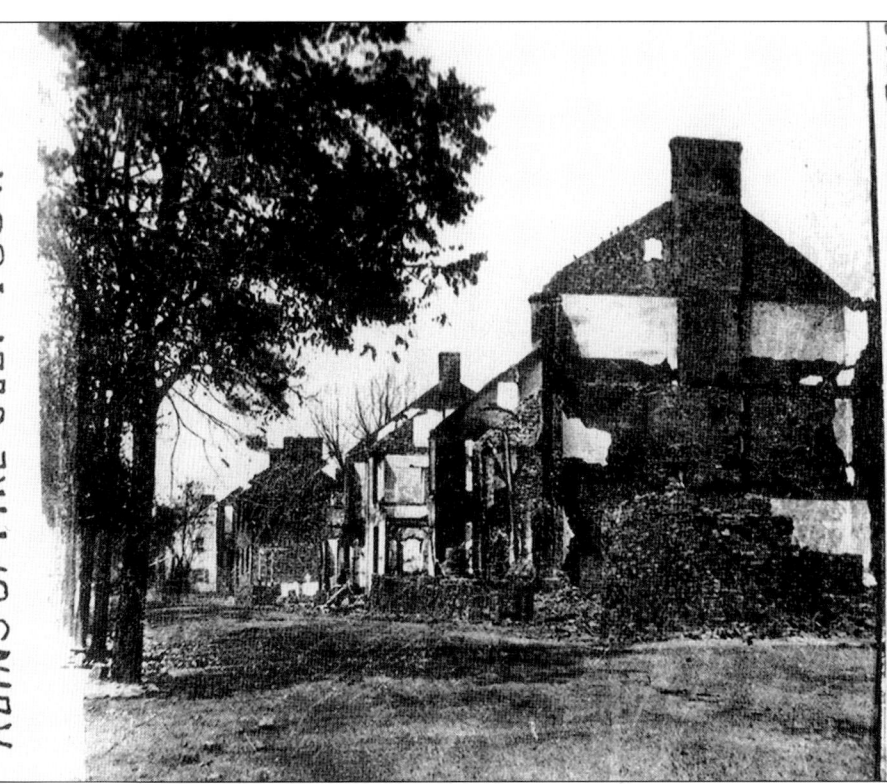

Main Street Looking North From Center Of Town. Ruins Of Fire July 1864. Zacharias Bros, Chambersburg, PA.

The view looking north on Main Street from the Diamond reveals the ruins of the July 30, 1864, burning. The burning was the third time that Confederate troops visited Chambersburg. The first was in October 1862, when Maj. Gen. J. E. B. Stuart swept into Chambersburg, taking horses, hostages, and supplies, cutting telegraph wires, and burning railroad shops. The second was in June 1863, when Confederate troops took control of Chambersburg. Over 65,000 troops—among them Confederate commander Gen. Robert E. Lee—camped in and around Chambersburg. Here Lee made the decision to move to Gettysburg to meet the Union Army and keep combat in the Northern arena. The Battle of Gettysburg resulted in nearly one-third of the Confederate's 75,000 men being killed, wounded, or missing.

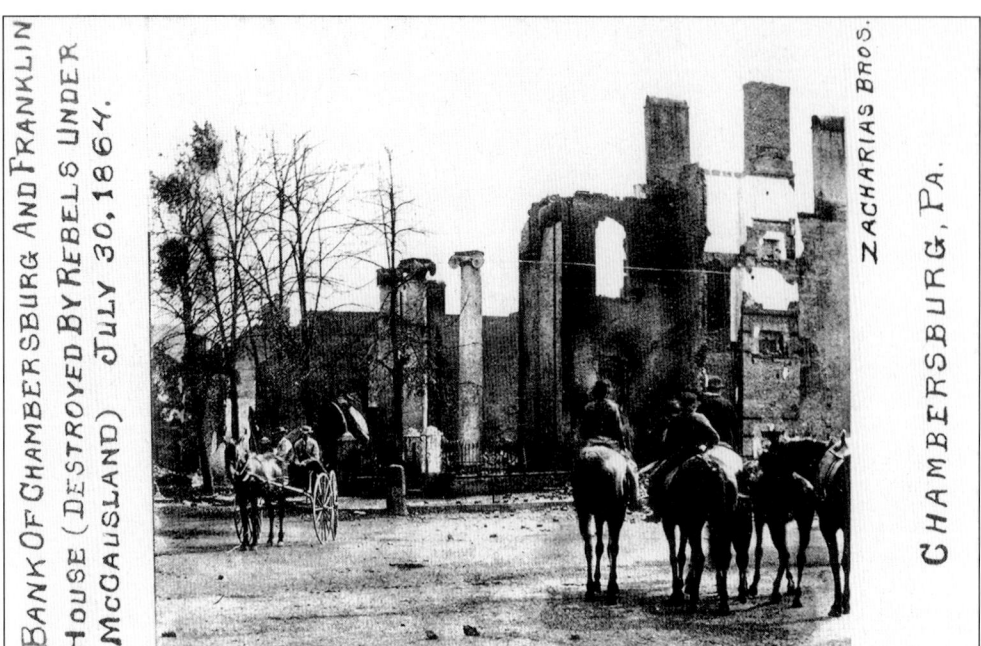

Onlookers view the damage Confederate troops inflicted on the Bank of Chambersburg and the Franklin House in the burning of July 30, 1864. Another bank was rebuilt on the site of the burned Bank of Chambersburg. Franklin Hotel was replaced by Central Presbyterian Church in 1868.

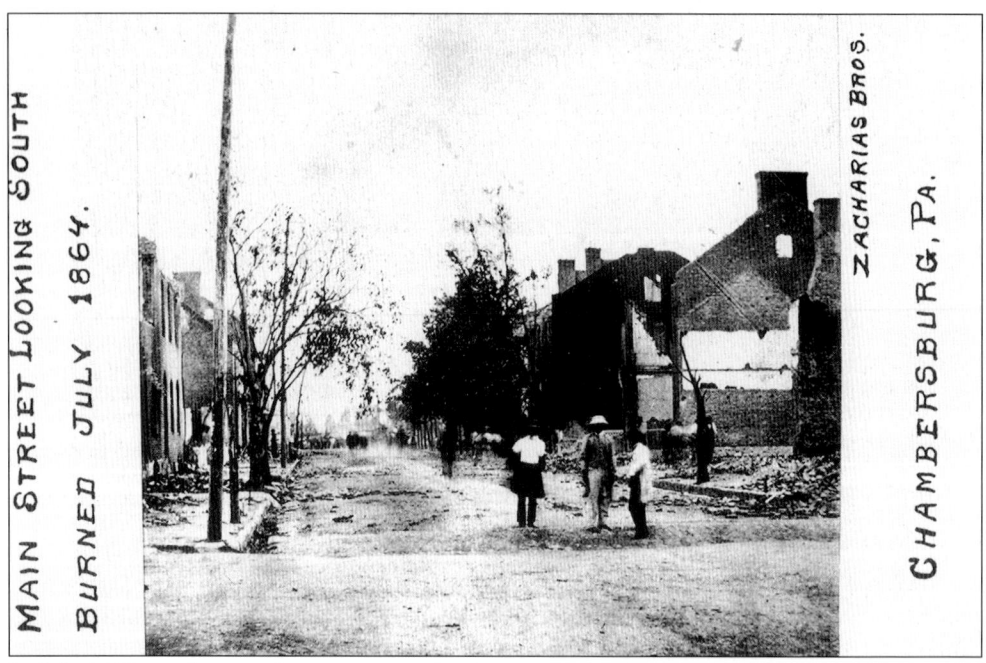

In July 1864, residents gather to inspect the destruction wielded by Confederate troops. In the background are the charred structures of South Main Street.

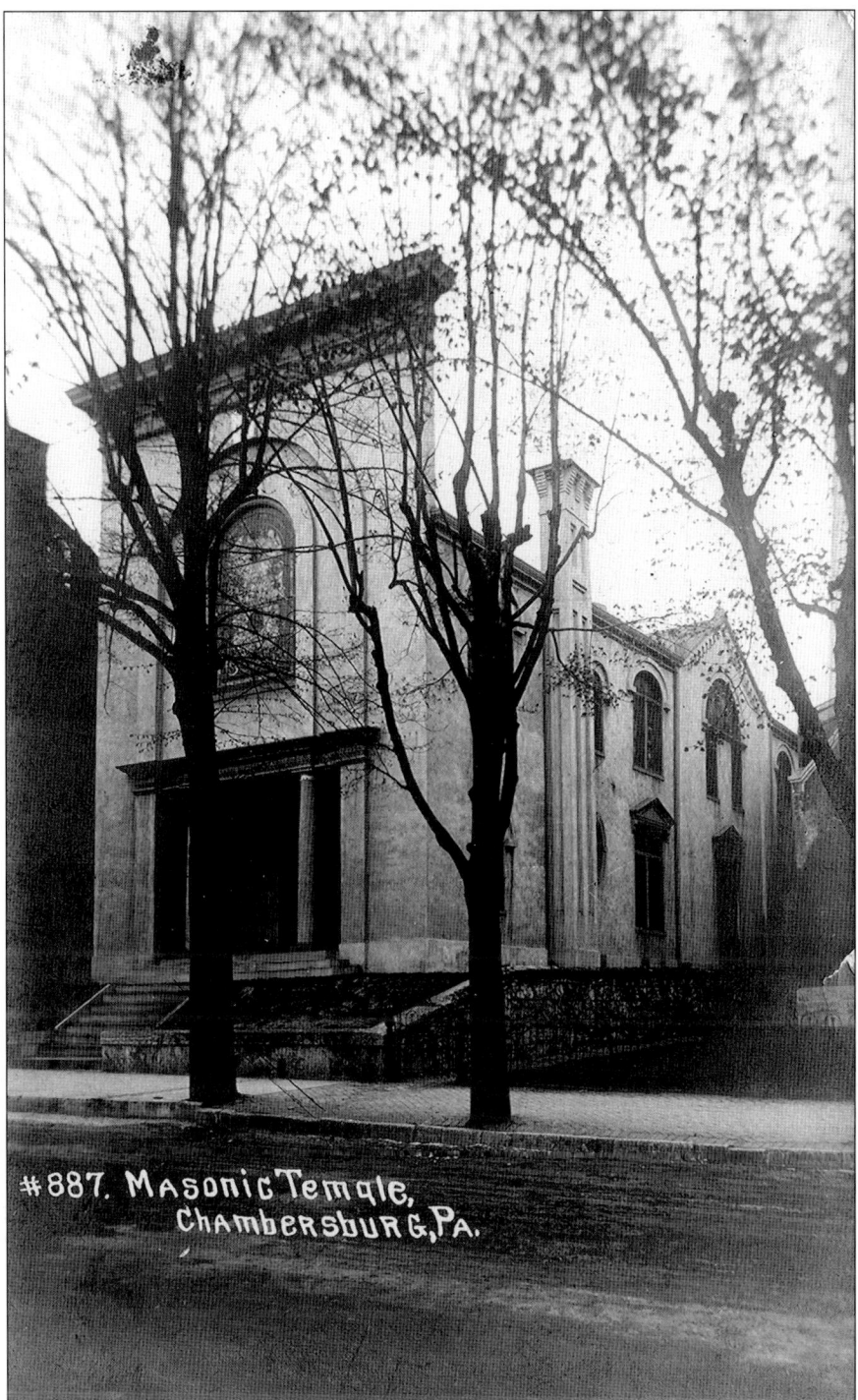

The Masonic temple on South Second Street was one of the buildings saved from the Confederate burning of Chambersburg in 1864. The building, whose cornerstone was laid in 1823, was constructed by Silas Harry. Listed on the National Register of Historic Places, it is the oldest building in Pennsylvania used for Masonic purposes.

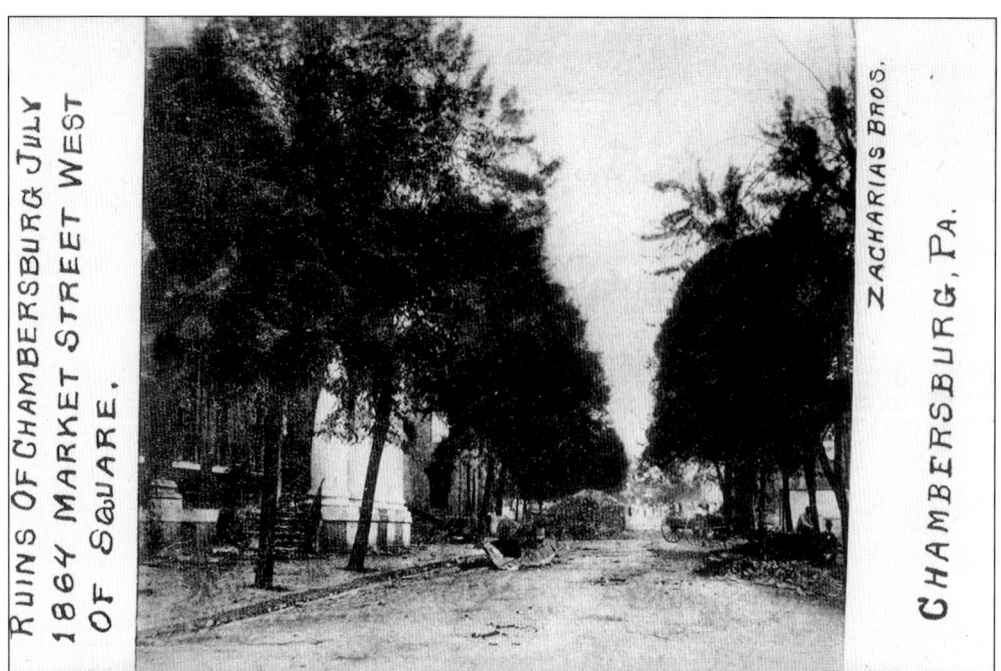

Residents on foot and in wagons examine the damage caused by the burning. Confederates burned Chambersburg in retaliation for Union depredations of the Shenandoah Valley.

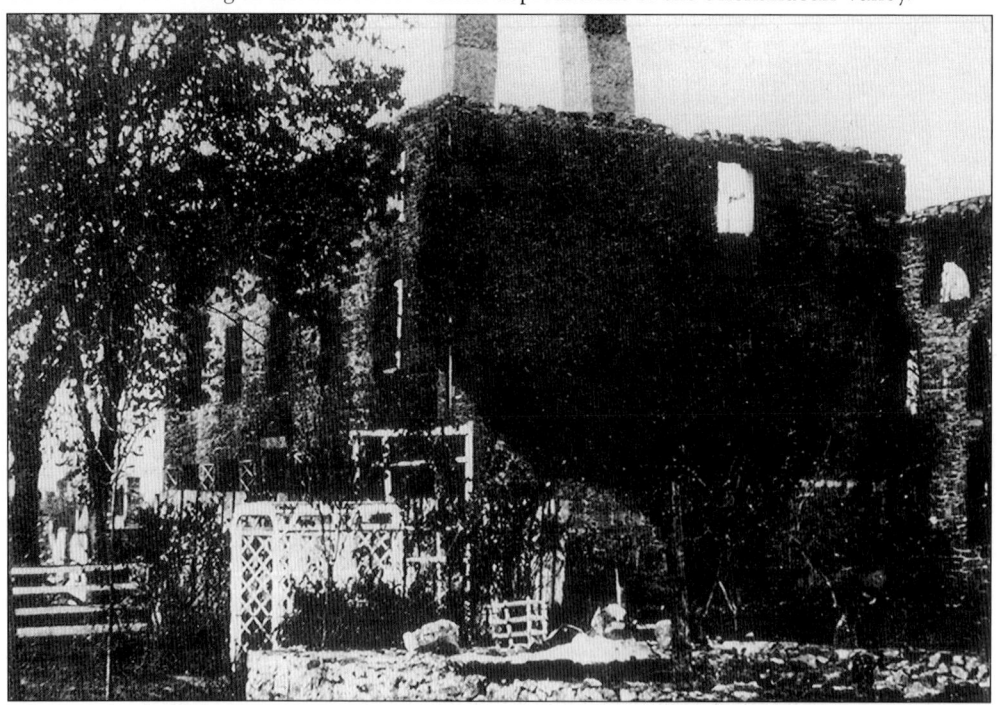

Shown are the ruins of the Rosedale Seminary for Girls after its destruction in the Great Fire. Later the Rosedale building was rebuilt and used for a variety of purposes. The most memorable was the Rosedale Theatre, which featured live entertainment as well as movies. The theater was torn down in the early 1960s; today this site is a parking area.

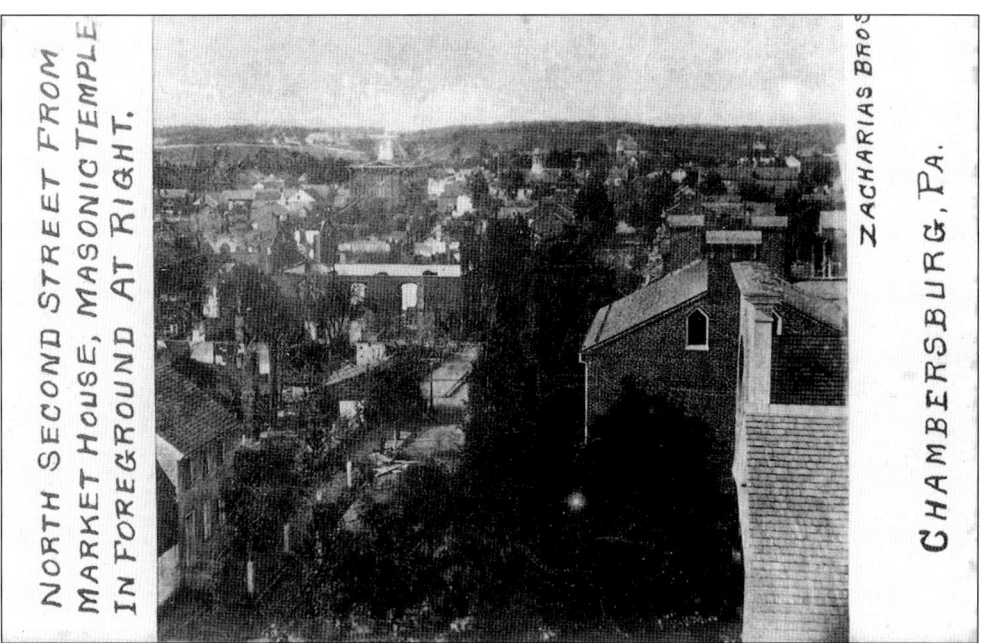

Photographed after the Great Fire, this panoramic view, taken from the Market House shows the Masonic temple on Second Street. In the distance, King Street School and the Old Jail are visible.

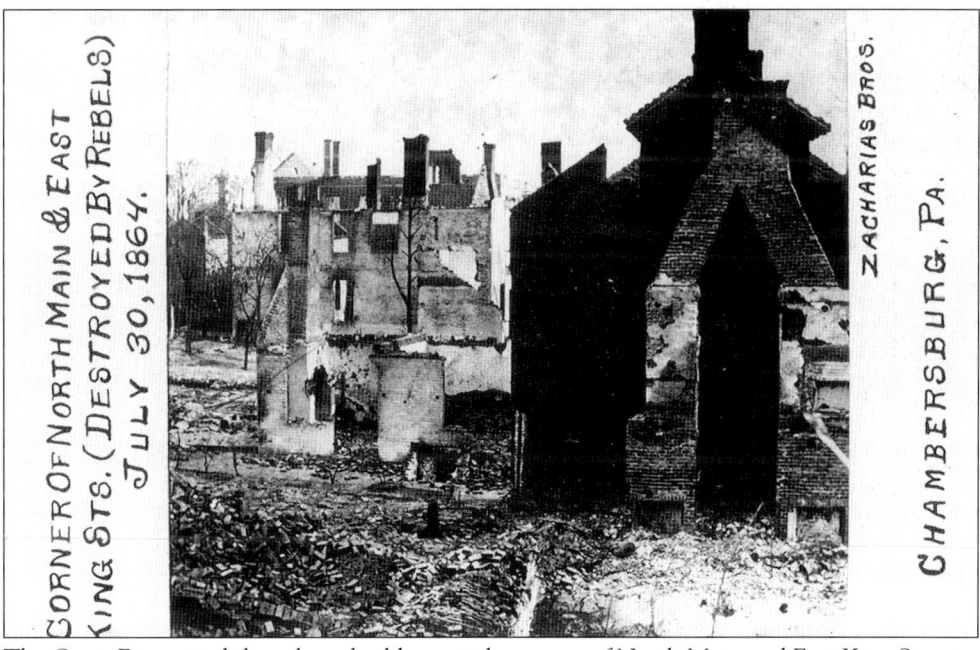

The Great Fire gutted these large buildings at the corner of North Main and East King Streets.

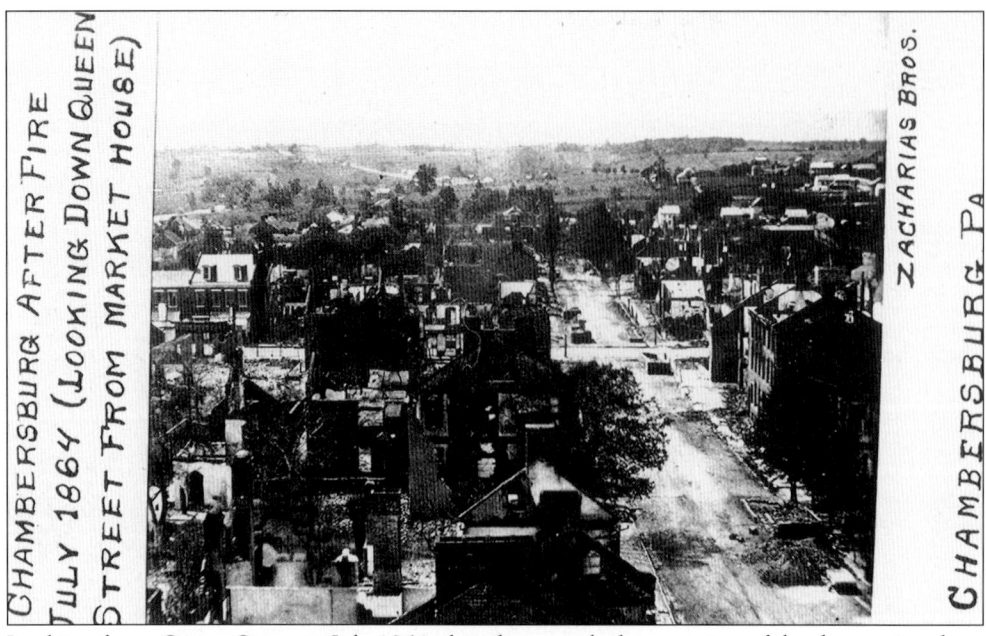

Looking down Queen Street in July 1864, this photograph shows a view of the destruction from the old Market House. The intersection at South Main and East Queen Streets looks deserted. On South Main Street, there are a few structures by an archway and alley that were spared.

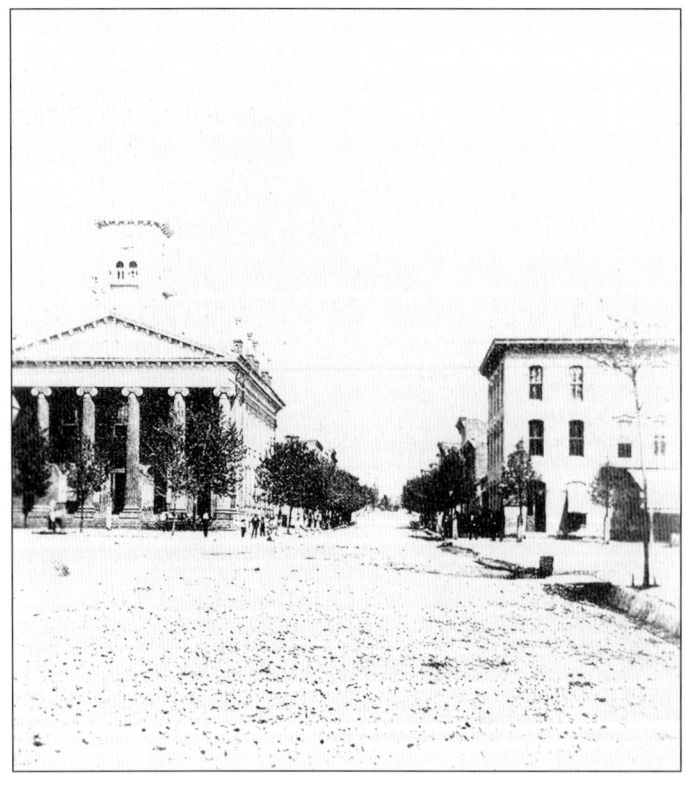

Taken in the early 1870s, this view of the Diamond shows the rebuilt Franklin County Courthouse and Valley National Bank Building. Visible on the courthouse dome is the new statue of Benjamin Franklin, completed by Frederick Mayer of Pittsburgh in 1865. The statue—gold leafed, eight feet tall, and more than 250 pounds—was removed from the courthouse in 1991 for restoration and is currently on display at the Chambersburg Heritage Center.

Dressed in their Sunday best, young lads pose at the arch and cannon of the Housum GAR Post in 1875. The GAR was a Union veteran's organization dedicated to securing legislation and benefits for veterans, supporting battlefield preservation, and honoring veterans.

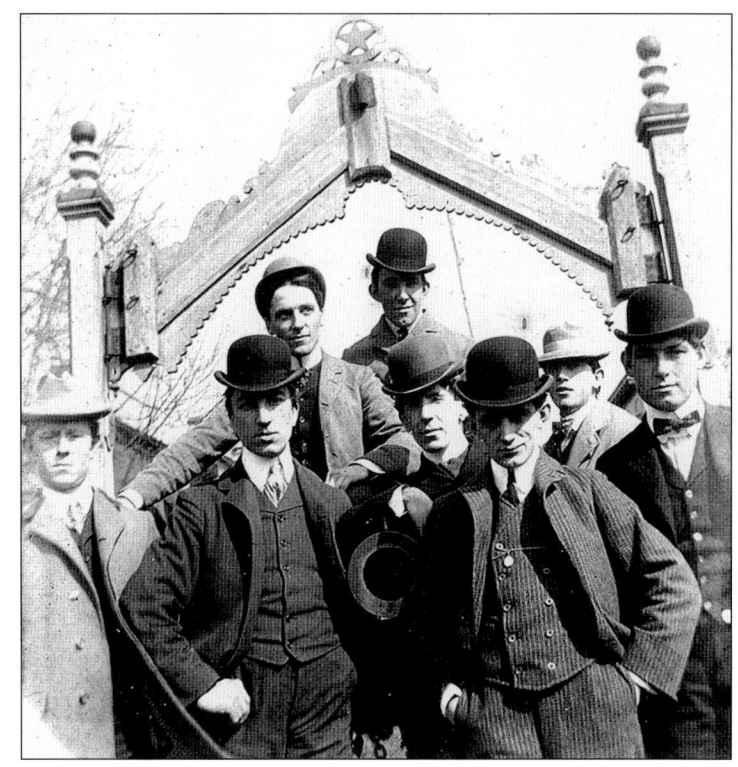

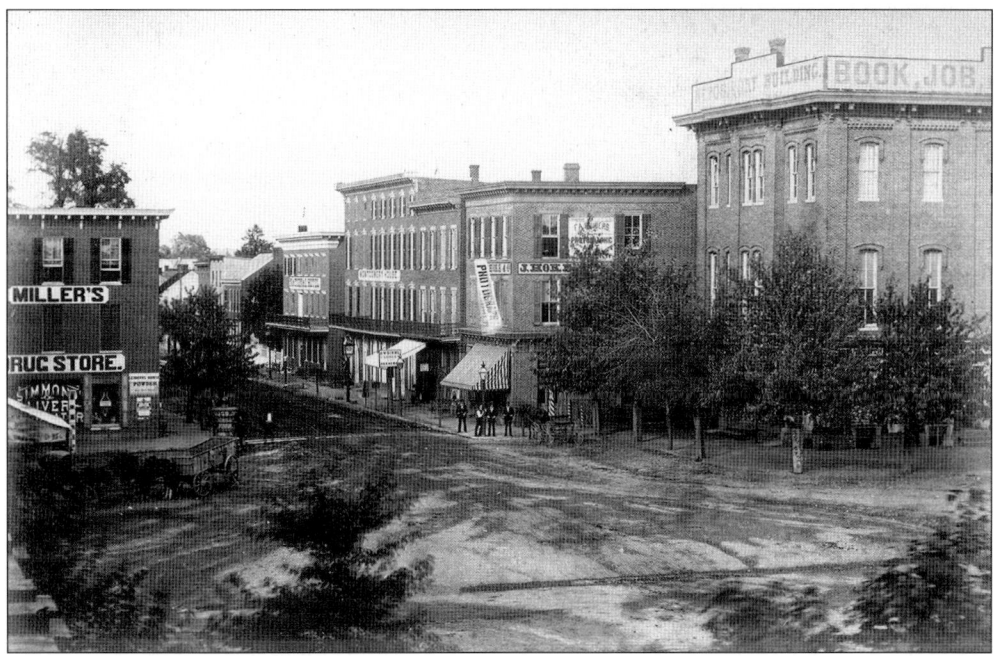

This c. 1870 photograph presents a rare view looking up North Main Street from Memorial Square before Memorial Fountain was erected. Notice the various businesses of the day, particularly the Repository Building, Jacob Hoke Building, Montgomery House, National Hotel, and the famous Miller's Drugstore with mortar and pestle.

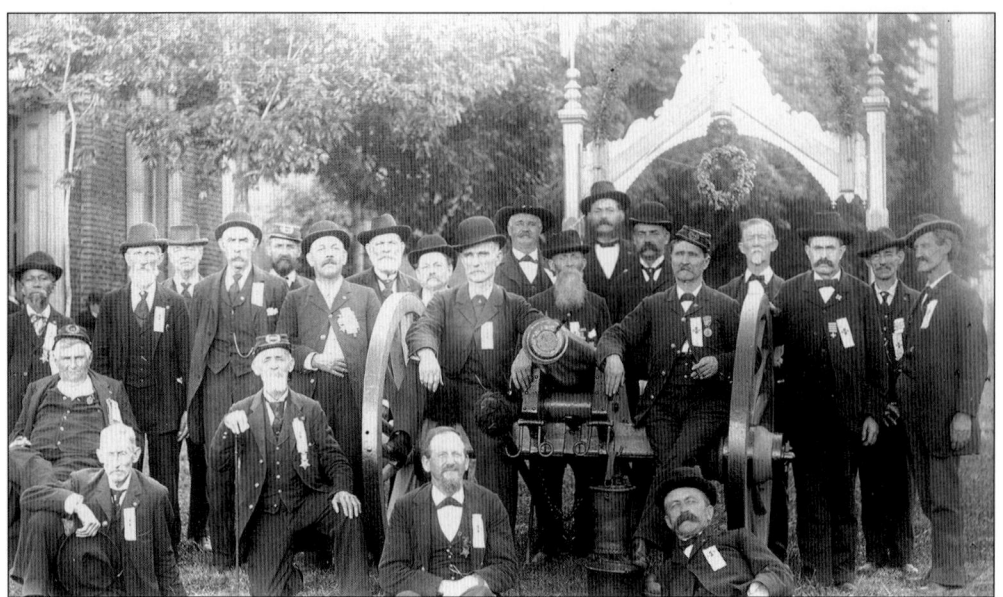
Proud Civil War veterans pose outside the Housum House on West Queen and Water Streets in 1885. The photograph was taken by H. Frank Beidel, an outstanding photographer of the day.

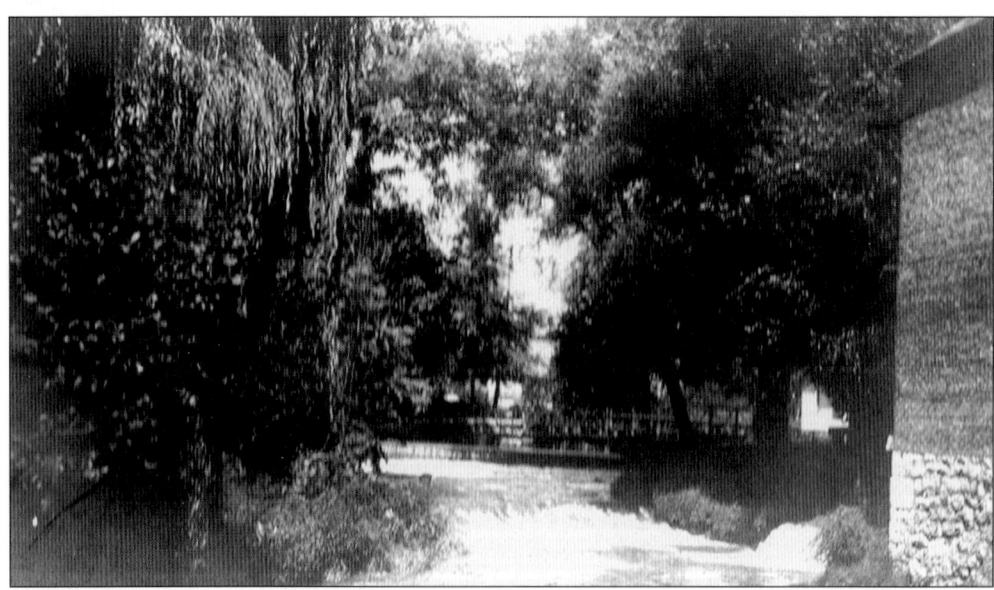
Taken around 1890, this picture shows a quiet time on the Falling Spring near King Street.

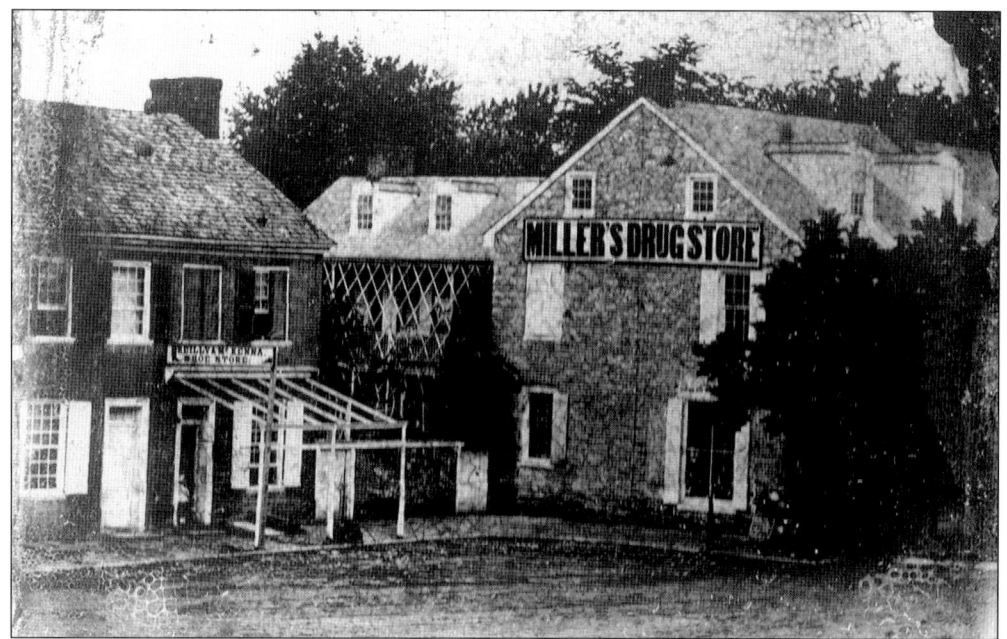

Miller's Drugstore stood on the northwest quadrant of the Diamond. On the left in this 1858 photograph is the Reilly and McKenna Shoe Store. Neither building survived the Great Fire. The brick buildings that replaced these businesses have housed many tenants throughout the years.

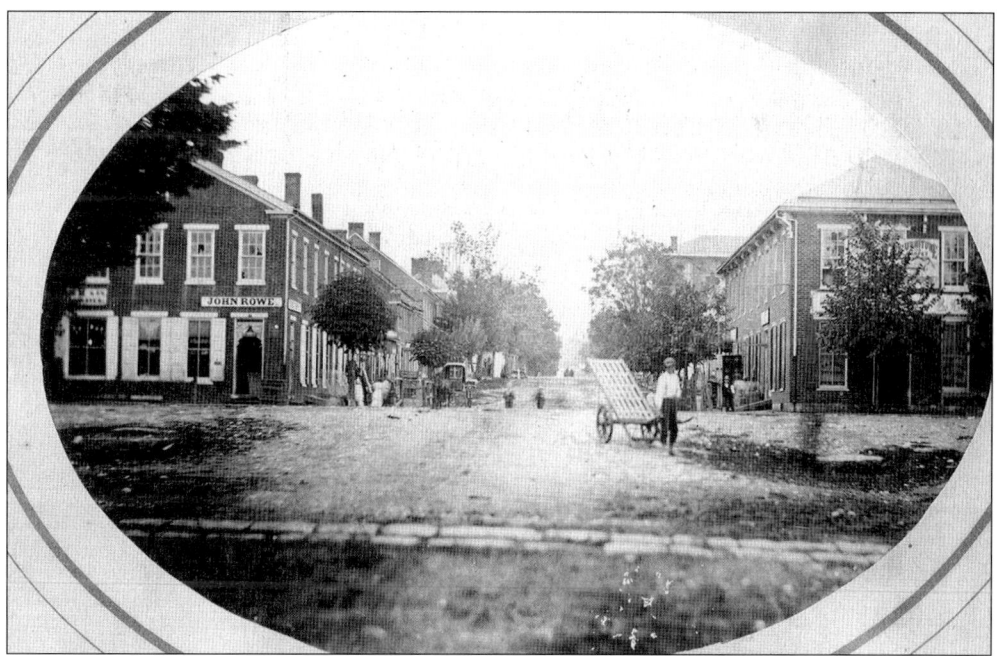

Looking south toward city hall in 1860, this peaceful pre–Civil War scene shows the intersection of Market and Second Streets.

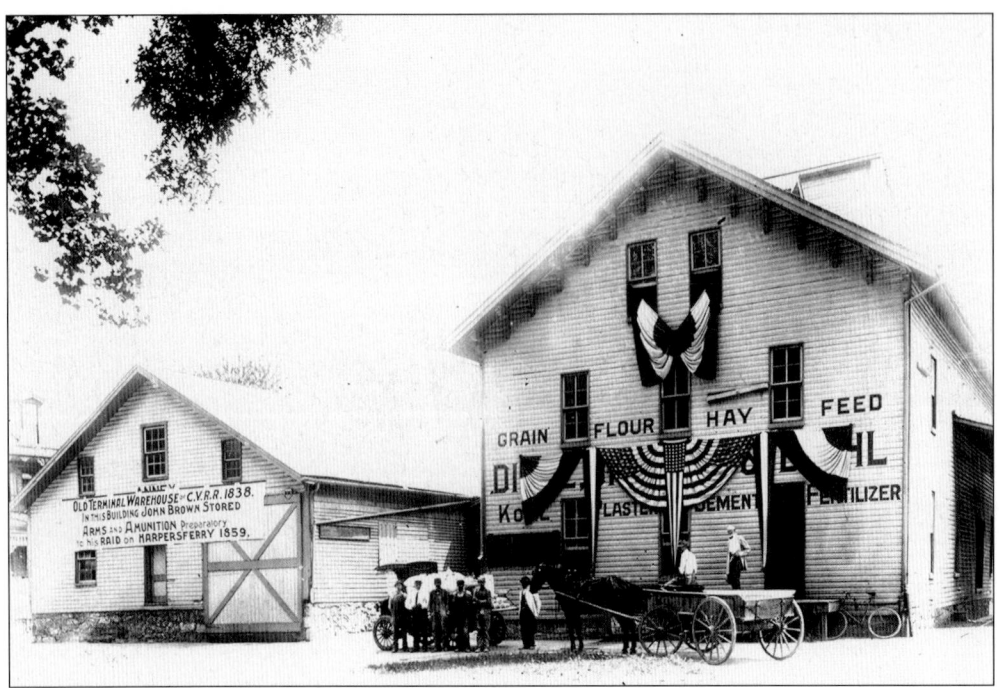

Taken in the early 1900s, this photograph shows the Diehl, Omwake, and Diehl mill and the Cumberland Valley Railroad Warehouse. At this location, abolitionist John Brown stored weapons for the planned capture of the federal arsenal at Harpers Ferry. Today this location is the site of United Towers.

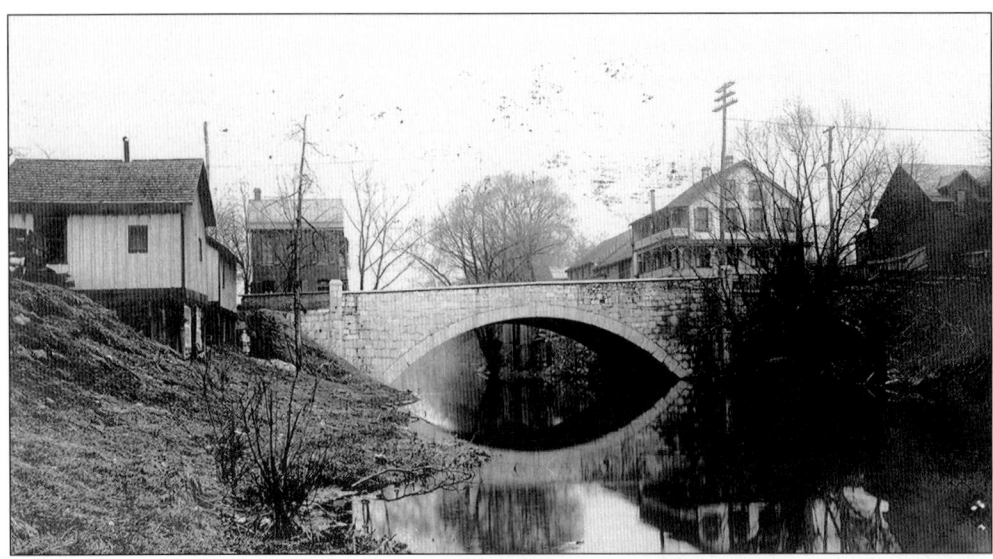

The beautiful old stone King Street Bridge was built by Silas Harry in 1828. All the surrounding structures in this view looking north on the Conococheague Creek have long been removed. The former Chambersburg Laundry building, which still stands, is on the right, and the old Western Maryland Railroad right-of-way is on the left.

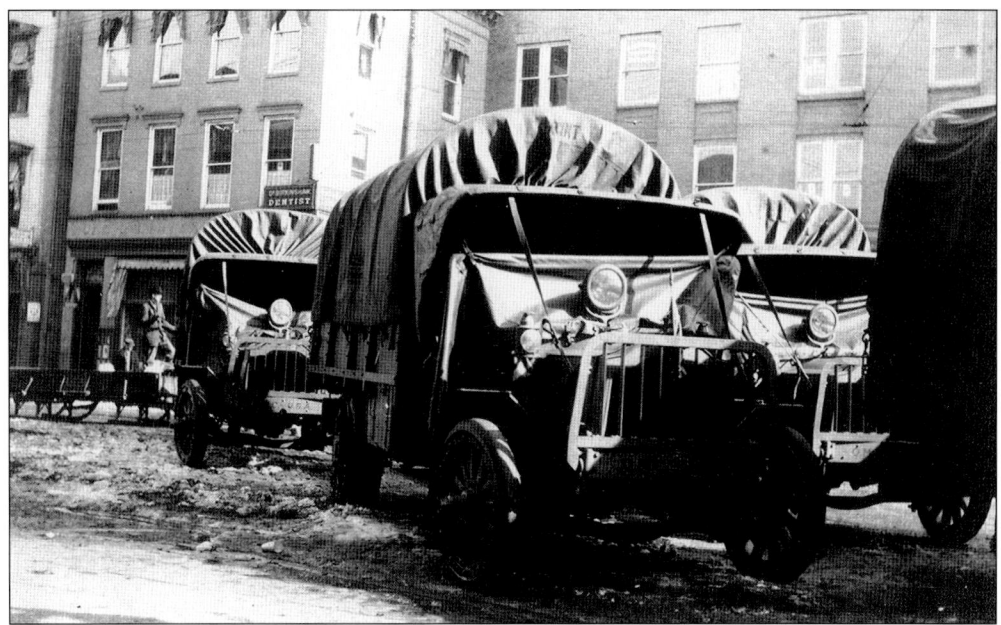

The troop train of Gen. John J. "Black Jack" Pershing halts on the Diamond in 1917. Pershing built American forces to 500,000 in World War I. Notice the horse-drawn flat sleigh to the left rear of the army truck. The Chambersburg Trust and Hoke Buildings are in the background.

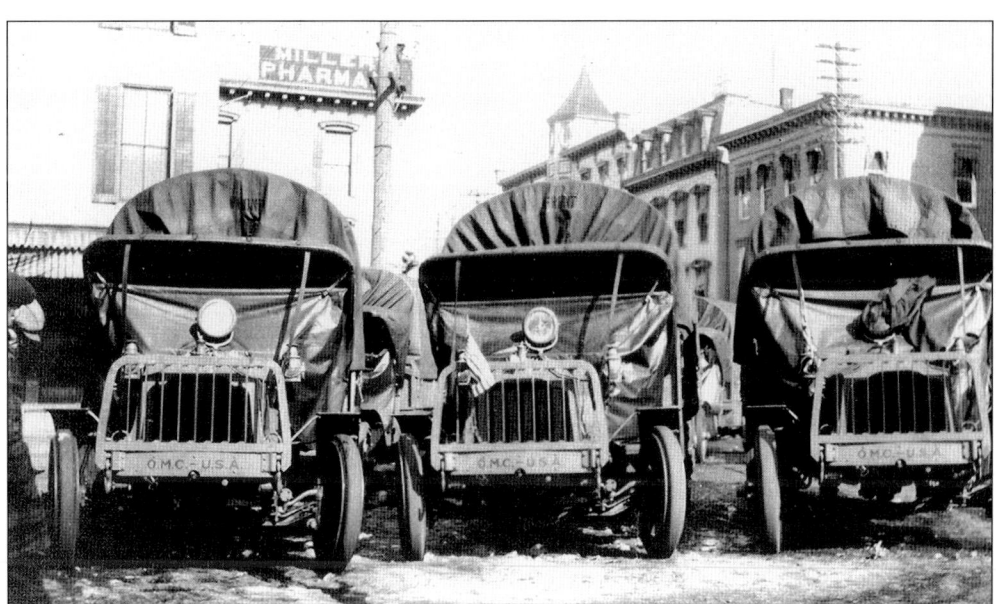

This image depicts another view of Pershing's troop transport on the Diamond. It was taken looking toward North Main Street, with the dome of the Hotel McKinley and the Miller's Drugstore building visible in the background.

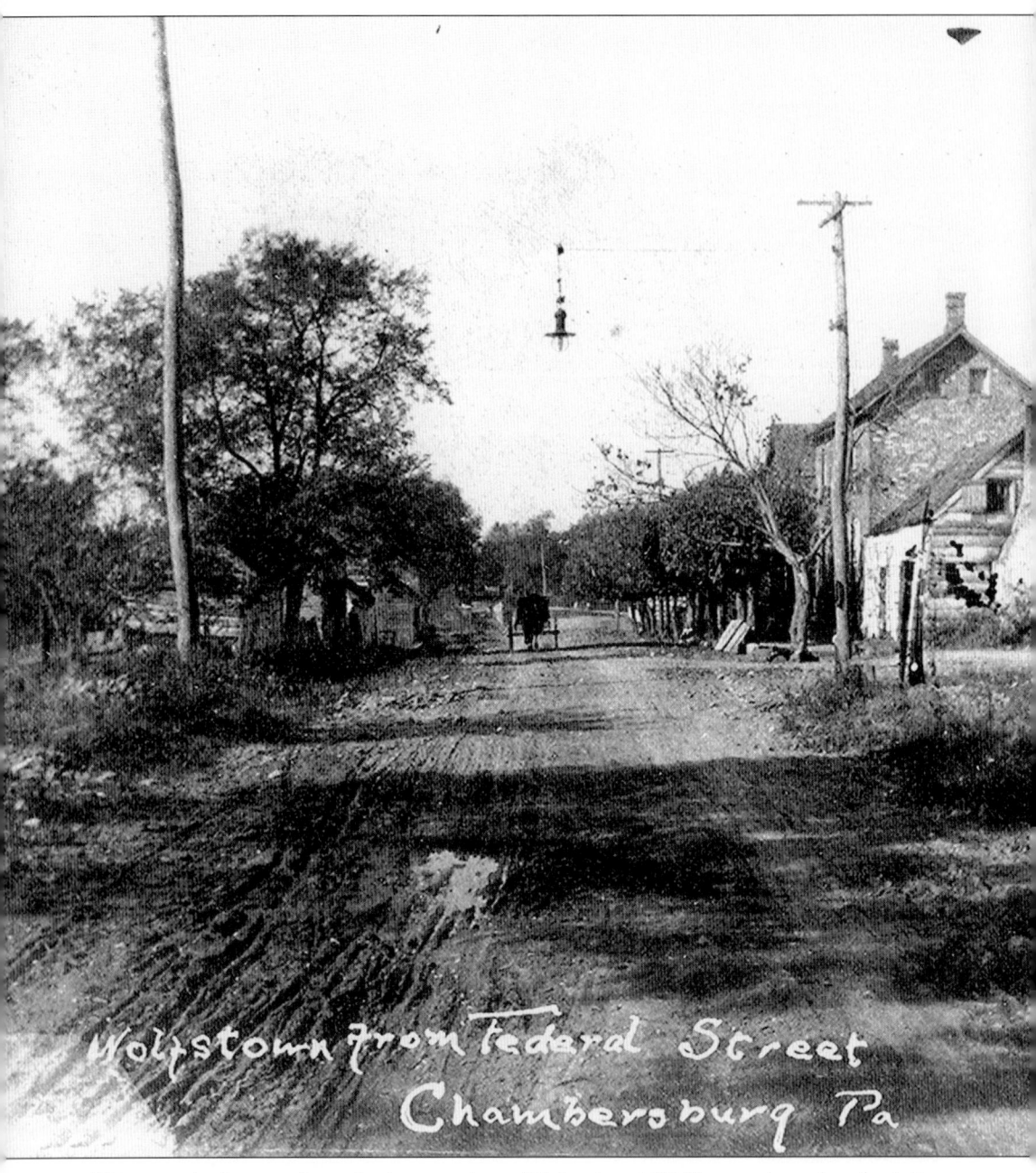

This view looks west from the intersection of Federal and Wolfstown (now Loudon) Streets. Note the early stone and log structures in the foreground. Today Southgate Shopping Center is adjacent to this area.

Two

LIFE ON THE DIAMOND

Benjamin Chambers designed the Diamond as a place for people to meet, to do business, and to find out the news of the day. He had large limestones hauled in to mark the entry points of the four main roads into town, and he sold plots of land along the Diamond. He also gave land for the courthouse. As the plots of land were sold, Chamberstown grew and the Diamond became the center of the community.

During the Civil War, thousands of troops, both Union and Confederate, passed through the Diamond. On July 27, 1863, Confederate commander Robert E. Lee met Confederate general A. P. Hill on the Diamond to discuss the crucial decision to move troops to Gettysburg. It was on the Diamond that Confederate general John McCausland demanded the ransom that was not met, thus leading to the town's burning.

Over the years, wagons, trolleys, and automobiles passed across the Diamond, bearing travelers north, south, west, and east. Residents from throughout Franklin County assembled on the Diamond for celebrations, parades, and special events. Festooned in lights or banners, by day or by night, the Diamond shines as the heart of the community.

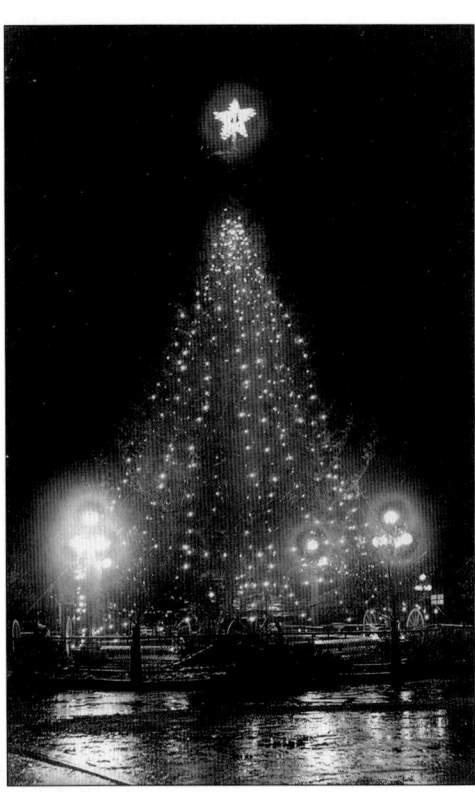

The fountain is swathed in lights to create the "first Christmas tree on the fountain" in 1914—a spectacular sight.

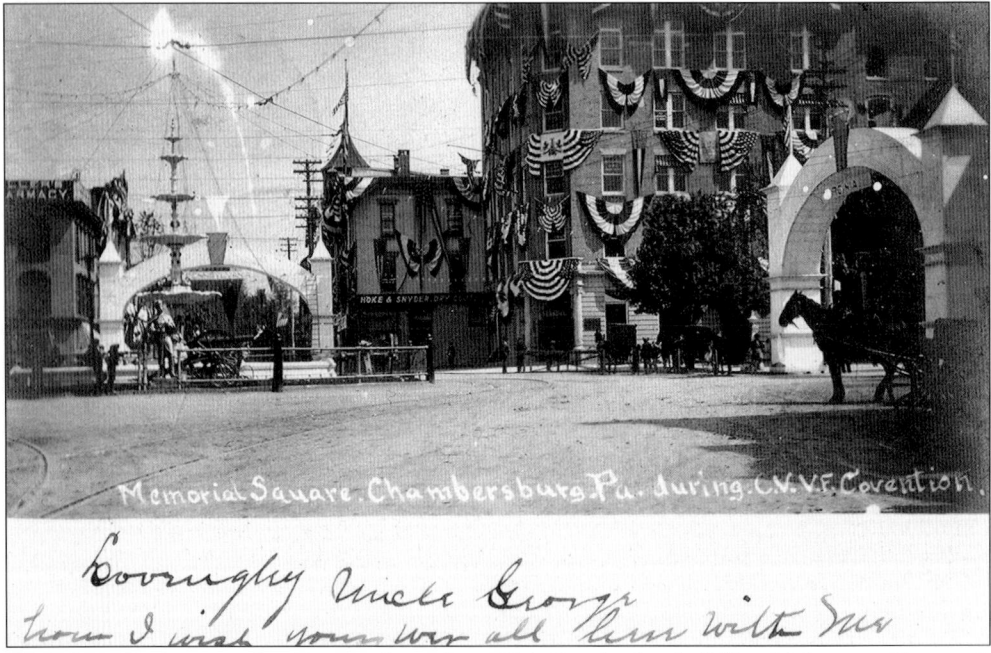

This festive time on the Diamond is the 1906 Cumberland Valley Volunteer Fireman's Convention. Wooden arches designate north, south, west, and east points on the Diamond. In the foreground, bunting decorates the Chambersburg Trust Building.

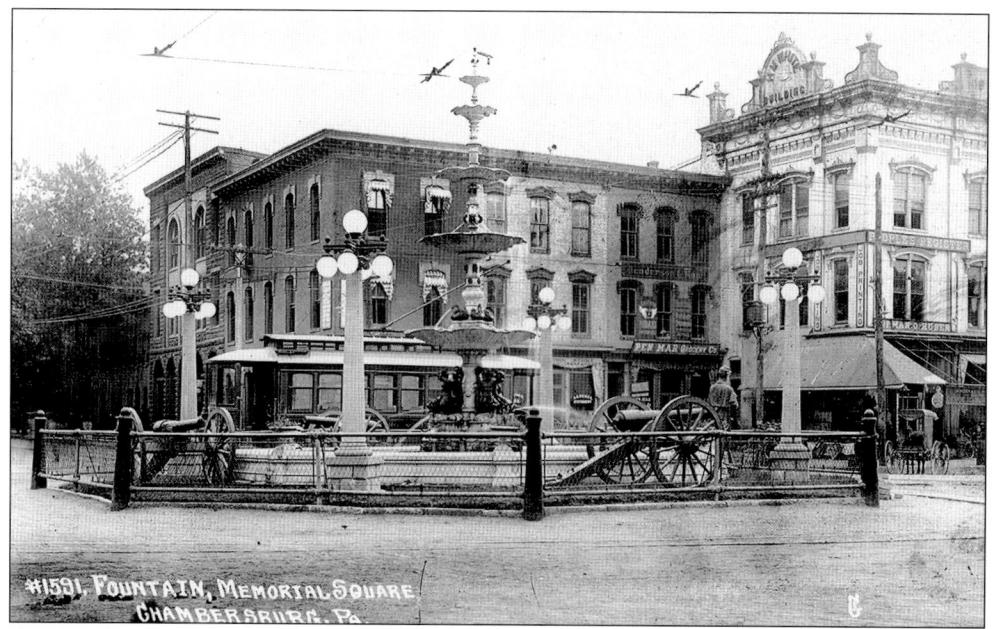

A Chambersburg and Gettysburg trolley car passes through the Diamond and around the fountain on December 31, 1914. Behind the trolley car is the old Valley National Bank building, the present-day site of the Chambersburg Heritage Center.

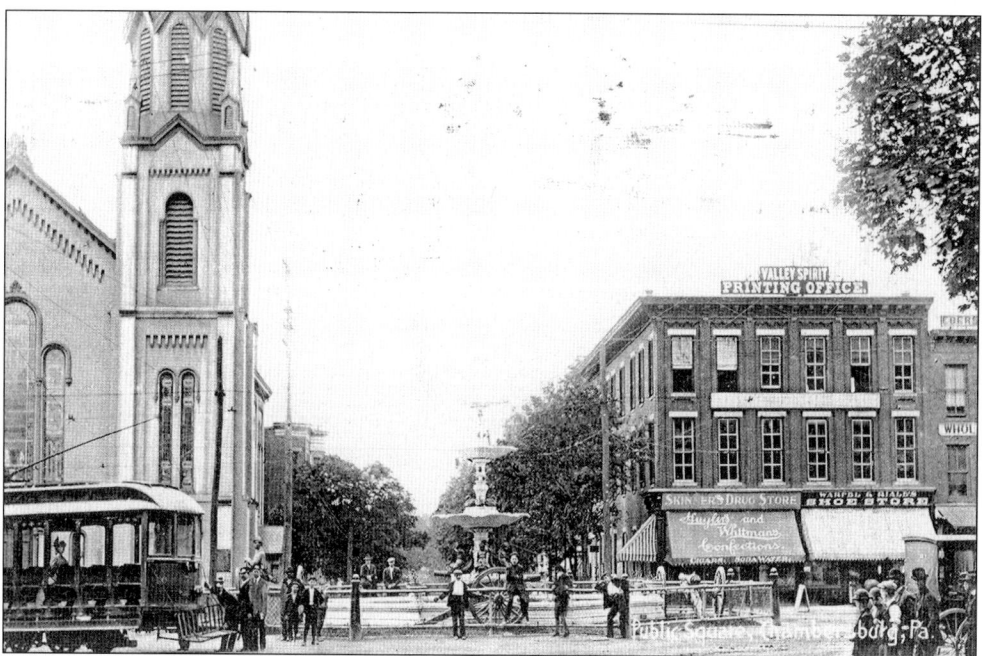

A Chambersburg and Gettysburg summer trolley car makes a stop on July 30, 1908, as citizens relax on the Diamond. This view of the Diamond was taken looking west on Market Street. On the southwest quadrant of Memorial Square is Central Presbyterian Church—a portion of its 186-foot spire can be seen. On the northwest quadrant is the Valley Spirit building, which houses Skinner's Drug Store.

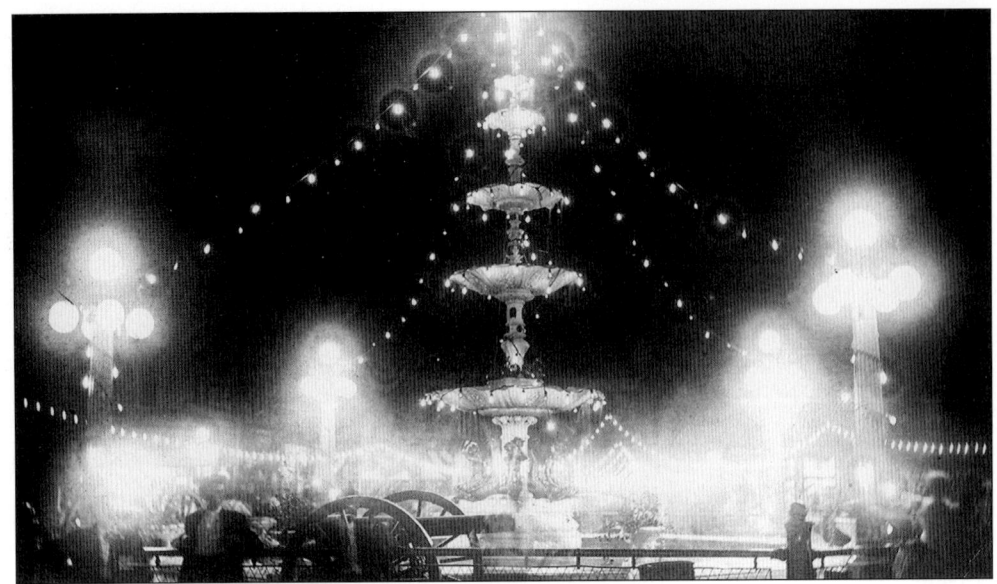

Memorial Fountain is illuminated for Old Home Week of 1914 and shows the new electric White Way lights.

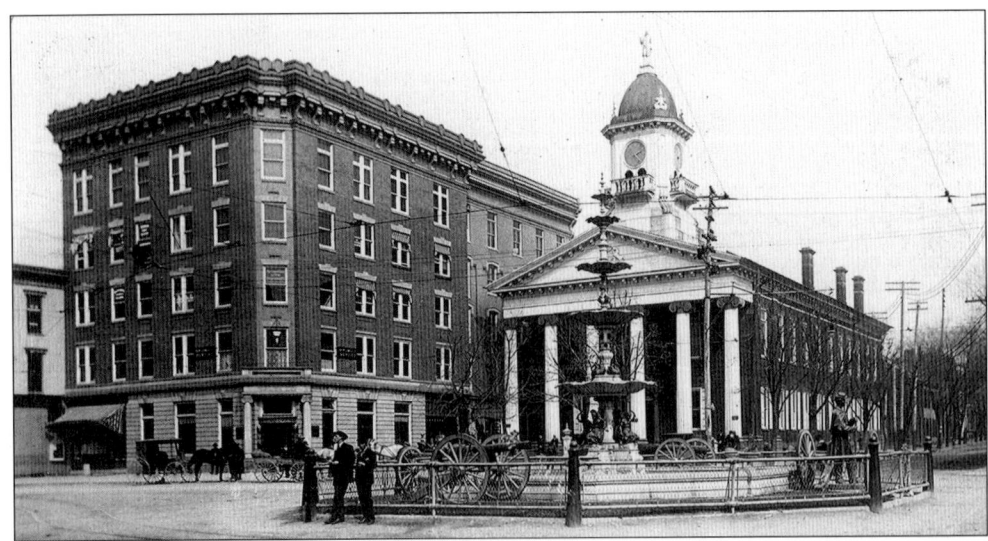

From the vantage point of West Market Street (now Lincoln Way West), this March 26, 1912, photograph preserves a distinguished view of the Franklin County Courthouse and the Chambersburg Trust Company building.

An appealingly decorated Chambersburg Trust Company building is prepared for the festivities of Old Home Week of 1914. The Chambersburg Trust Company building was constructed in 1905.

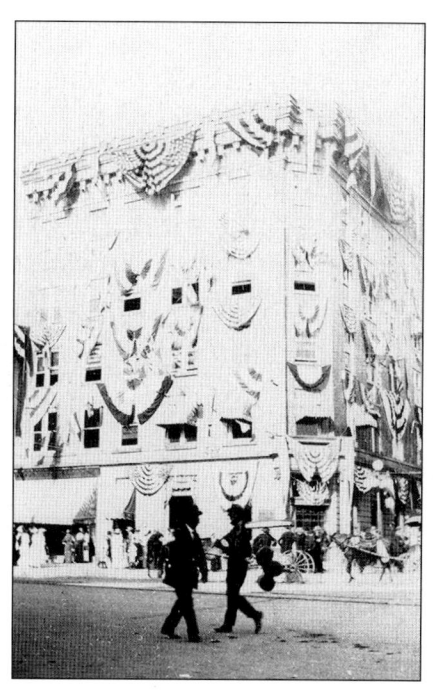

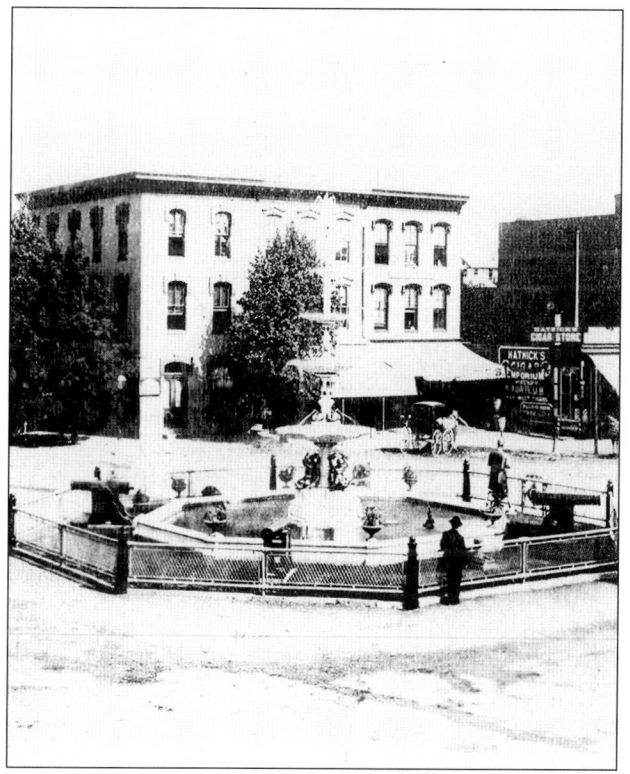

Taken in the early 1880s, this open view of the Diamond shows the original home of the Valley National Bank building. The location has housed a bank since 1809 when Edward Crawford opened a one-room bank in his home. The building was replaced in 1915 with the marble Valley National Bank building, designed by the Philadelphia architectural firm of Furness, Evans, and Company. In August 2003, the Chambersburg Area Development Corporation undertook the refurbishment of the marble bank building, and on July 16, 2004, the Greater Chambersburg Chamber of Commerce opened its offices and the Chambersburg Heritage Center. Also of note in this photograph are the original stationary fortification guns around Memorial Fountain.

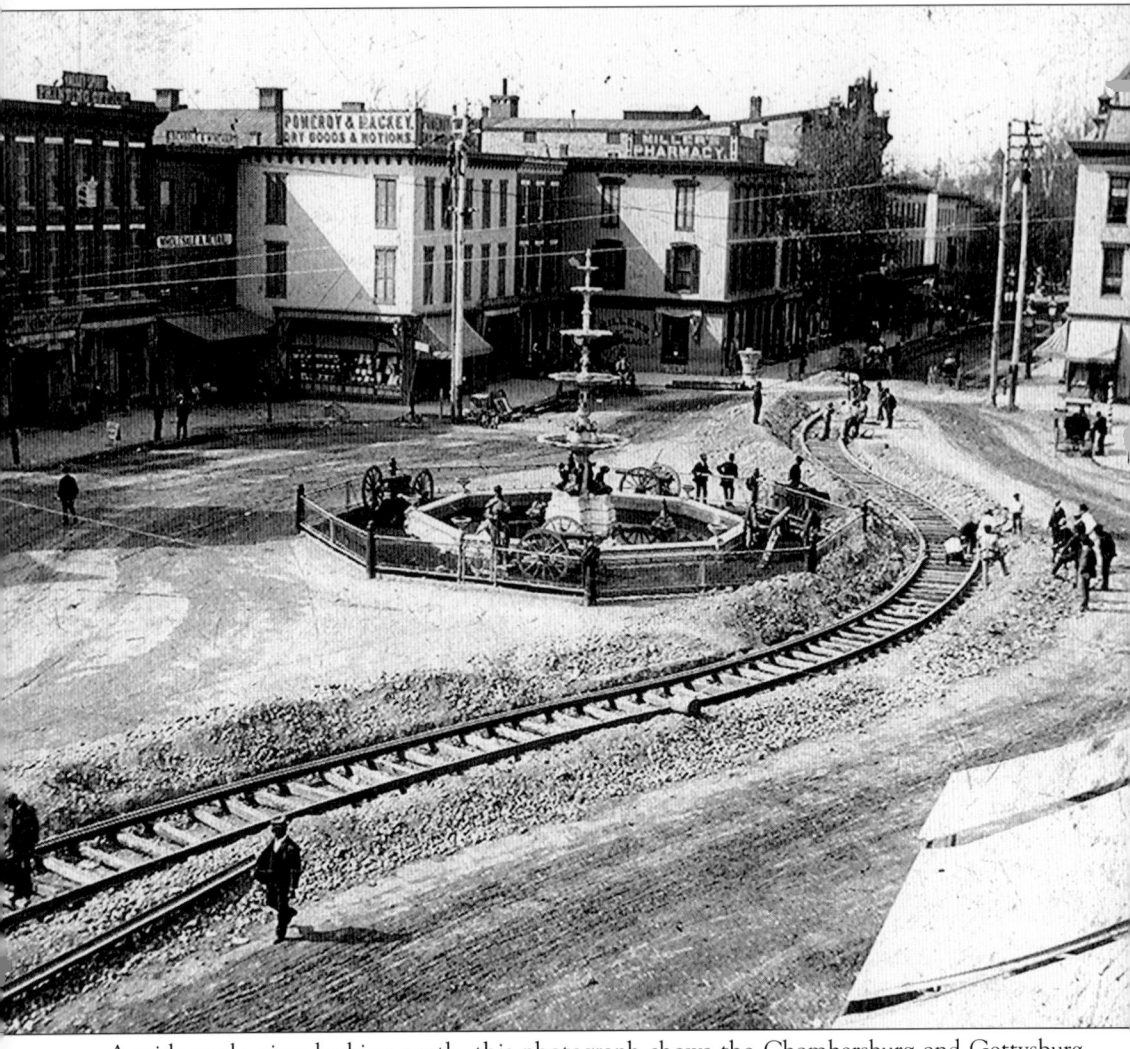

A wide-angle view looking north, this photograph shows the Chambersburg and Gettysburg Railway laying trolley car tracks through the Diamond in 1900. Visible in the background are numerous advertisements of local businesses.

This 1897 view of the fountain shows a metal cover over the basin to protect it from the elements.

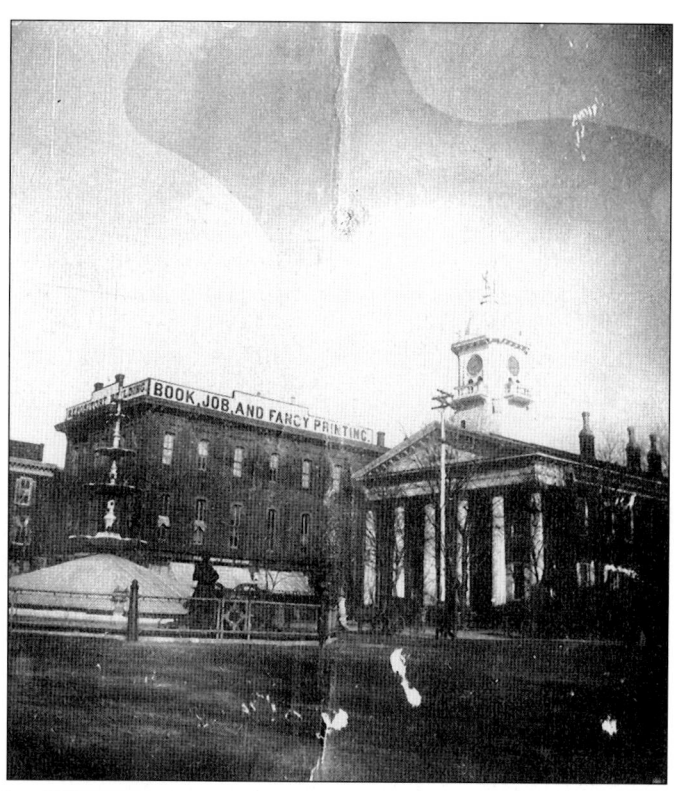

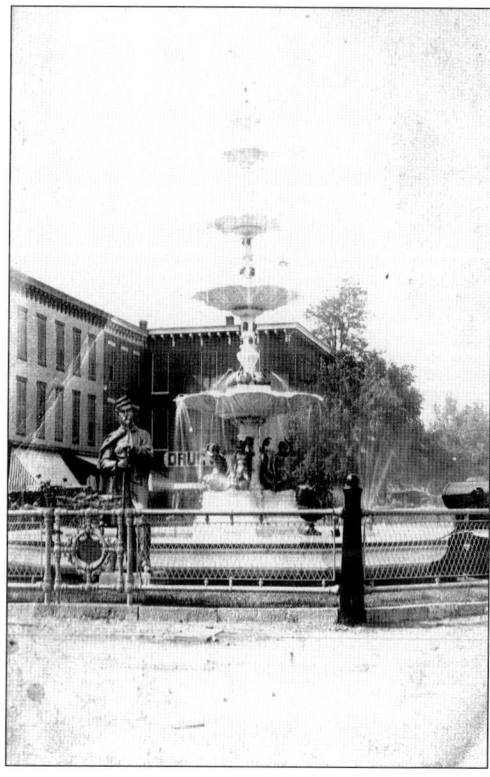

Taken from South Main Street, this 1880s photograph shows the fountain. A breeze picks up the flowing water and creates a fine mist.

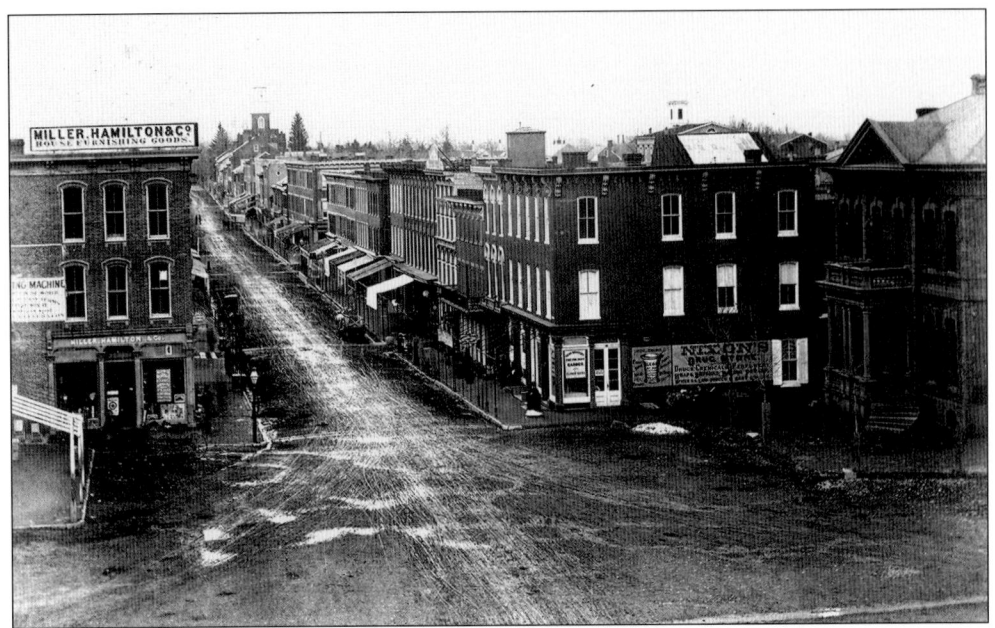

This view of South Main Street shows a quiet day in the early 1870s. The spire of the Zion Reformed Church is visible in the distance. Zion Reformed is one of Chambersburg's three rose rent churches, those for which Benjamin Chambers gave land. As payment, a rose is given yearly to a descendant of the Chambers family. The other two rose rent churches are Falling Spring Presbyterian and First Lutheran.

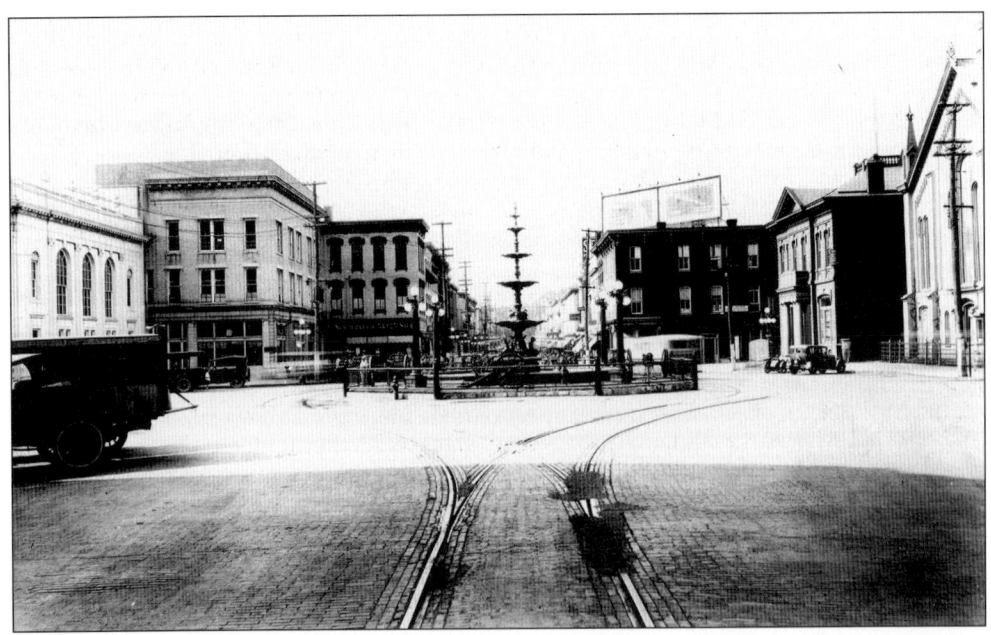

As time passed, the identity of the Diamond evolved into Memorial Square. This 1936 picture captures a more contemporary presence on the Diamond, with the once-used trolley tracks and the automobiles that made them obsolete. Other features of note are the National Bank, the Central Presbyterian Church, the advertising billboards, and the bricked roadway.

Three

TRAINS, TROLLEYS, AND AIRPLANES

Transportation has always helped Chambersburg thrive. In the days of the toll road, Chambersburg was a principal stop on the way west to Pittsburgh. When the railroad came to town in 1837, Chambersburg was again a key junction. An 1839 Cumberland Valley Railroad poster advertised: "Leave Chambersburg at 4 o'clock in the morning. Arrive at Harrisburg at 8, at Lancaster at 12, at Philadelphia before 6 PM. Returning: leave Harrisburg as soon as the cars from Philadelphia arrive, about 5 o'clock in the evening, and arrive at Chambersburg at 10 PM." Travelers to Pittsburgh could transfer from rail to stagecoach in Chambersburg for the ride west.

At the beginning of the 20th century, trolleys provided Chambersburg residents with another alternative to travel to adjoining communities. The Chambersburg and Gettysburg Electric Railway Company laid trolley track, and the line, which was intended to link the judicial seats of Franklin and Adams Counties, met the resistance of the Cumberland Valley Railroad. A court order, granted in favor of the railroad, prevented the trolley line from passing across Cumberland Valley Railroad tracks at Third and Queen Streets and at the western edge of Fayetteville. Travelers desiring to continue past these points were required to disembark, walk a few hundred feet, and board another trolley to continue their trip. This situation persisted until 1905, when control of the trolley passed to the Cumberland Valley Railroad.

Although the Cumberland Valley Railroad maintained a competitive attitude toward other transportation modes, it was an important factor in Chambersburg's vitality. It provided the technology to facilitate Franklin County's first telegraph, telephone, and electrical systems and contributed aid to societies and volunteer organizations. By 1900, the railroad employed nearly 1,800 people.

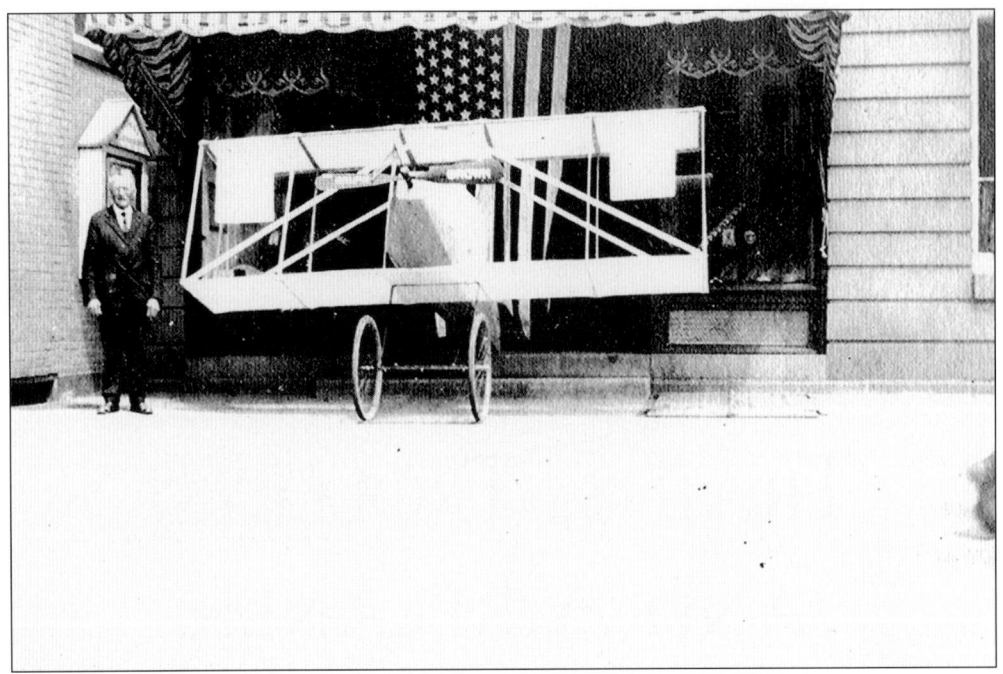

The owner of Ludwig's Jewelers, Walter Ludwig, sports a replica of a World War I airplane in front of his business on South Main Street to honor Ralph Brown, one of his employees, who was serving with American Expeditionary Forces.

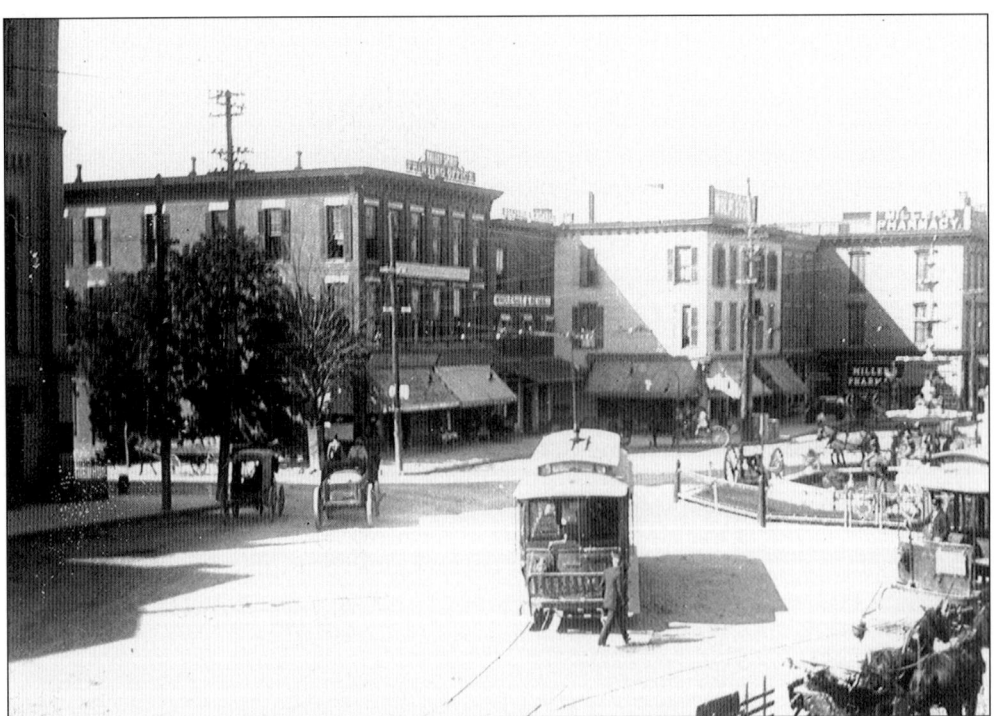

Two Chambersburg and Gettysburg trolley cars meet on the square in 1909, as numerous wagons transport people and goods.

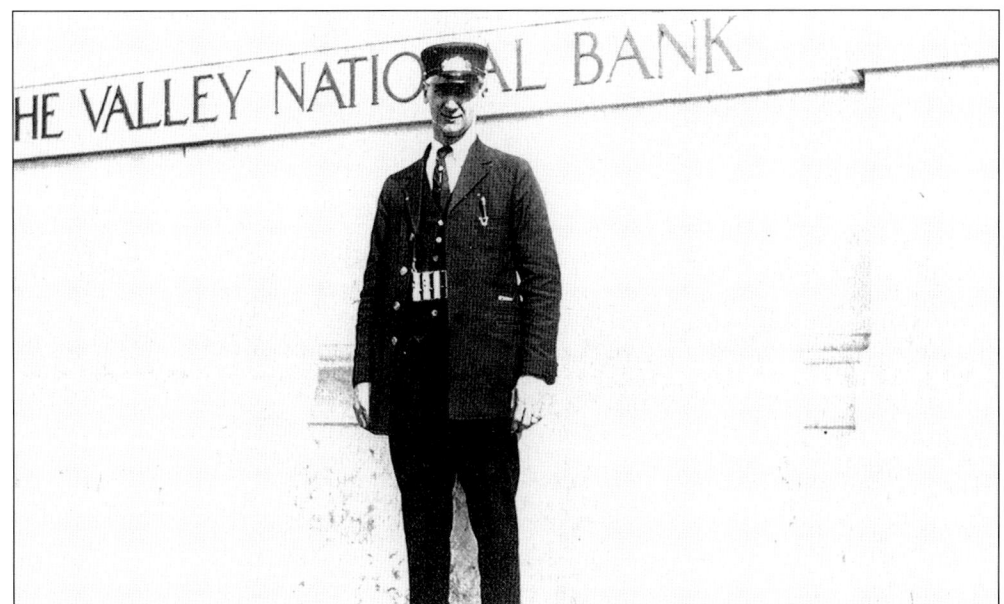

Chambersburg and Gettysburg Railway conductor Charles Dessem stands in front of the newly completed Valley National Bank. Today this 1915 white marble building houses the Chambersburg Heritage Center, an interpretive center that focuses on the frontier, Civil War, Underground Railroad, architecture, and transportation history of Franklin County.

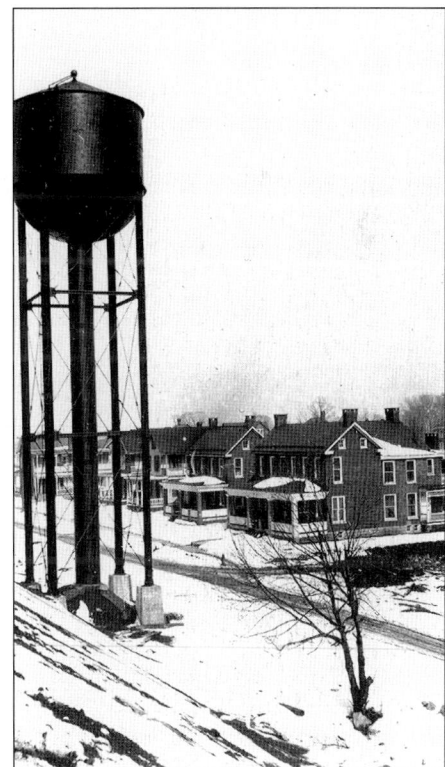

The Cumberland Valley Railroad water tower had just been completed when this photograph was taken on February 28, 1914. The homes in the background are on North Fourth Street. The tower was razed in December 2004.

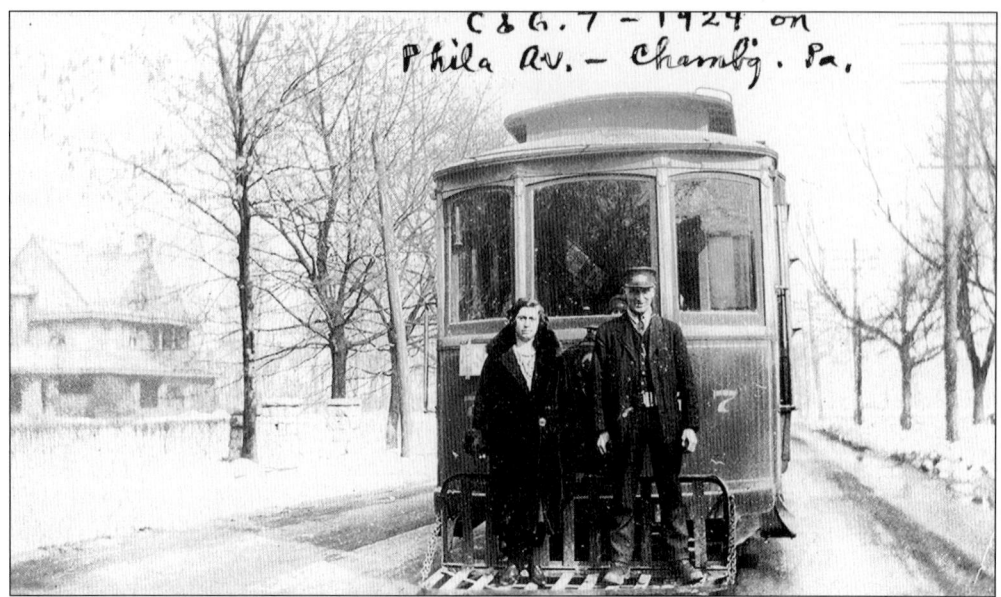

Mr. and Mrs. Calvin Senseney stand on the cowcatcher of Chambersburg and Gettysburg Car No. 7 in 1924. The trolley car is heading south on Philadelphia Avenue. In the periphery is the Sharpe home, now Sharpe House on the Wilson College campus.

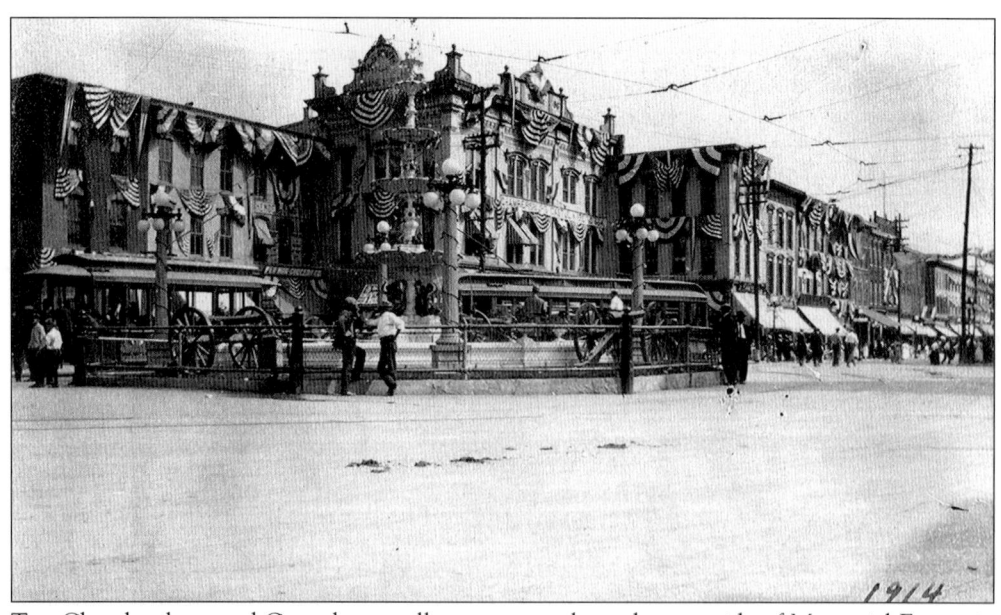

Two Chambersburg and Gettysburg trolley cars pass along the east side of Memorial Fountain during the Old Home Week celebration of 1914.

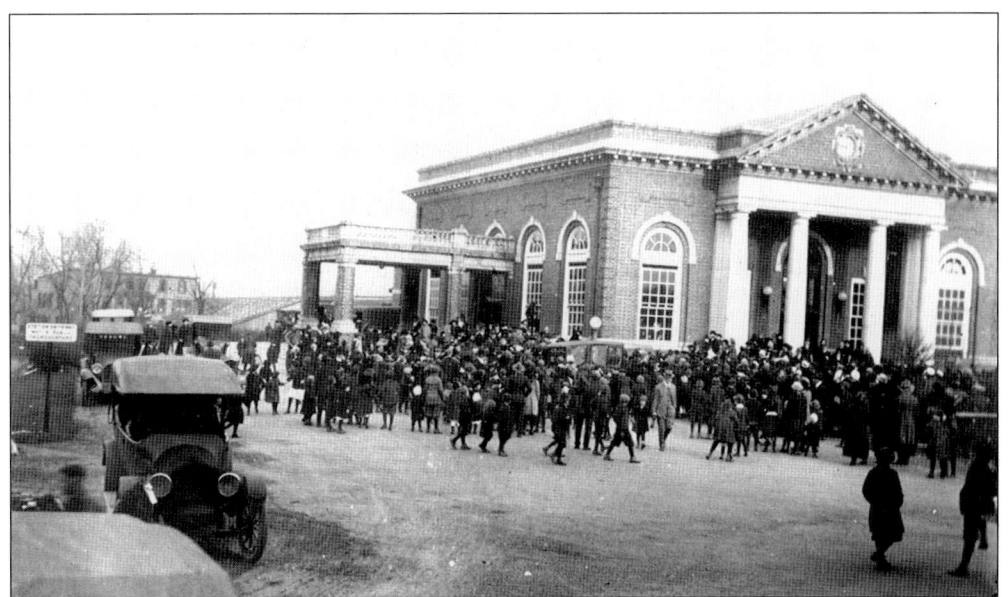

A large crowd gathers at the former Cumberland Valley Railroad Station on Penncraft Avenue on December 10, 1921, to see Santa Claus.

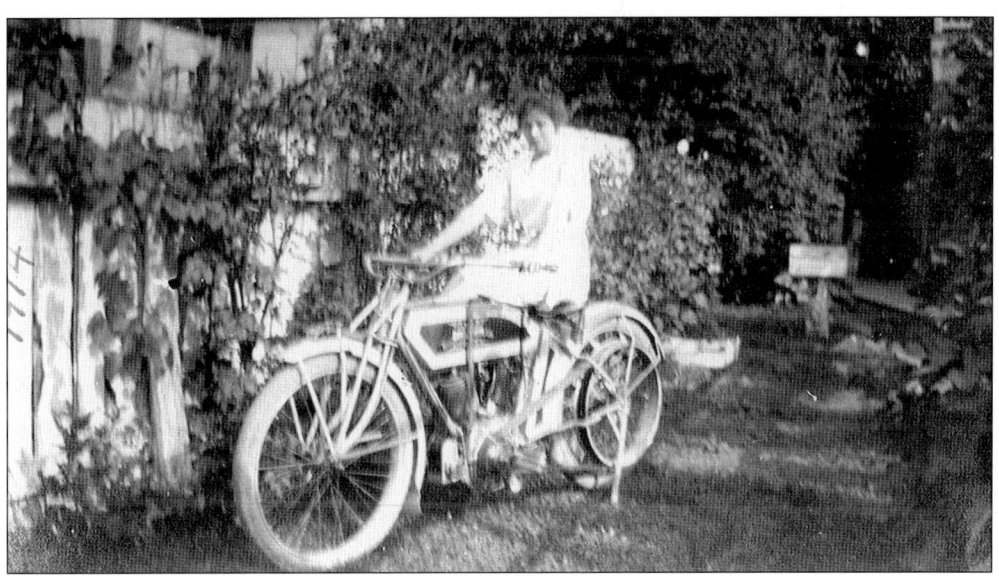

A young lady sits on an early motorcycle in a yard on South Second Street in the summer of 1914.

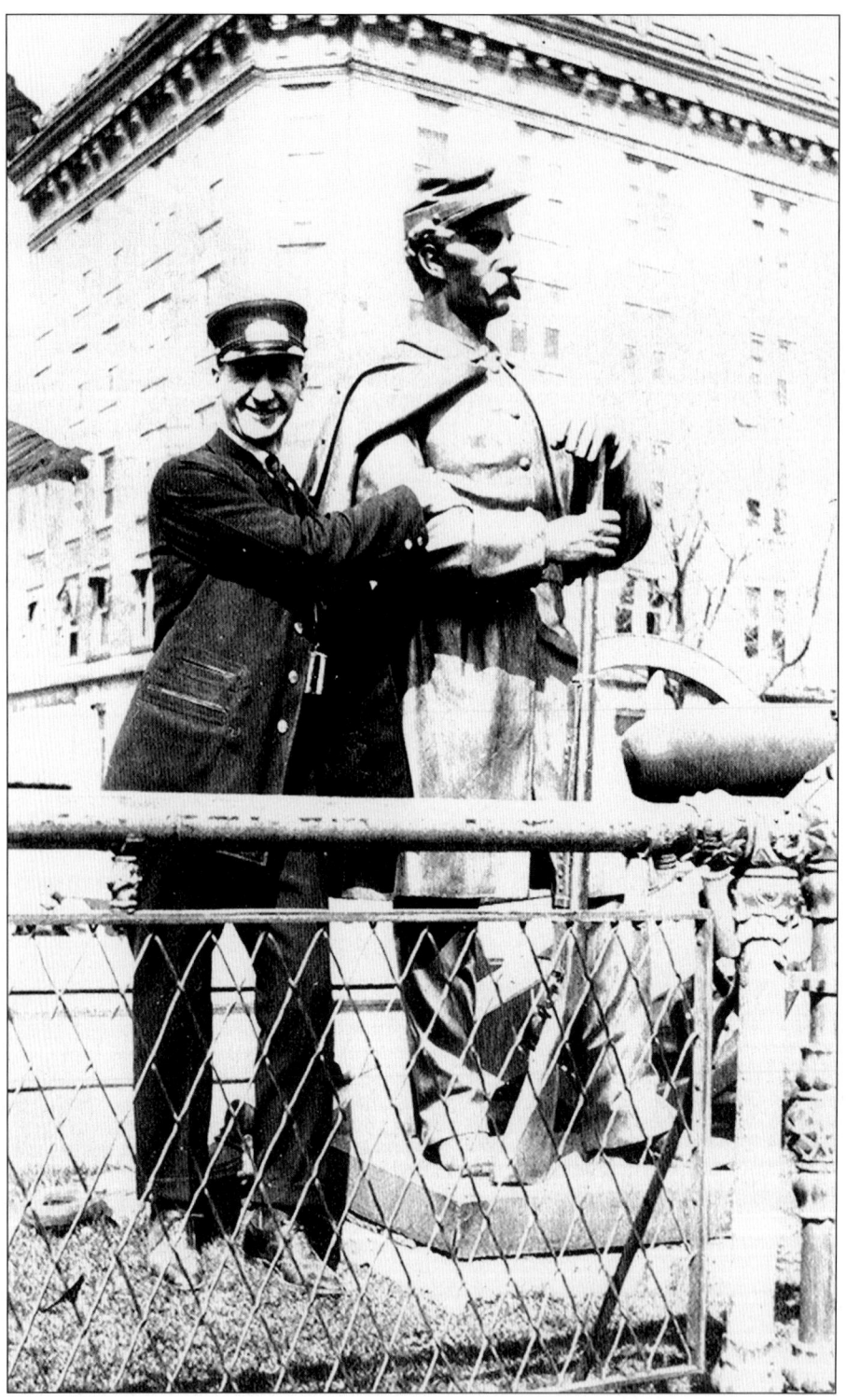

Chambersburg and Gettysburg Railway conductor Charles Dessem makes a new friend on the Diamond in 1915.

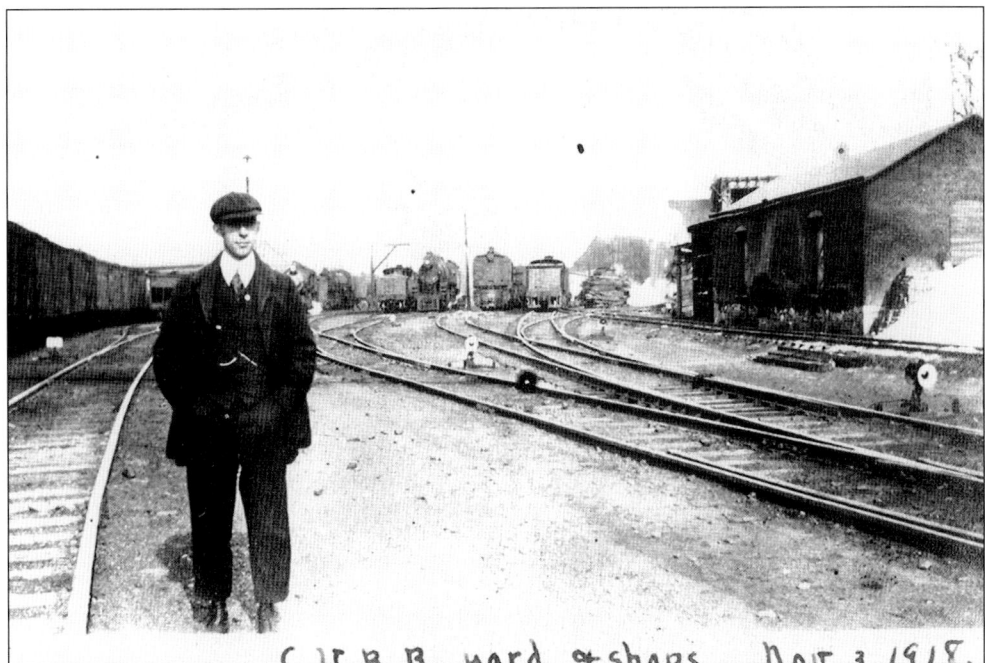

Taken on November 3, 1918, this photograph shows the Franklin Yard of the Cumberland Valley Railroad with its trains and shops. The Cumberland Valley Railroad was absorbed into the Pennsylvania Railroad system in 1919.

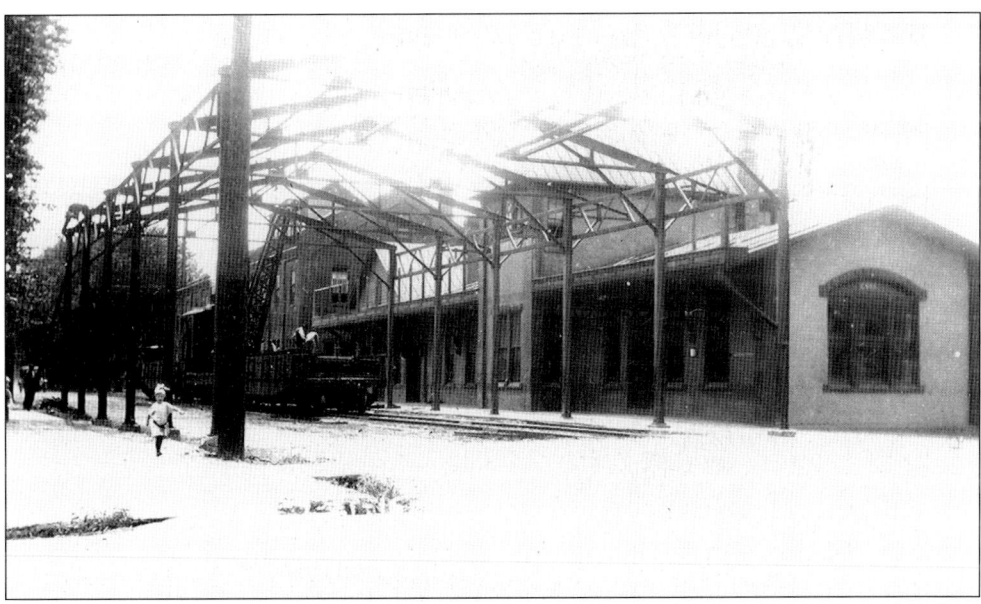

Pictured are the old Cumberland Valley Railroad Station and train shed on North Third Street. The train shed was dismantled in 1916. Today the Public Opinion occupies the Third Street Station.

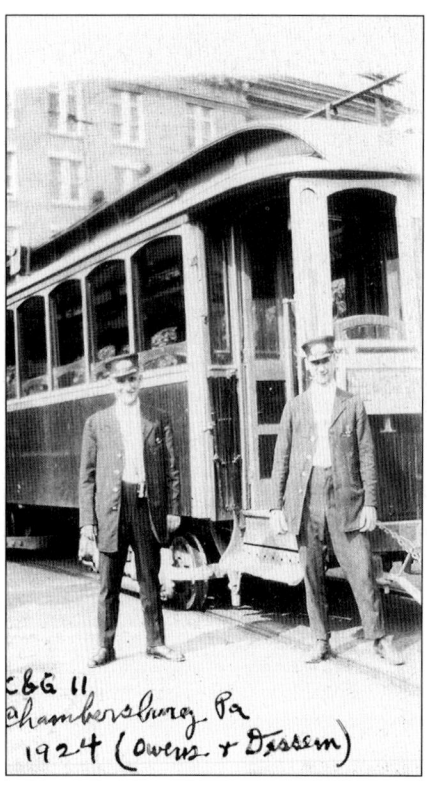

Chambersburg and Gettysburg Railway employees Mr. Owens and Charles Dessem stand by Car No. 11 on the square in 1924. By this time, automobiles had increased in popularity. Although the trolley was still employed as transportation to the pleasure parks in warmer weather, seasonal patronage was not enough to maintain operations. The last trolley ran on December 21, 1926.

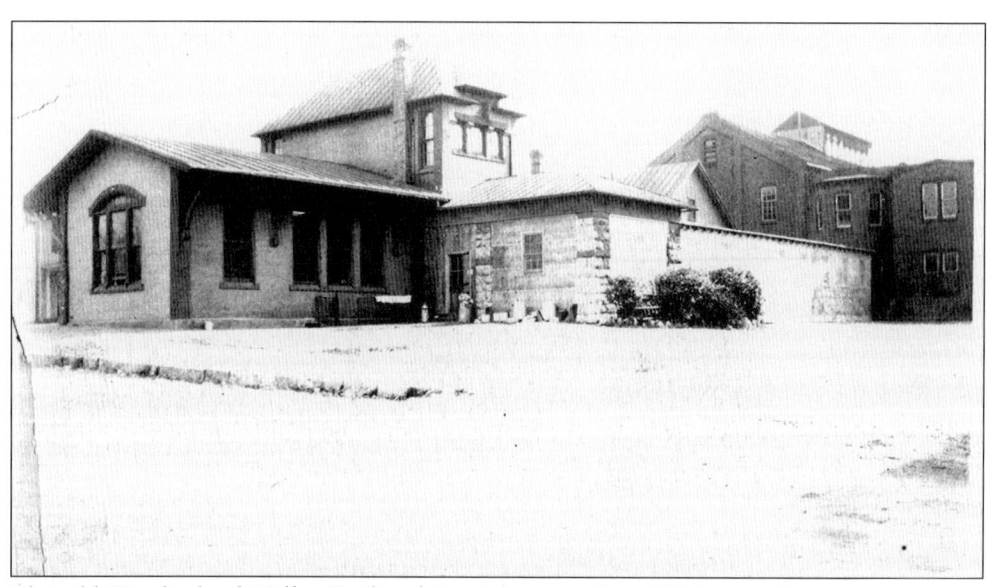

The old Cumberland Valley Railroad Station, retired in 1914, served as an emergency hospital during the influenza epidemic of 1918. This rear view of the station was taken from East King Street.

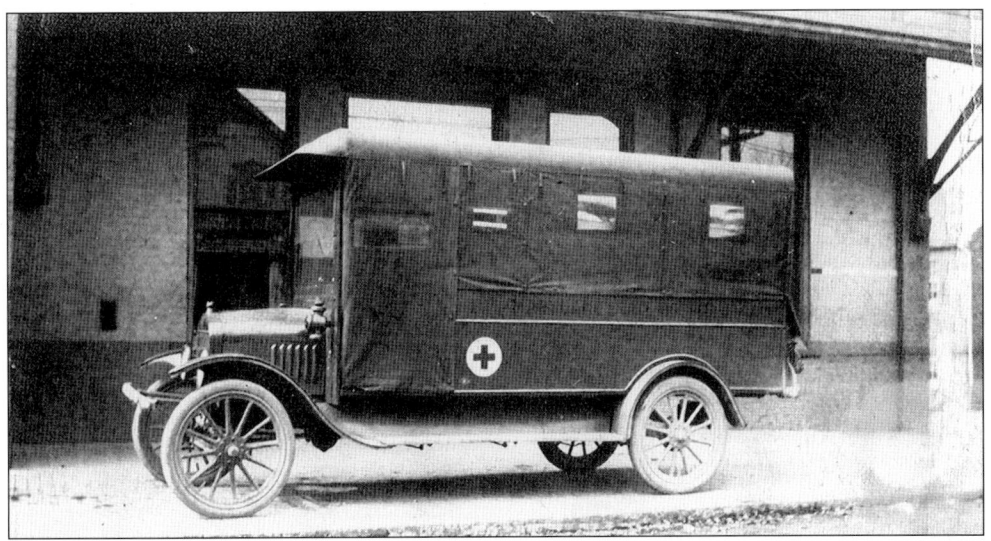

An American Red Cross ambulance is parked on the sidewalk during the 1918 influenza epidemic. This view of the old Cumberland Valley Railroad Station was taken from North Third Street.

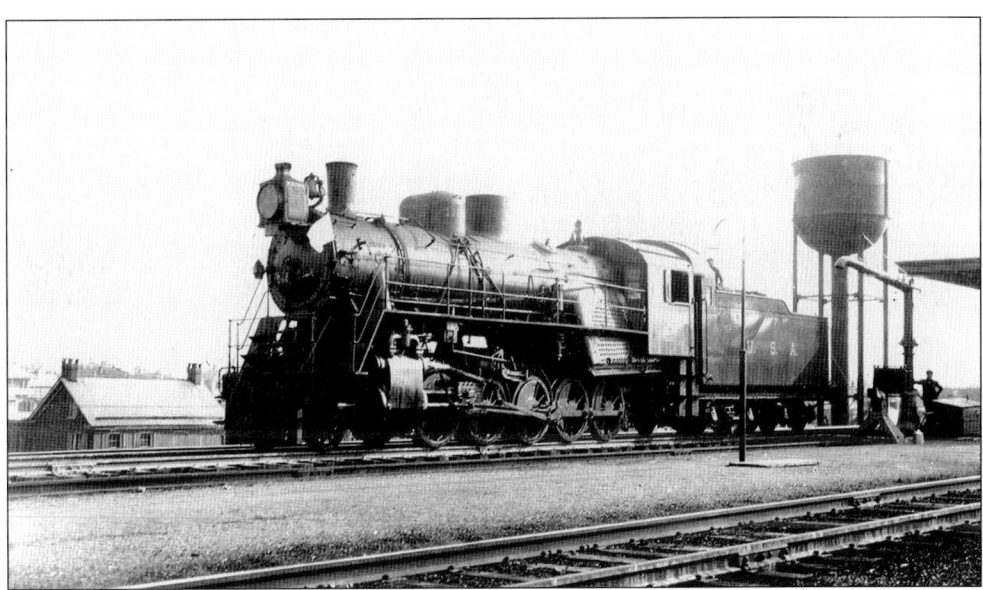

U.S.A. steam engine No. 1124 stops to fill its tender with water on March 5, 1918, before heading north. Fourth Street is in the background.

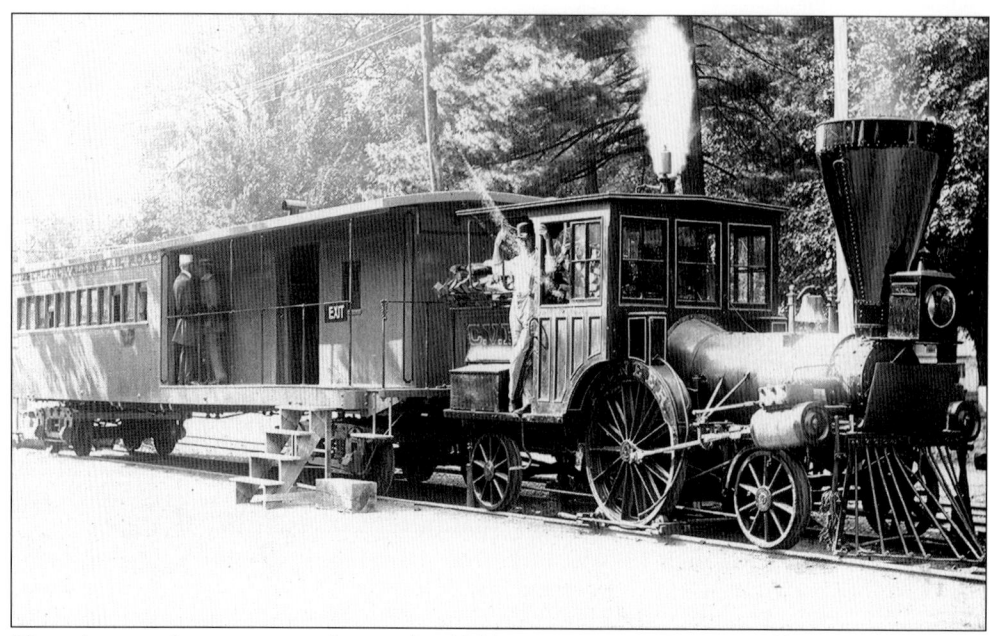

This photograph captures a classic, the 1851 steam engine *Pioneer* pulling a combination car. Combination cars carried half freight and mail and half passengers. The Smithsonian Institute restored the *Pioneer*, and the combination car is displayed at the Railroad Museum of Pennsylvania at Strasburg. The *Chambersburg*, designed by Cumberland Valley Railroad employee Philip Berlin, was the first sleeping car built in Chambersburg. The special excursion train ran from Chambersburg to Mont Alto in 1909; the engineer was John Siebert.

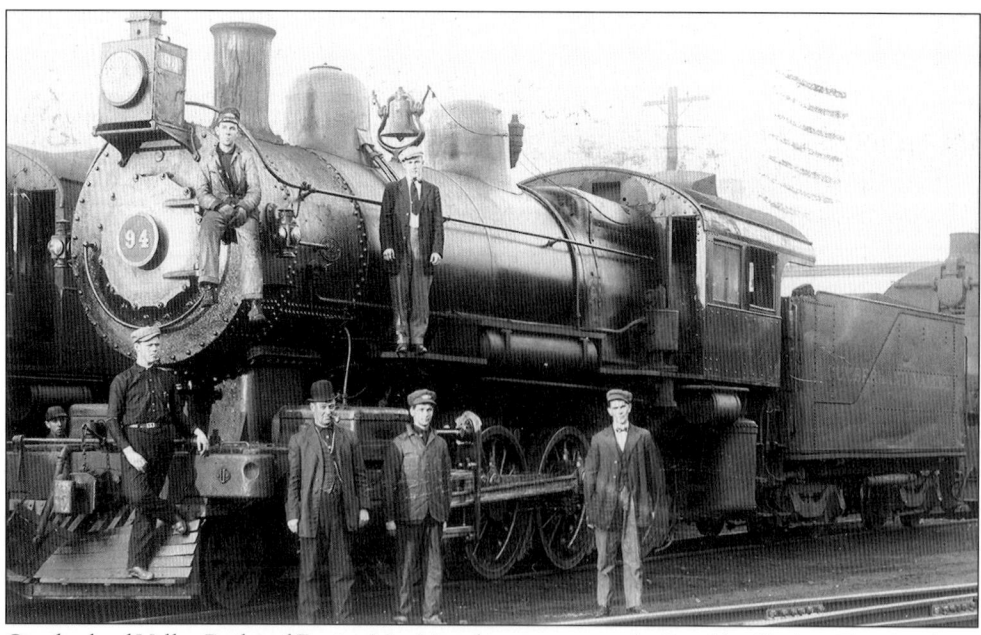

Cumberland Valley Railroad Engine No. 94 and its crew are at the Franklin Yard in Chambersburg in 1911.

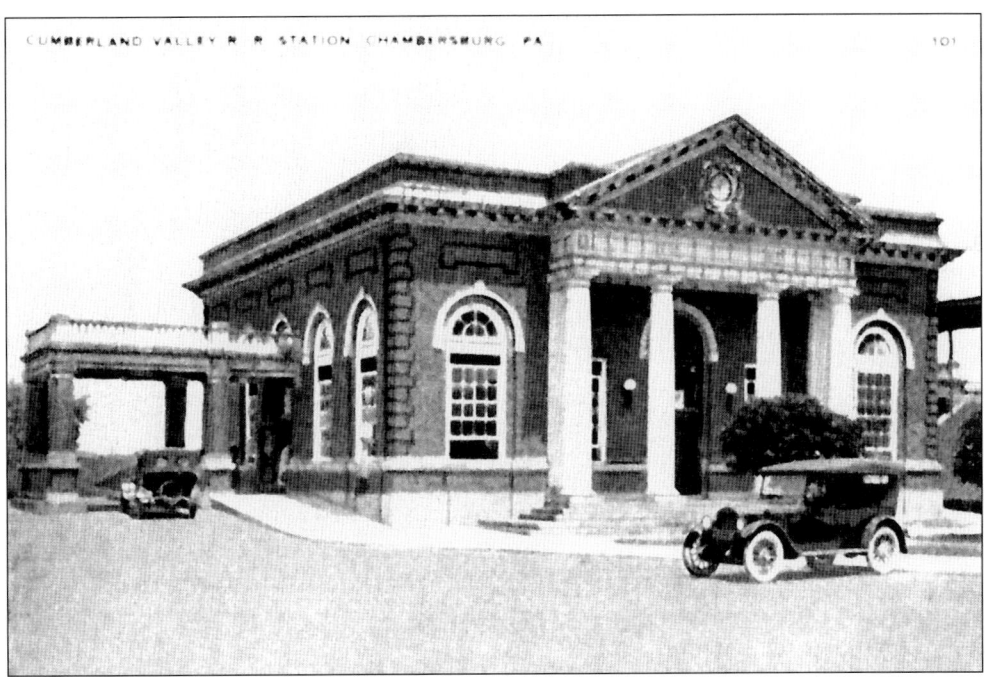

Completed in 1914, the Cumberland Valley Railroad station on Penncraft Avenue featured an elevated boarding area between the tracks on the Chambersburg High Line. As beautiful as it was functional, the rail station served the community into the 1960s.

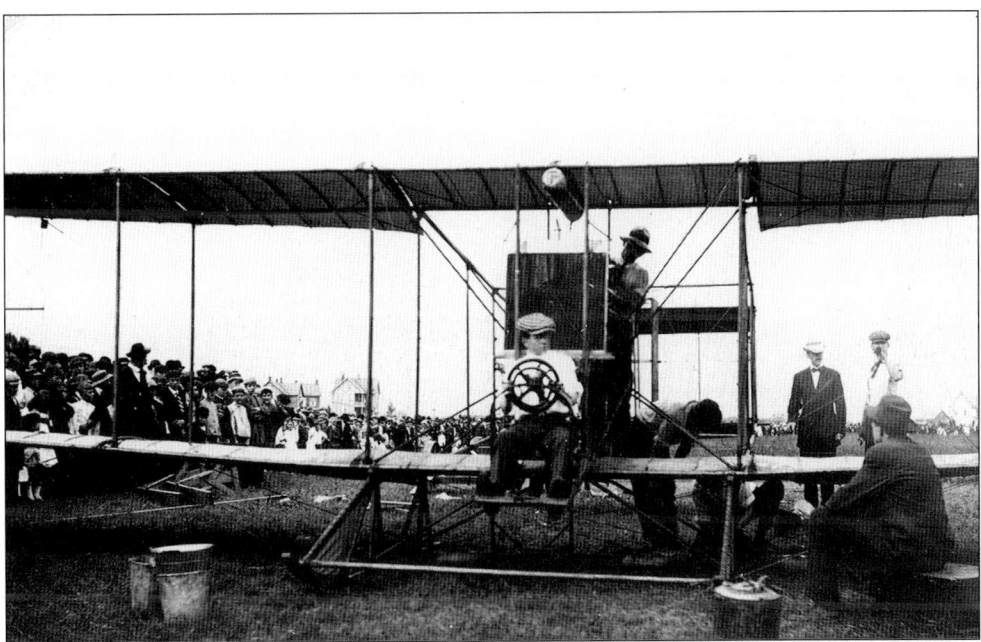

Young pioneer aviator Paul Peck prepares his Rex-Smith biplane for the first flight over Chambersburg on September 23, 1911. This experimental aircraft was shipped by rail and assembled on location for the flight. The Chambersburg Businessmen's Association paid Peck $1,000.

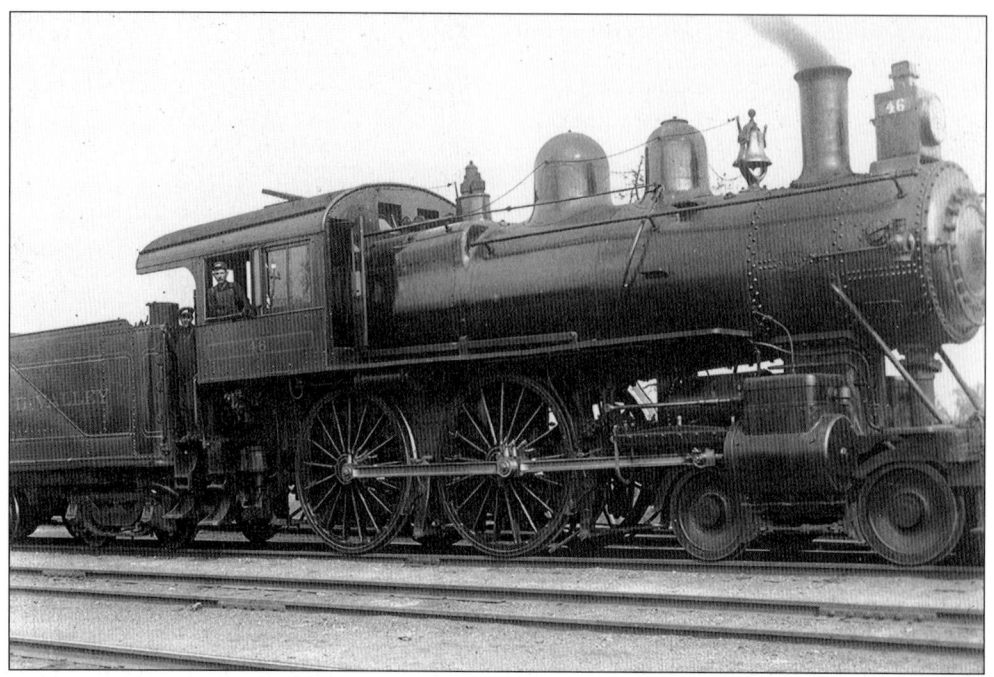

Ready for the next run, Harry B. Shaffer sits in the cab of Cumberland Valley Railroad Steam Engine No. 46 in Franklin Yard on July 6, 1914.

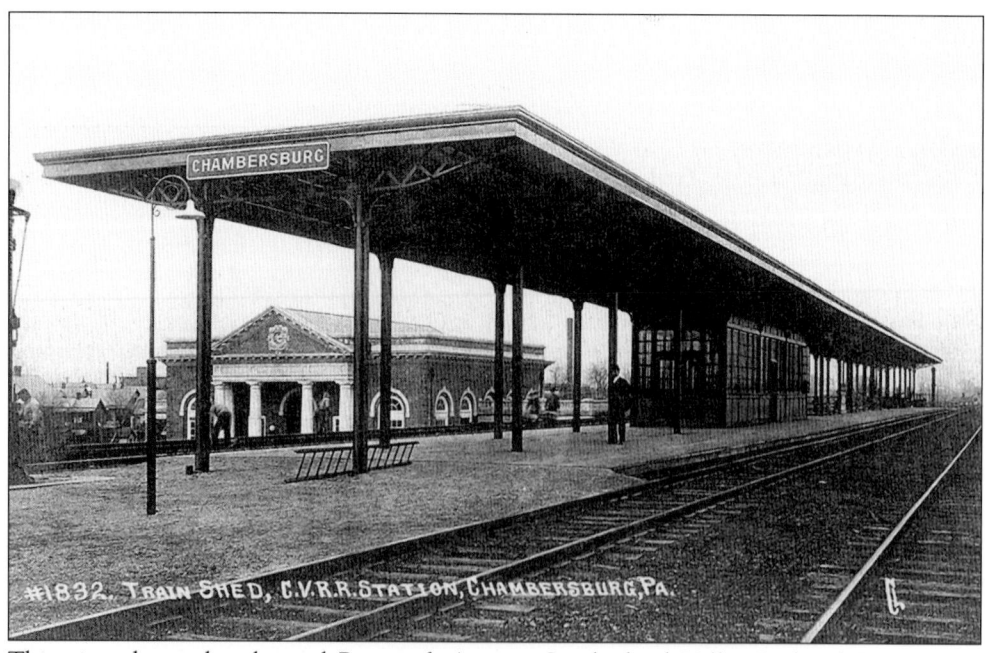

This view shows the elevated Penncraft Avenue Cumberland Valley Railroad Station and platform in 1915.

The first airship to fly over Chambersburg was piloted by Paul Peck on September 23, 1911. Peck safely completed his journey this day, but unfortunately he died in a plane crash in Chicago in 1912 at the age of 22.

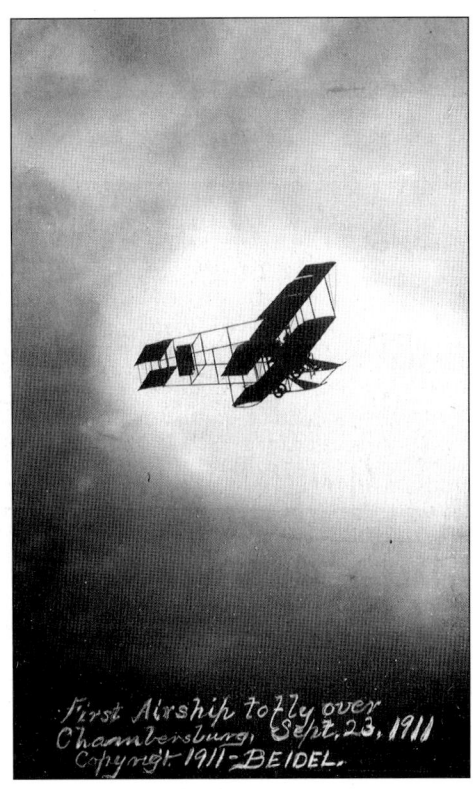

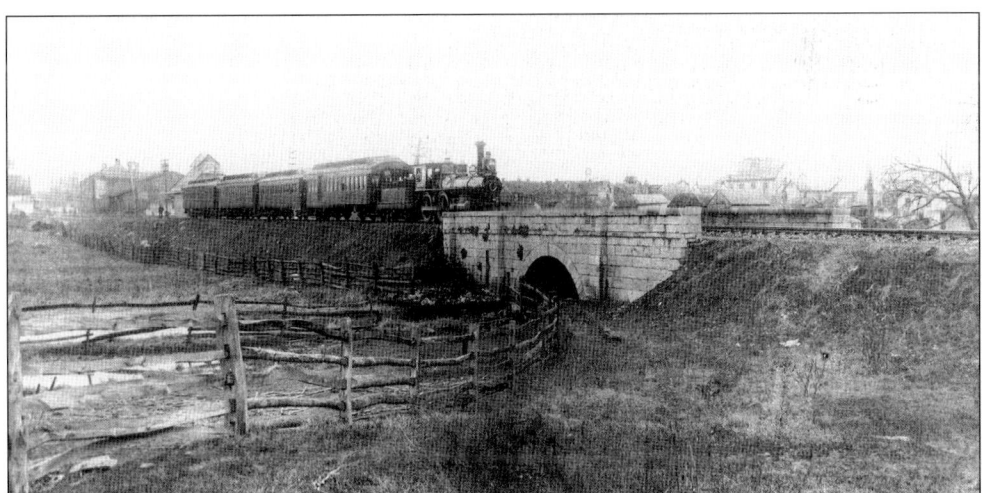

A Cumberland Valley Railroad passenger train heads north from Third Street in the 1890s. The old stone bridge still stands. The pasture and fence were replaced by the former Ice and Cold Storage Building at the intersection of Grant and Kennedy Streets.

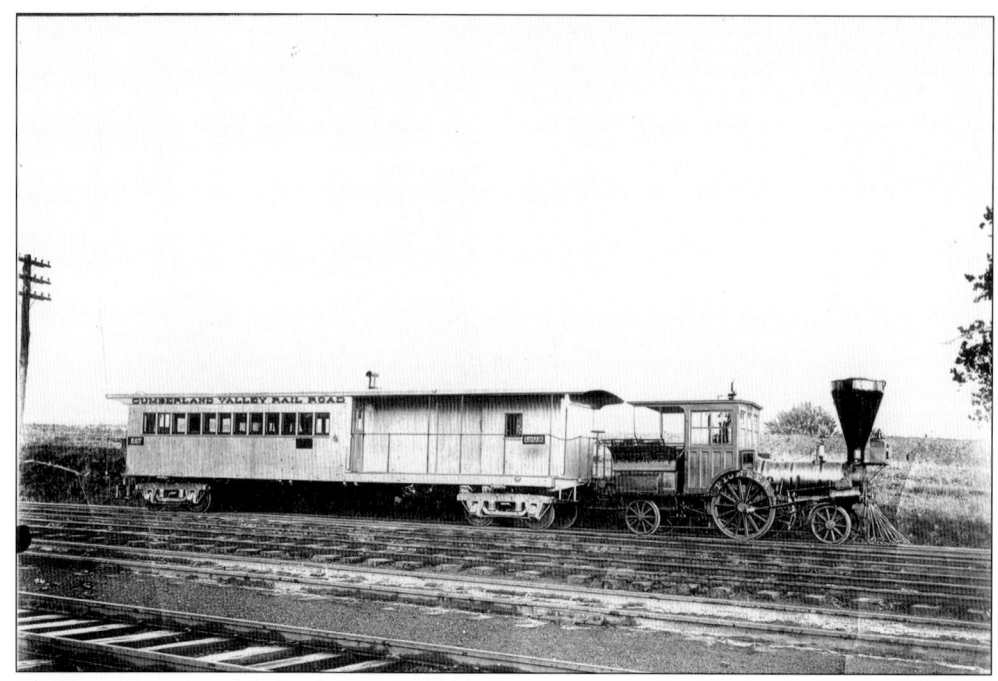

The *Pioneer* engine and the combination coach are shown at the Cumberland Valley Railroad yard in 1910. The *Pioneer*, purchased in 1851 by the Cumberland Valley Railroad, was one of the first light locomotives; it could reach a speed of 40 miles per hour while pulling two cars.

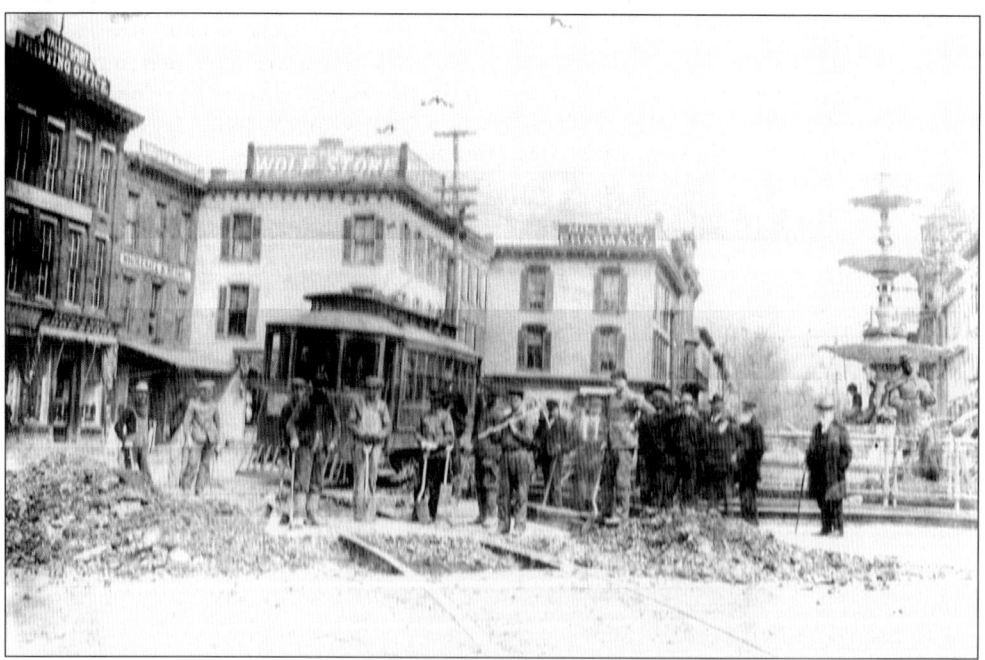

The Chambersburg and Gettysburg trolley car has stopped on the Diamond for some track replacement in 1910. Workers take a break while the photographer takes the shot. Note the Valley Spirit Printing office on the left and Miller's Pharmacy in the background.

Four

CIRCUSES, PARADES, AND AMUSEMENTS

In the early 1900s, Chambersburg residents anticipated the excitement of the big top with a parade of animals, the circus band, and an assortment of cotton candy, peanuts, popcorn, and pink lemonade. The circus was a fantastic spectacle. Residents enjoyed the entertainment and the chance for community fellowship. Parades were another type of community celebration that attracted people from all parts of the county for relaxation and enjoyment.

Pleasure parks and amusement parks were other leisure destinations. In 1900, industrialist Augustus Wolf created a lake. Wolf owned the Wolf Company, which produced machinery and metal components, and the Lakeview Milling Company, which displayed the machinery his other company produced. The overflow of water from his lake provided the power source to generate electricity for his businesses, and the lake became a wonderful diversion for the enjoyment of Wolf Company employees and Chambersburg residents alike. Boating was a main attraction, with over 50 boats, including some naphtha-powered launches, available for rent. Naphtha, a form of petrol, was used in place of steam to eliminate the need for a legally licensed steam engineer to operate the boats. Swimming was also popular. Wolf's Lake included a bowling alley, athletic fields, shuffleboard court, a dance pavilion called Dreamland, and a 10-story, 100-foot-high tower to lodge visitors.

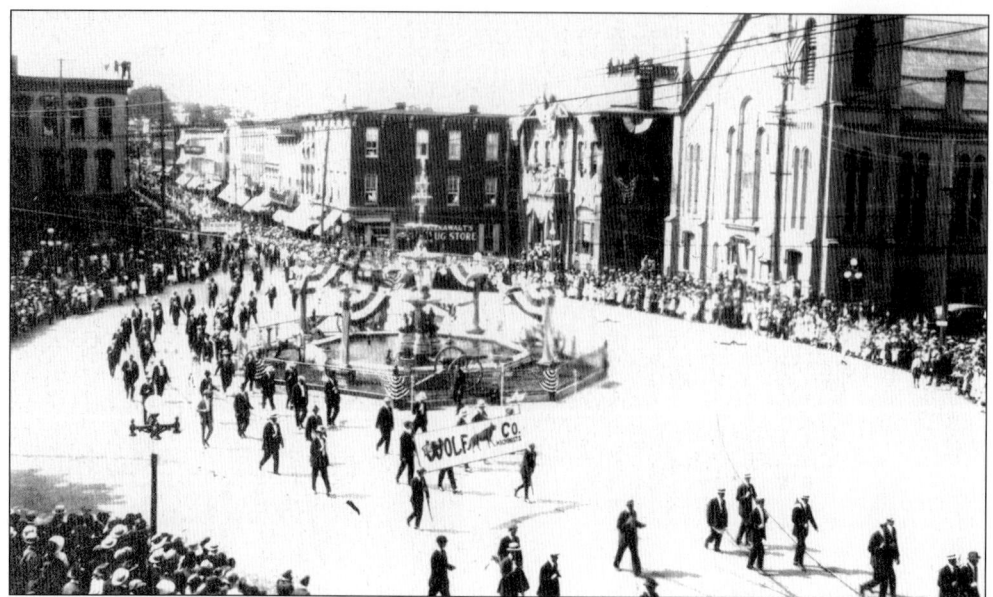
Wolf Company employees sport a fancy banner rounding the Diamond during the Industrial Parade in 1914, one event in Old Home Week.

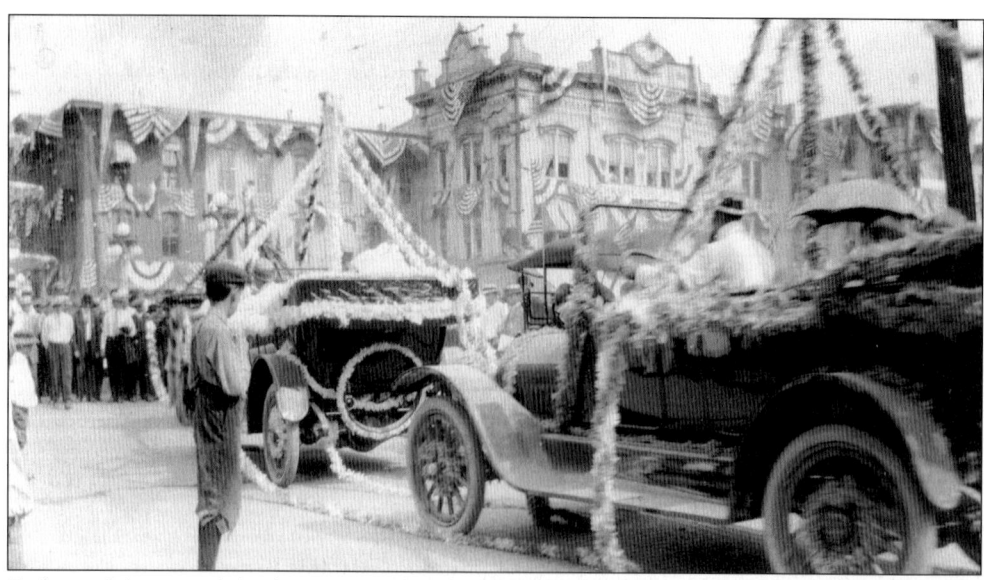
Early-model automobiles line up on Lincoln Way West for the Auto Parade held during Old Home Week of 1914. This view faces east toward the square. A variety of community events were staged during Old Home Week, bringing old and new residents together for enjoyment.

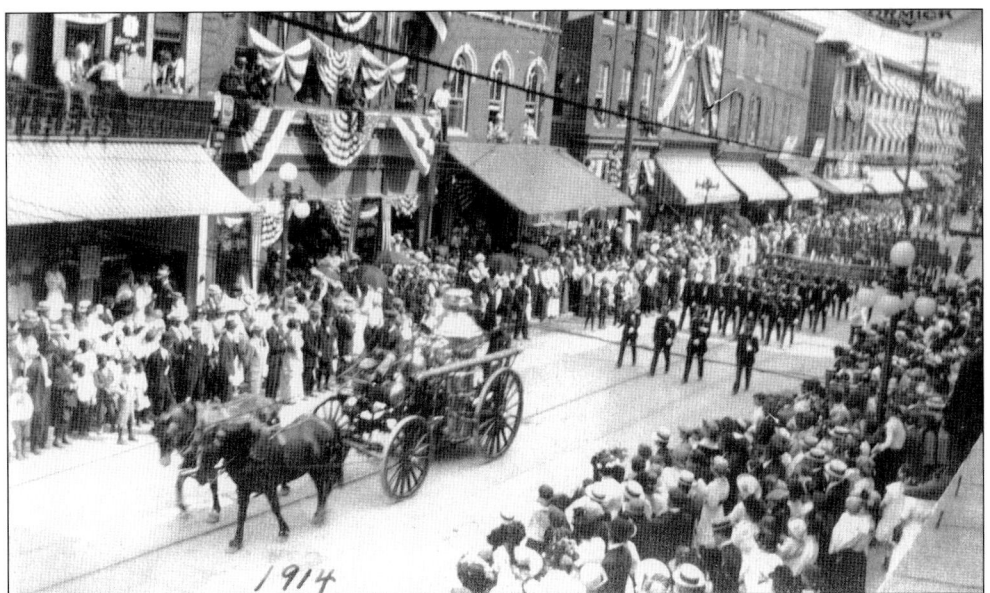

The Goodwill Steam Fire Engine and Hose Company No. 3 of Chambersburg, with its 1892 LaFrance steam engine, proceeds north from South Main Street in the Firemen's Parade held during Old Home Week of 1914.

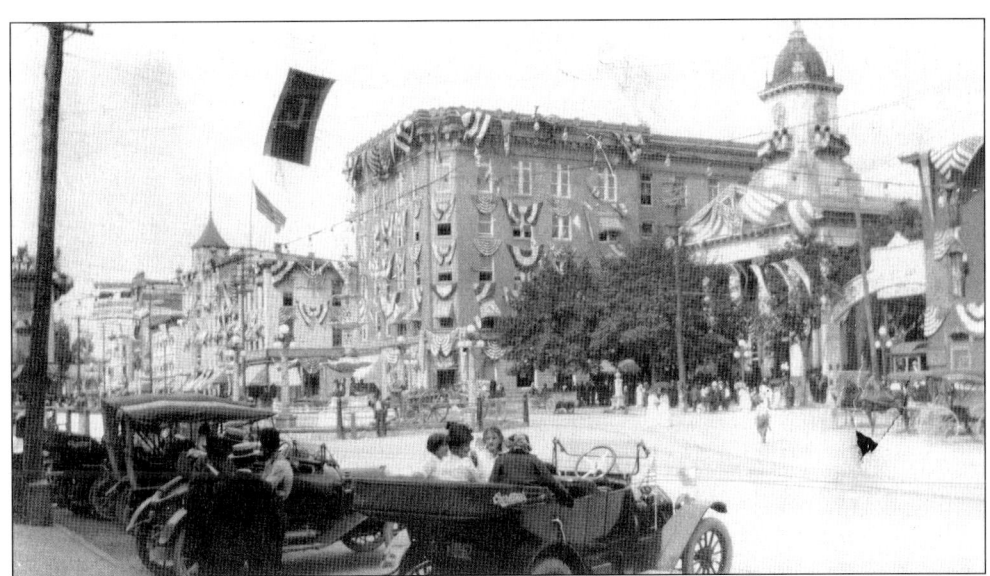

The Diamond is decorated for the celebration of Old Home Week of 1914.

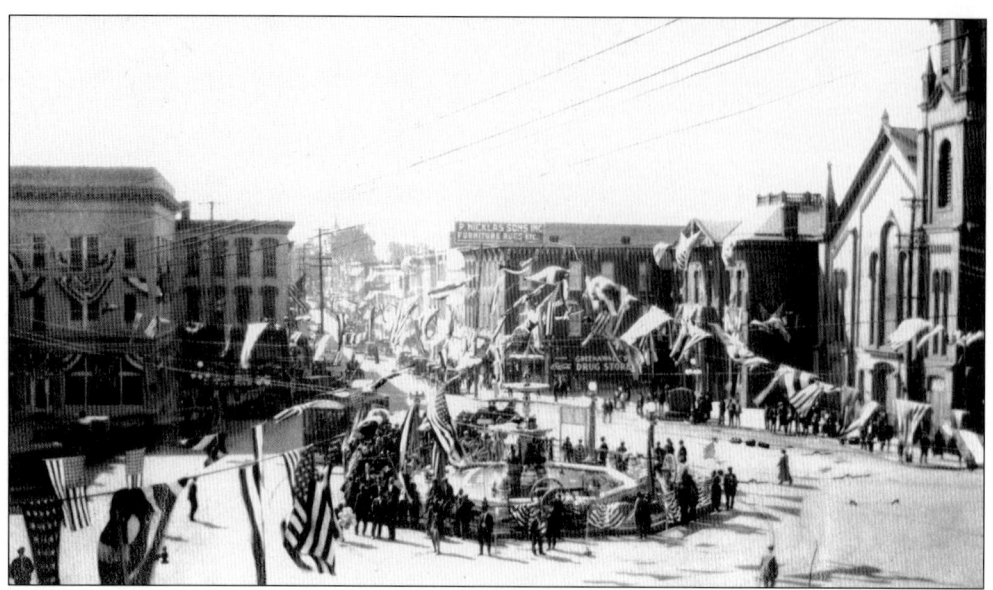
A lone trolley car passes around Memorial Fountain during the Lincoln Highway celebration held on October 4, 1921. Wind has the flags and banners waving in all directions.

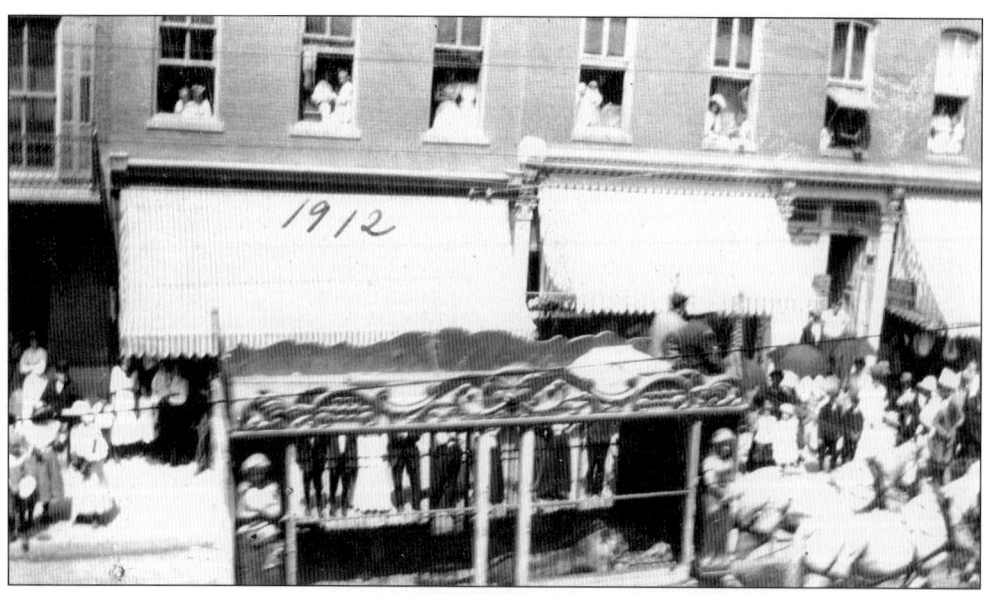
The Barnum and Bailey Circus lion wagon heads north on South Main Street in the 1912 Circus Parade.

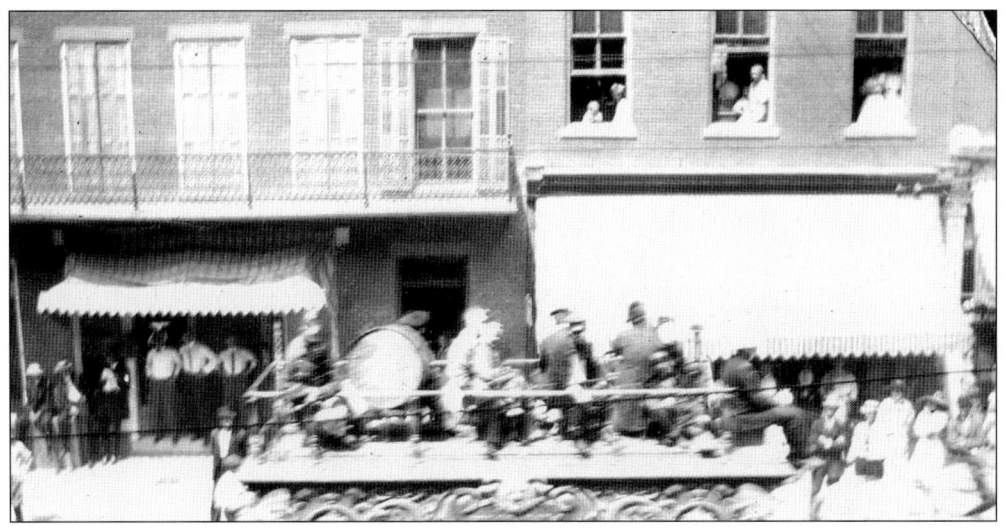
The Barnum and Bailey Circus Band performs for the citizens en route to Wolf's Lake in 1912.

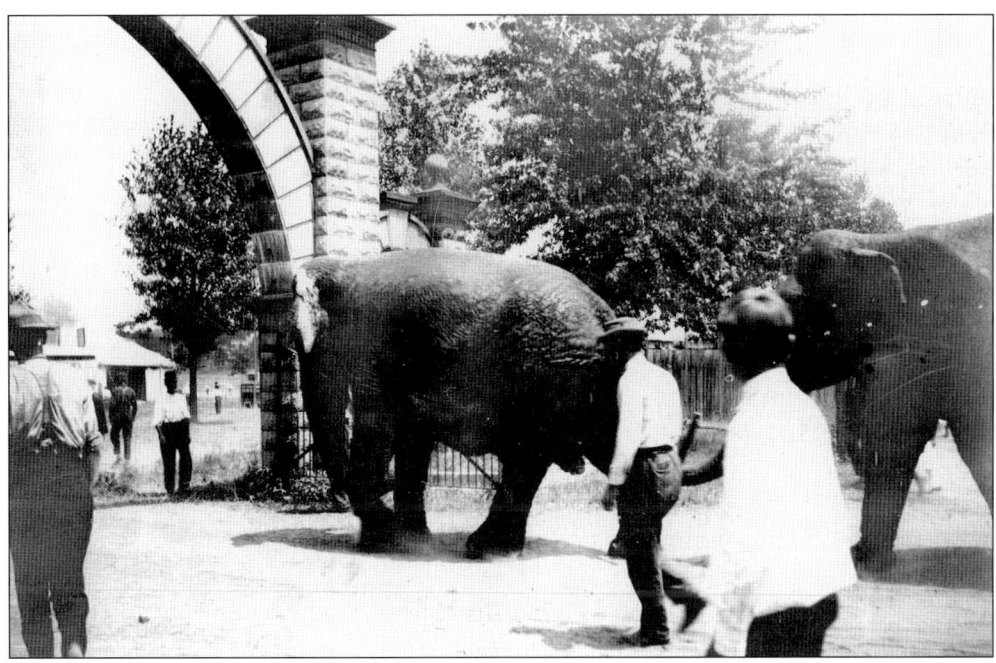
The circus elephants pass through the Dreamland arch at the Wolf's Lake amusement park in 1909.

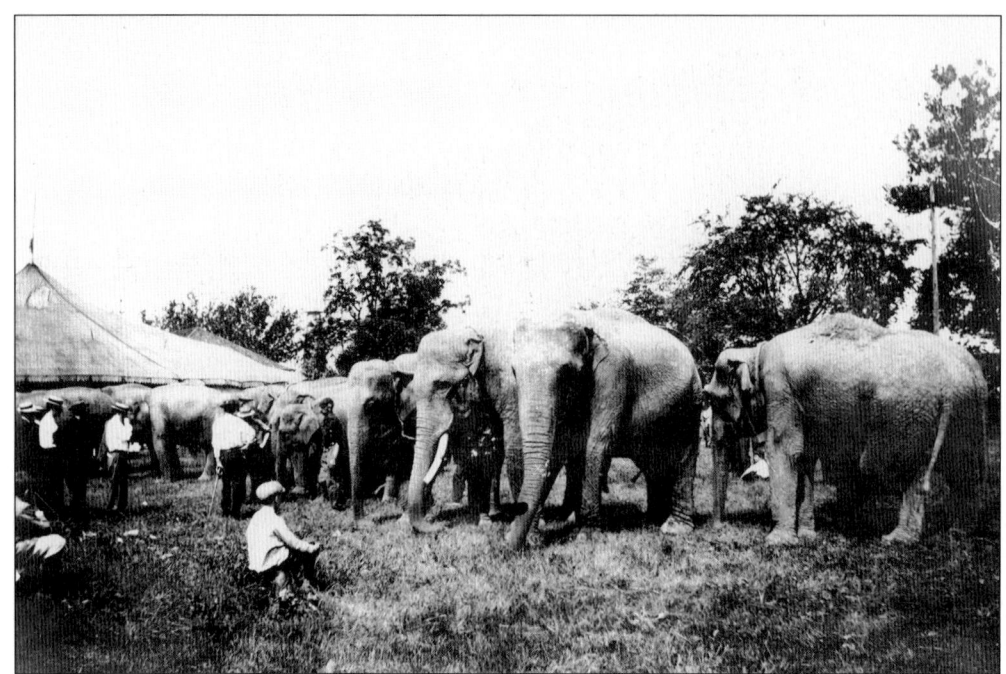
The circus elephants are ready for review at Wolf's Lake in the summer of 1909. One elephant has large ivory tusks.

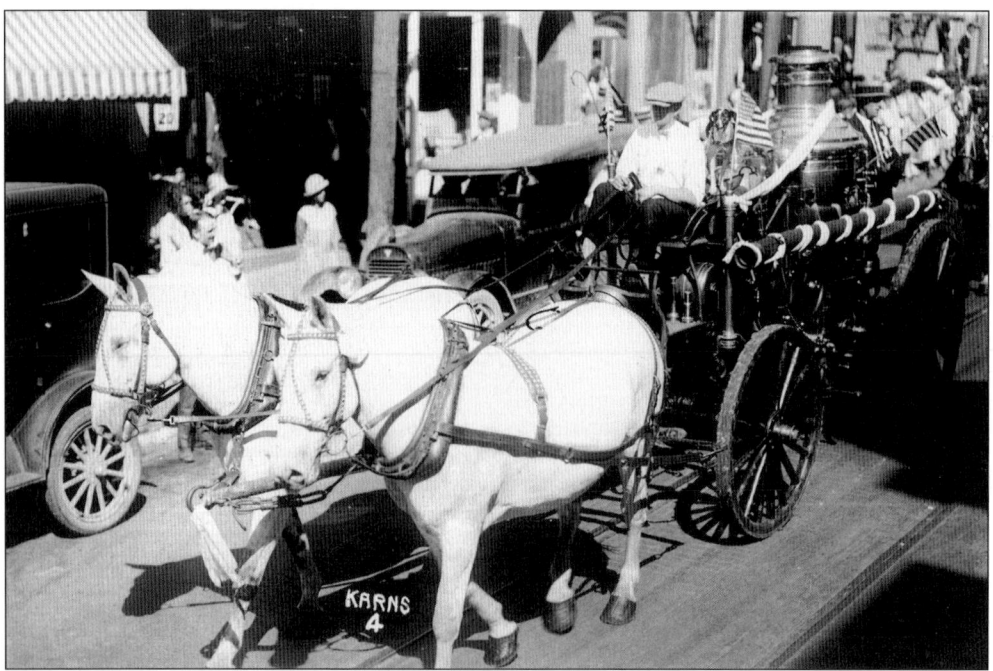
In the 1917 Firemen's Parade, the Cumberland Valley Hose Company No. 5 of Chambersburg heads down Lincoln Way West with its 1903 American LaFrance steamer being pulled by Pat and Charlie, two white horses trained by George Stake.

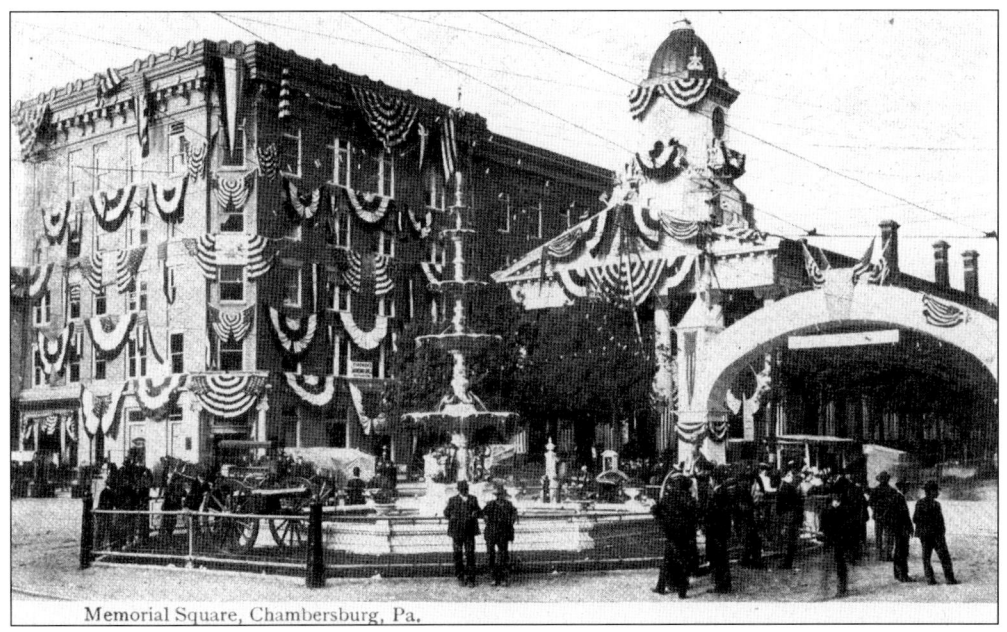

Citizens gather around the fountain during Old Home Week of 1906. Note the authentic Civil War field pieces around the fountain.

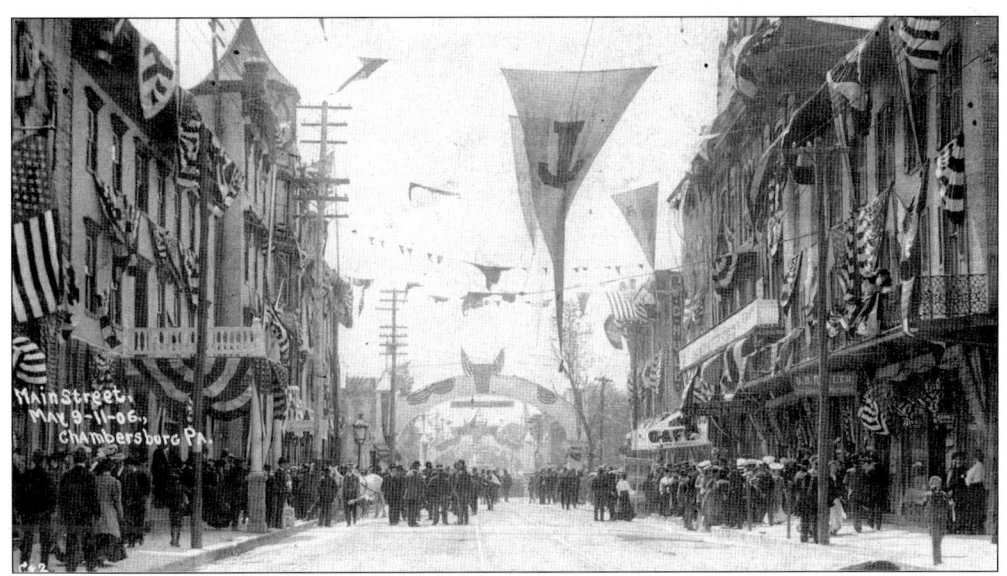

In this view facing Memorial Square, the sidewalks of North Main Street are busy with residents and visitors during Old Home Week of 1906. Flags and banners are being swept about by the wind.

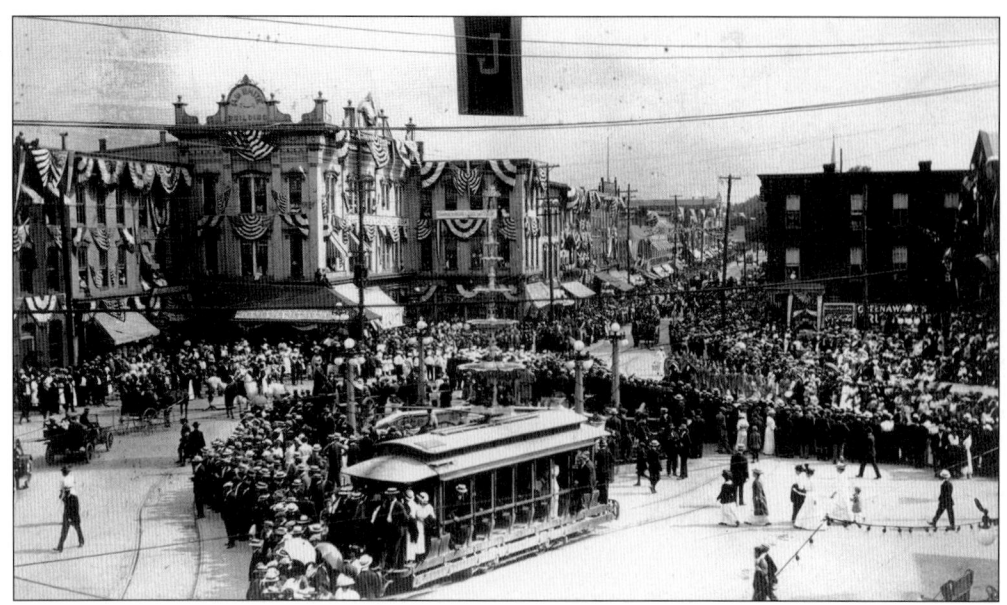

A passenger-filled Chambersburg, Greencastle, and Waynesboro summer trolley car parks on the Diamond for a good view of the Firemen's Parade during Old Home Week of 1914. The sidewalks of South Main Street overflow with spectators.

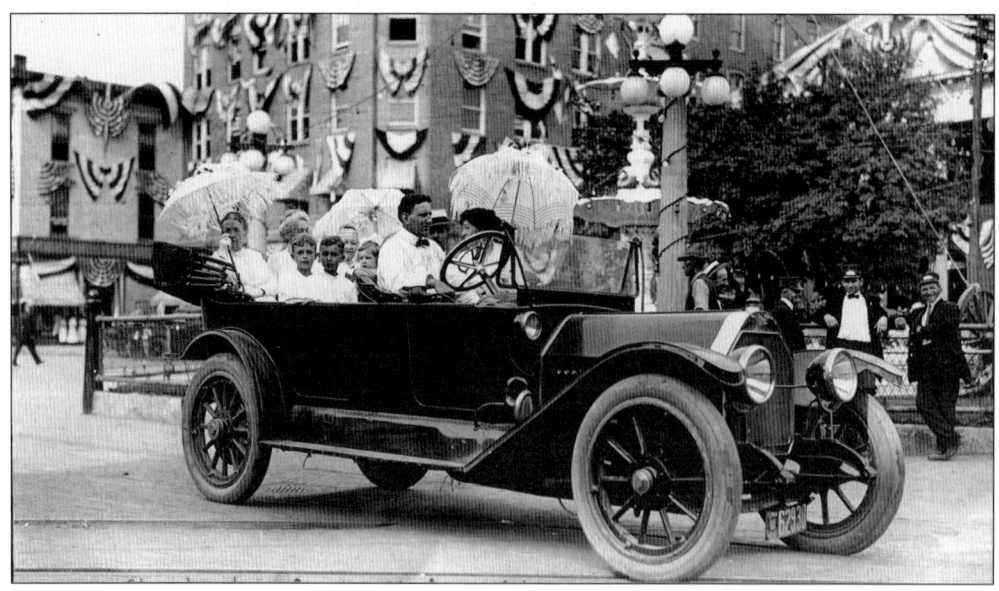

A participant and his family pass the fountain in the Auto Parade held during the Old Home Week celebration of 1914.

THIS IS TO REMIND YOU

That You Are Going to

WOLF'S LAKE
Thursday Eve, July 26

DANCING 8 TO 1:30

Admission 20 Cents.   George Jones, Mgr.

The area's largest attraction for many years was the Wolf's Lake Amusement Park in Chambersburg. This advertisement card was intended to remind the bearer of dancing at Wolf's Lake.

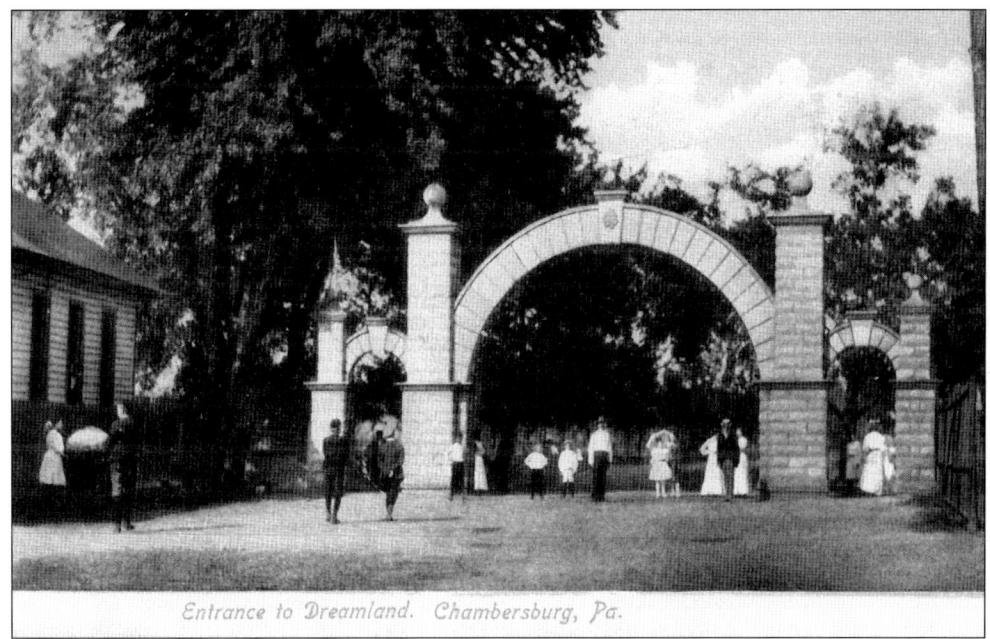

This 1907 view depicts the Dreamland Arch at Wolf's Lake.

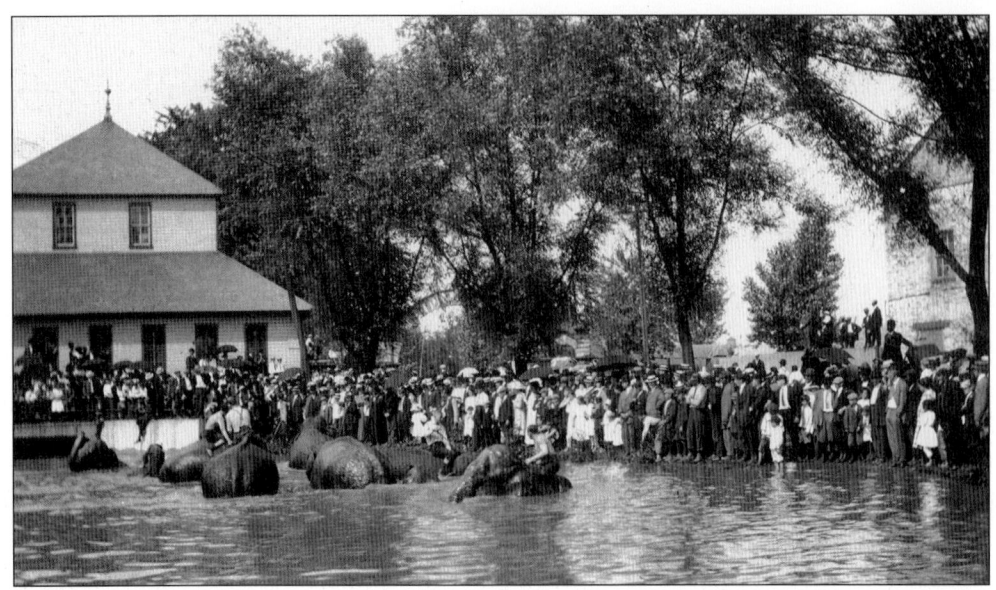
A huge crowd turns out to see the Barnum and Bailey Circus elephants cool off in the millrace at Wolf's Lake in 1914.

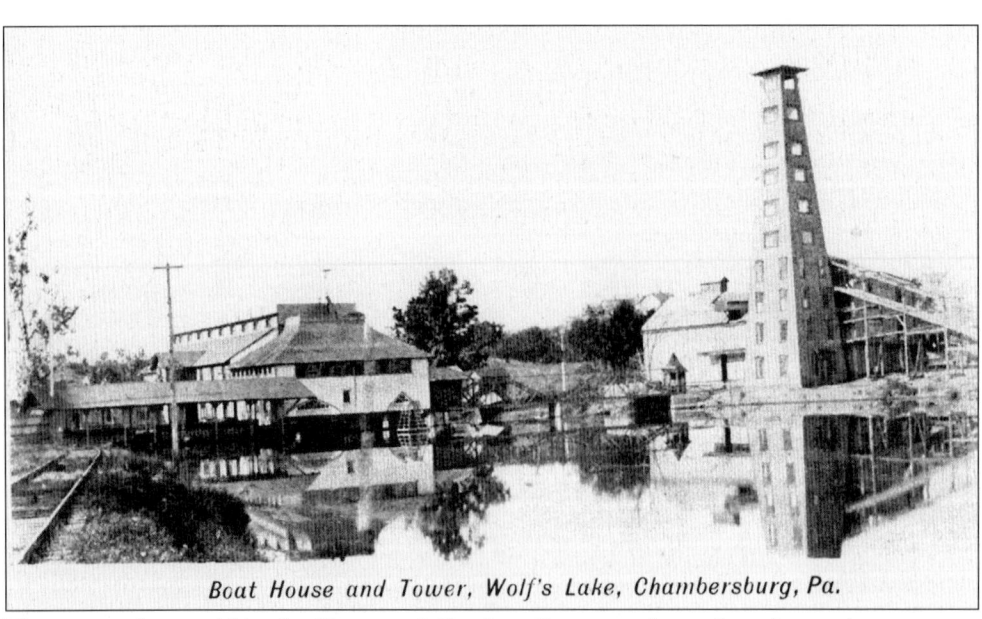
This postcard was sold by the Greenawalt Brothers Drugstore, located on the southwest corner of Memorial Square, in 1906. It shows the boathouse and the 10-story tower at Wolf's Lake.

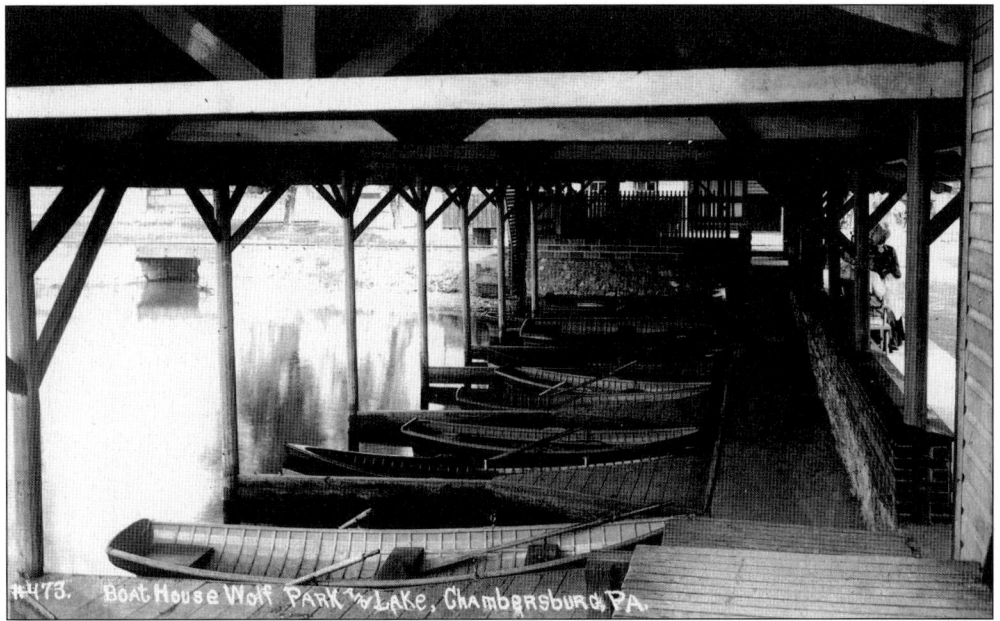
Boating was a popular way to relax in the early 1900s. The boathouse at Wolf's Lake offered over 50 boats for rent in 1908.

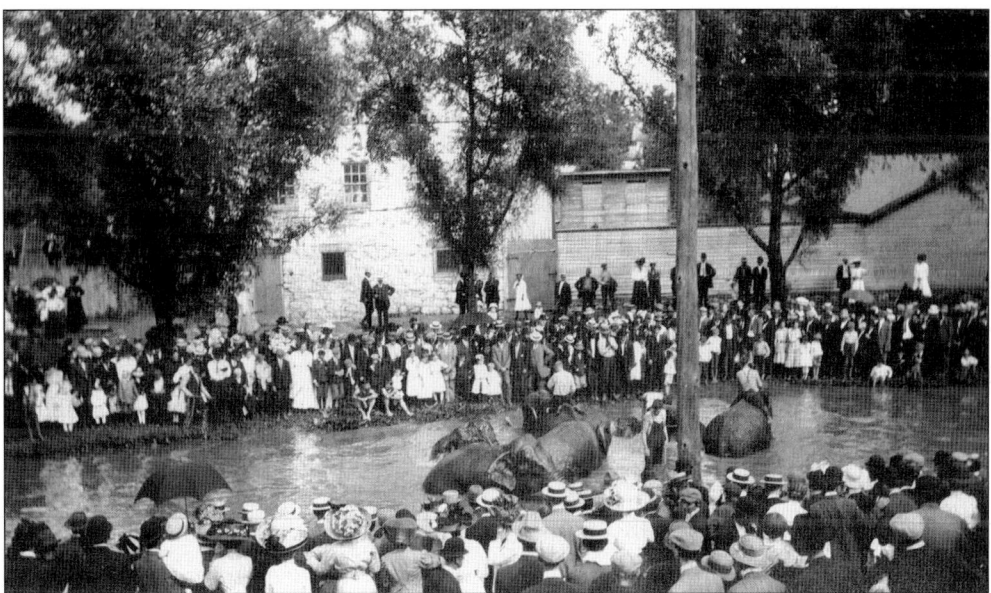
This 1914 view of the Barnum and Bailey Circus elephants in the millrace shows how many adults and children came to watch the elephants.

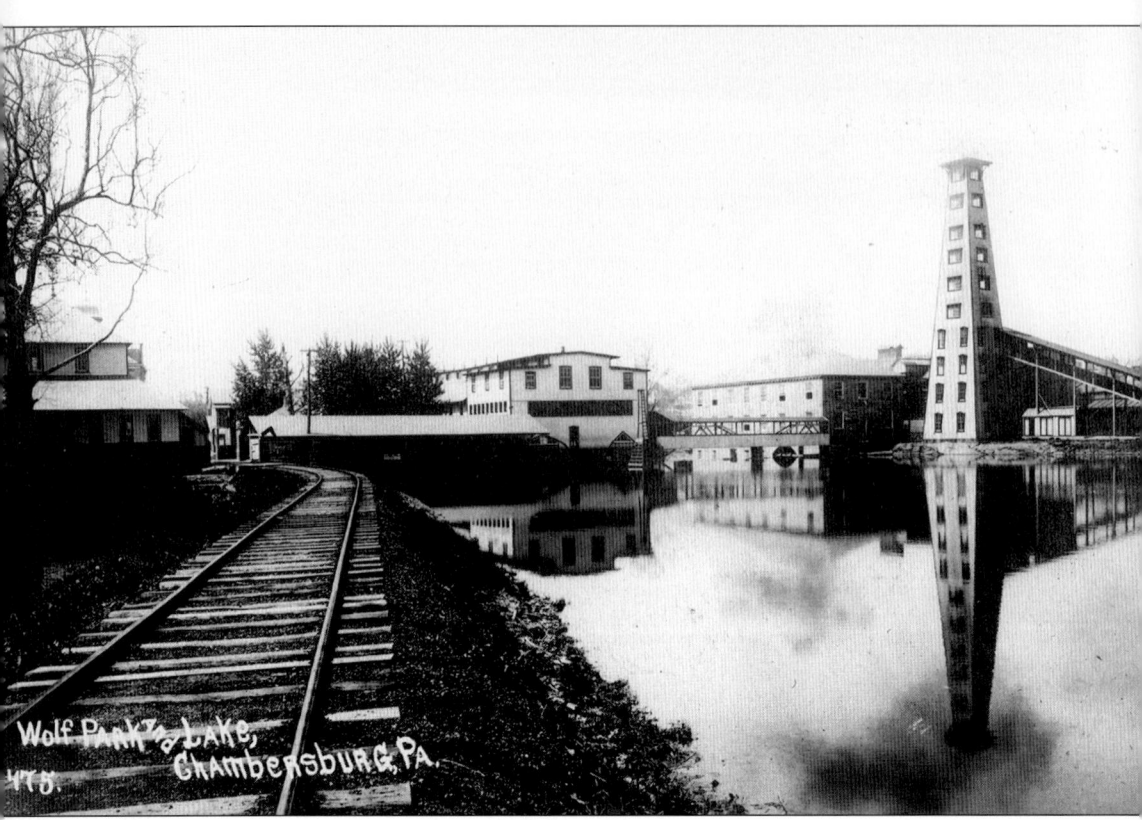

This photo postcard shows the view from the Cumberland Valley Railroad tracks, looking toward the boathouse and tower at Wolf's Lake in 1908. It was manufactured by C. A. Laughlin, a well-known local photographer from Shippensburg.

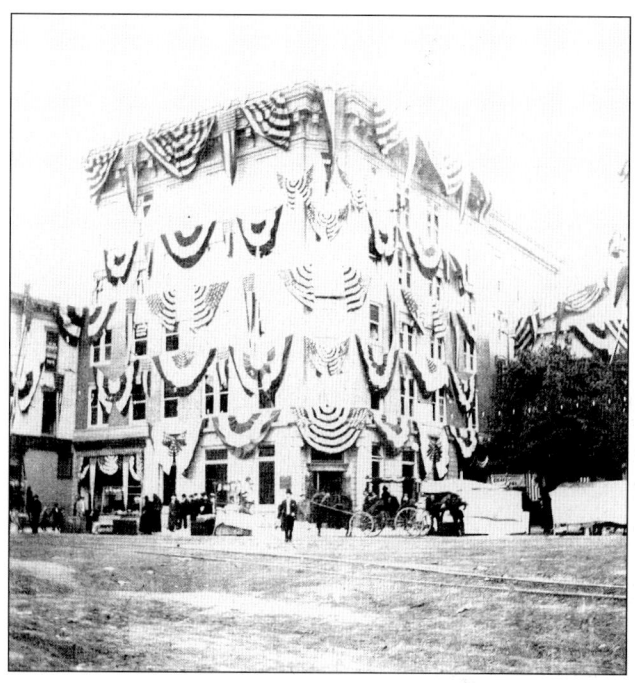

The newly built Chambersburg Trust Company building is bedecked for Old Home Week in 1906.

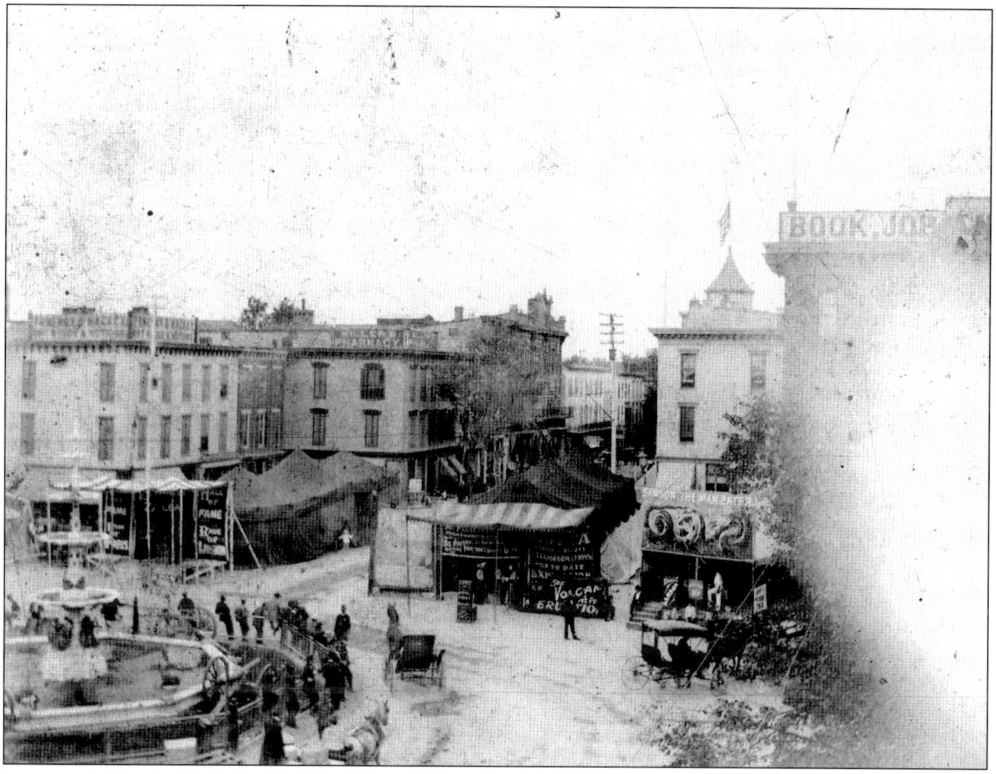

Tents fill the street during a street fair held in 1900. This view was taken from the former White Building (now F&M Trust Company), looking north toward North Main Street.

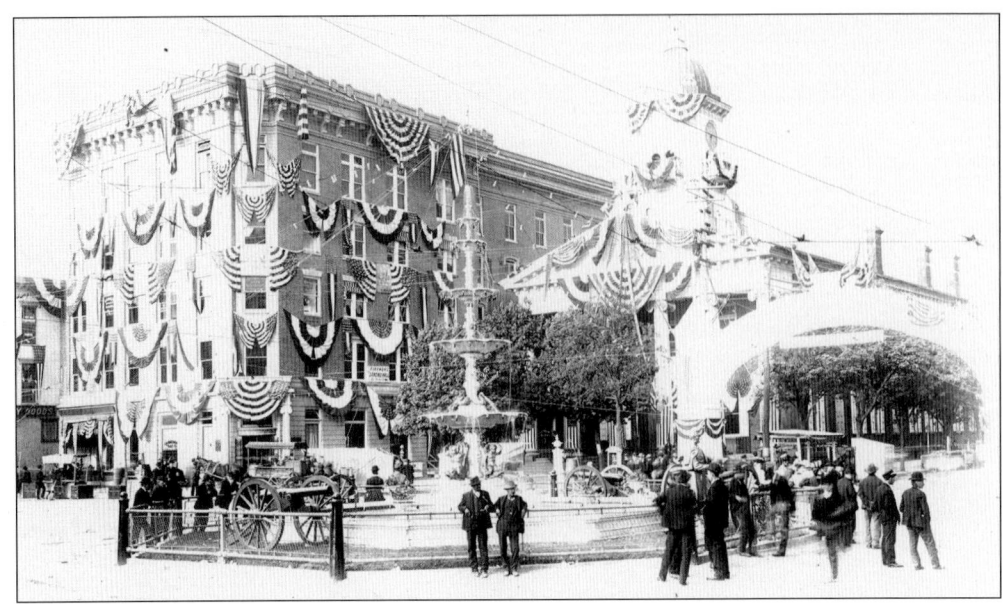

This H. Frank Beidel photograph of Memorial Square shows the newly constructed Chambersburg Trust Company building, the Franklin County Courthouse, and Memorial Fountain during the Old Home Week celebration of 1906. Beidel was a respected local photographer.

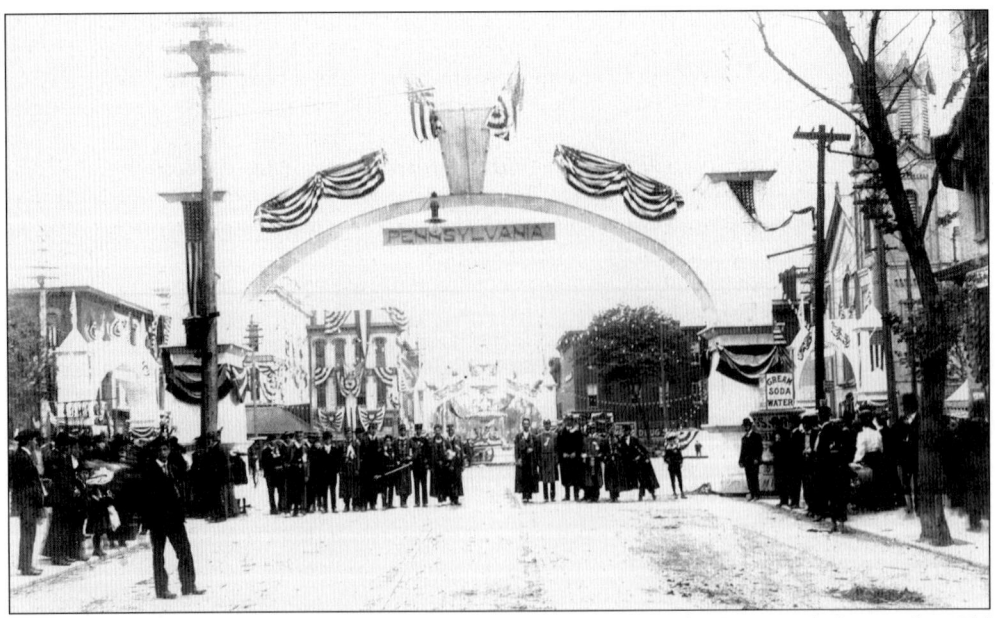

Another Beidel photograph of North Main Street looks into the Diamond during the Old Home Week of 1906. All four wooden arches are visible. Some firefighters are gathered, perhaps waiting for a trolley car.

Five

SNOWSTORMS, FLOODS, AND FIRES

Federal and state emergency management agencies recognize Pennsylvania as one of the most flood-prone states in the country, and over the years, Chambersburg has shared some of that legacy. The unexpected and extreme aspect of nature that manifests itself in extraordinarily fast-rising water levels or massive snowstorms cements itself in the mind. It is difficult to forget water rushing past the Chambersburg power plant or seeping under the doorway of city hall.

Not all events are acts of nature like floods and snowstorms. Great fires also have a similar longevity in the mind. In just a few hours, fires can change communities forever or can rally communities together in the struggle to prevent unwanted destruction. Certainly the Great Fire of 1864 qualifies as such a triumph. Closer to contemporary history is the 1938 Central Presbyterian Church fire, which was contained by local firefighters. The main structure was preserved and the roof rebuilt. The 186-foot-high peak still rises today as a hallmark of central Chambersburg. Be it fire, flood, or snowstorm, larger-than-life occurrences create a marker of time that is retained for generations

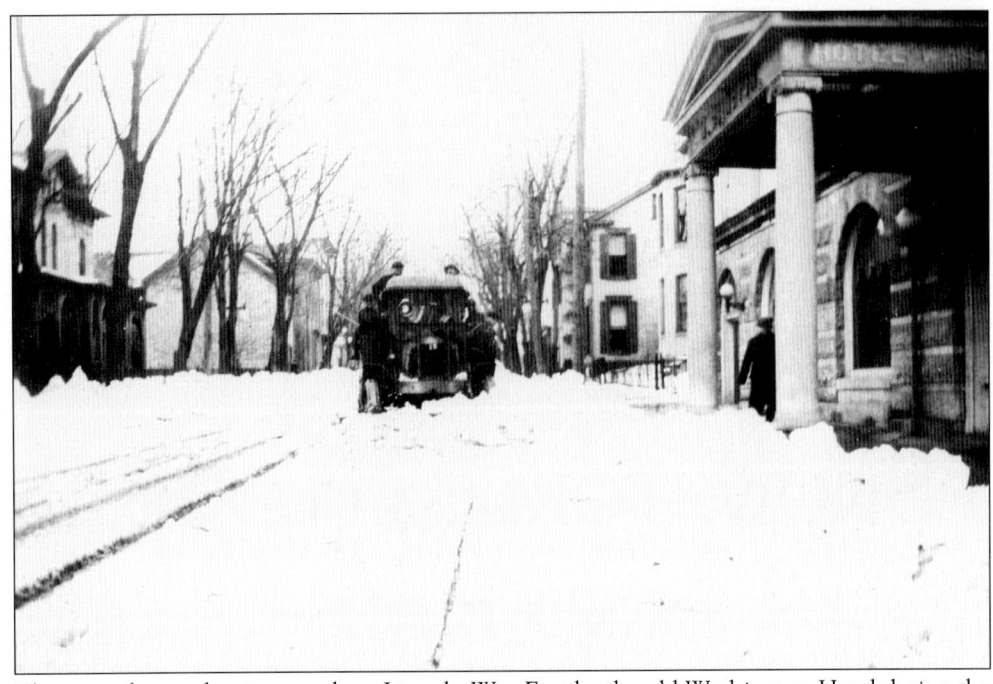

The snowplow makes its way along Lincoln Way East by the old Washington Hotel during the winter of 1914. The trolley car has made a path in the snow.

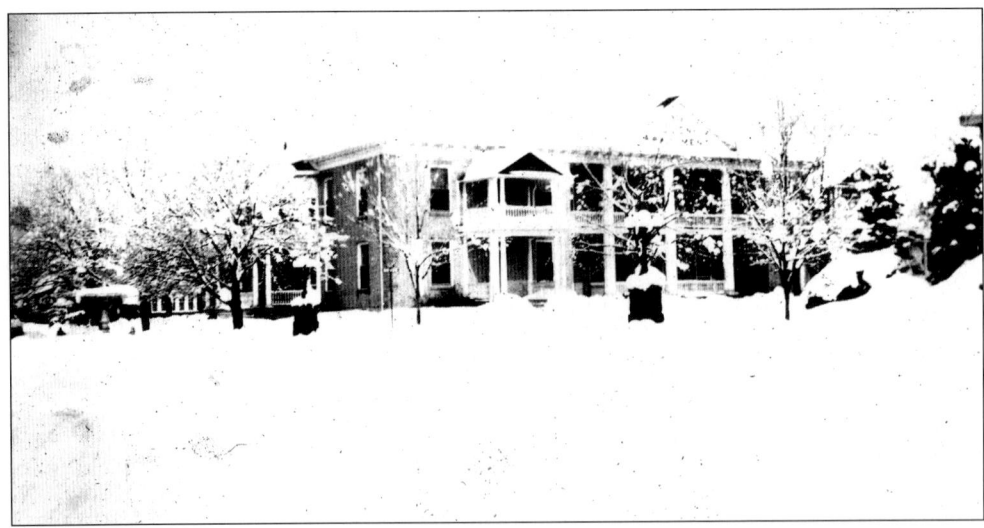

Residents of Glen Apartments on Glen Street appear to be snowed in during this snowfall in 1914. Built by Diederick Allday, Glen Apartments was the first apartment complex in Chambersburg. The Glen Street residential development was also designed by Allday; it featured brick homes, a private sewer system, and electric lines in the alleys behind the homes.

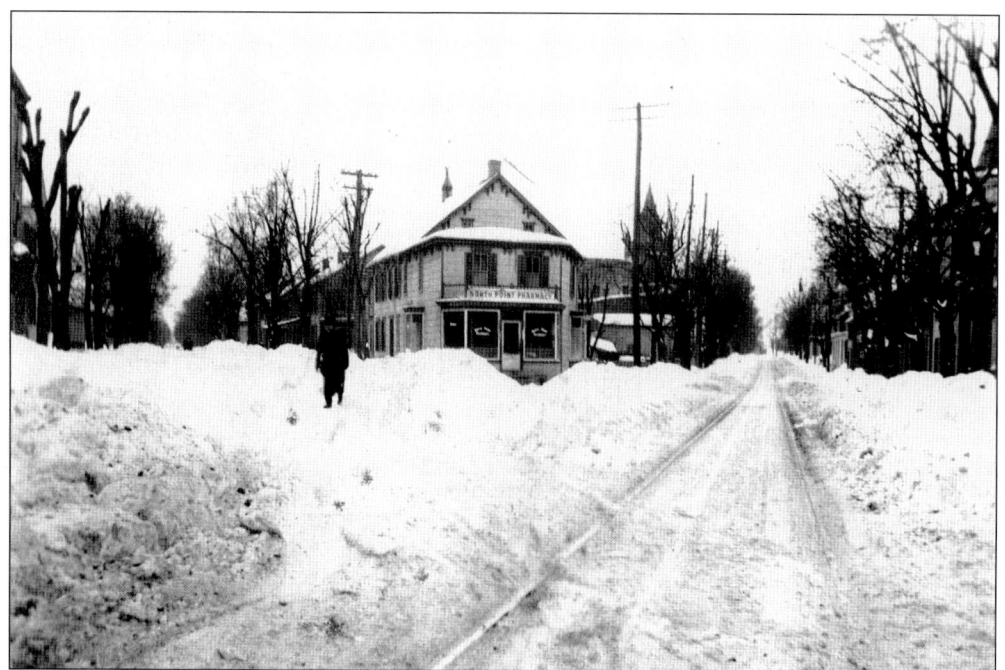

This is North Second Street and Philadelphia Avenue at the north point in the winter of 1914. The old North Point Pharmacy can be seen in the background.

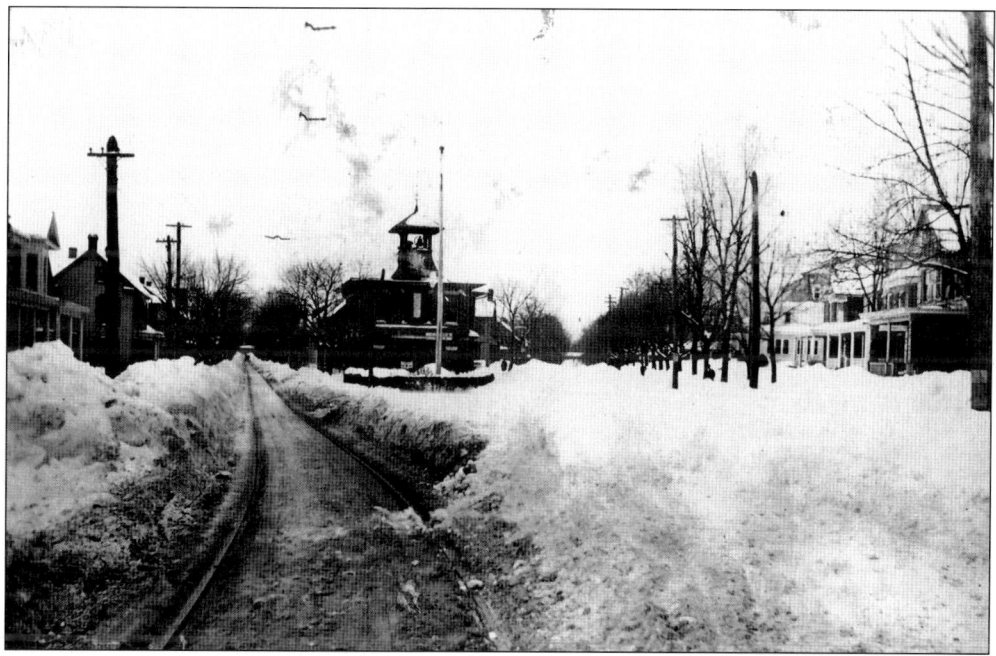

The snowy scene shows the trolley tracks that have been cleared on East Queen Street and Lincoln Way East at the East Point during the winter of 1914. The Friendship Engine and Hose Company No. 1 Firehouse can be seen in the background. This firehouse was built in 1911 as a two-story building; a third floor was added in 1938.

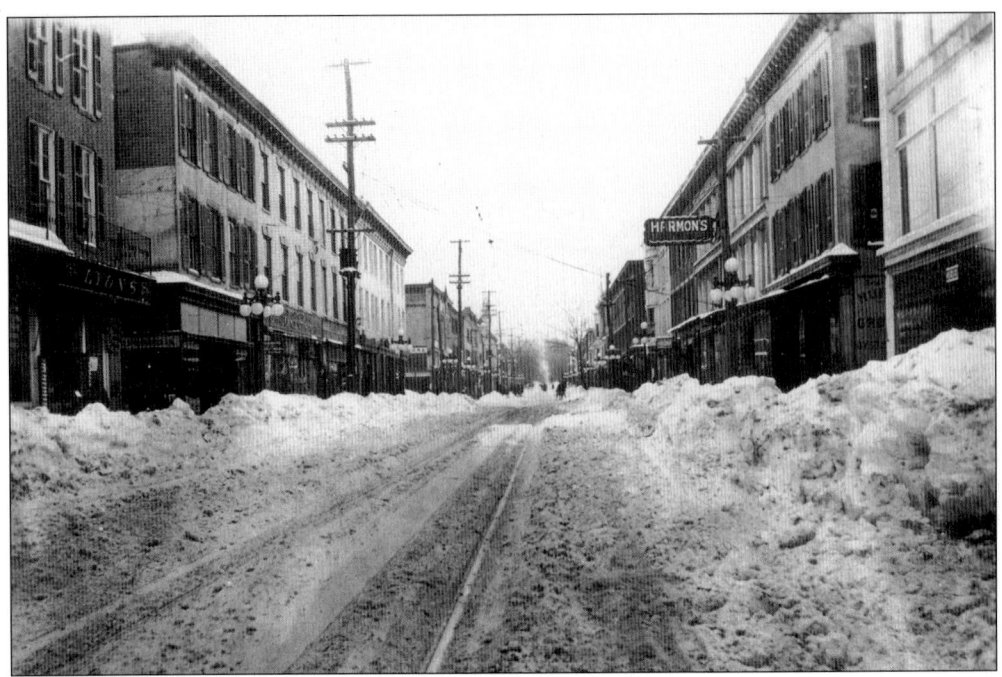

Taken from the square, this 1914 photograph looks down a snow-covered South Main Street toward Queen Street.

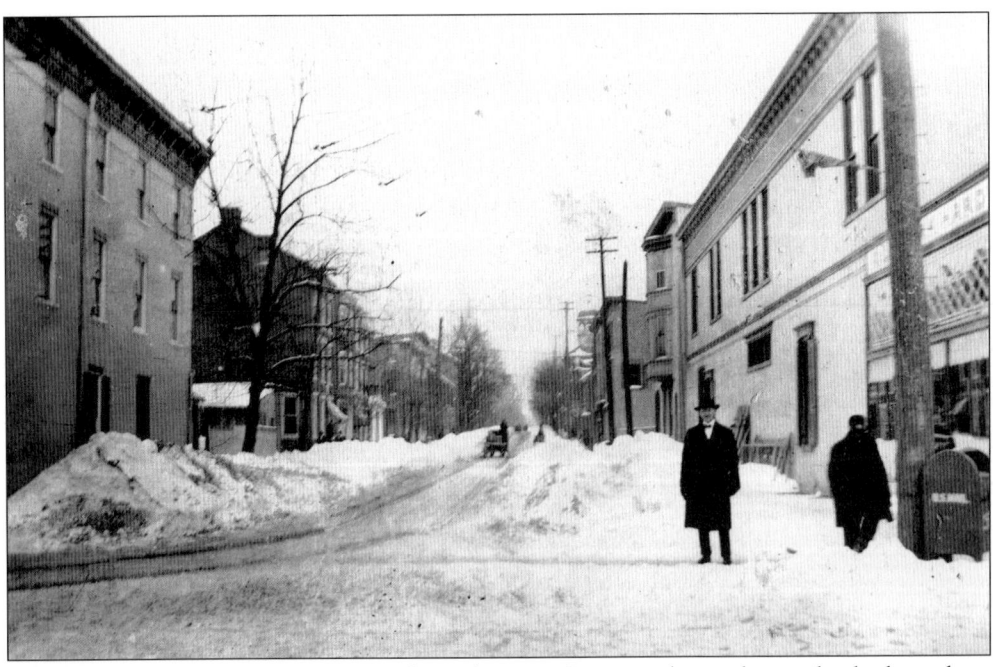

At the intersection of East Queen and South Main Streets, a horse-drawn sleigh slogs along toward city hall in the winter of 1914.

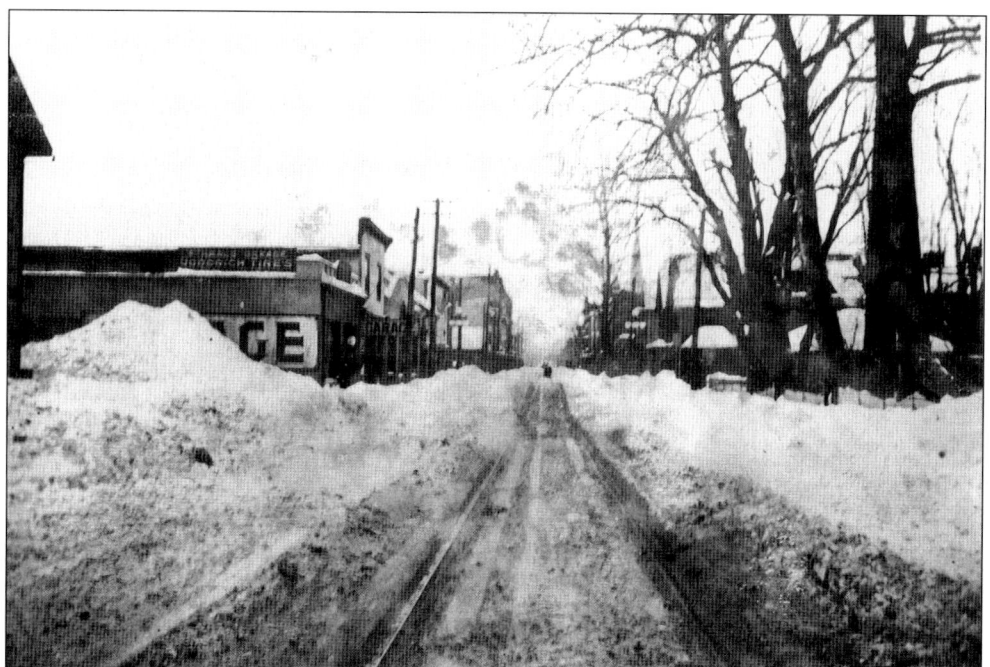

Snow covers North Main Street near the intersection of King Street in 1914. Note Schaals Garage in the foreground and the steeple of the Central Presbyterian Church in the distance.

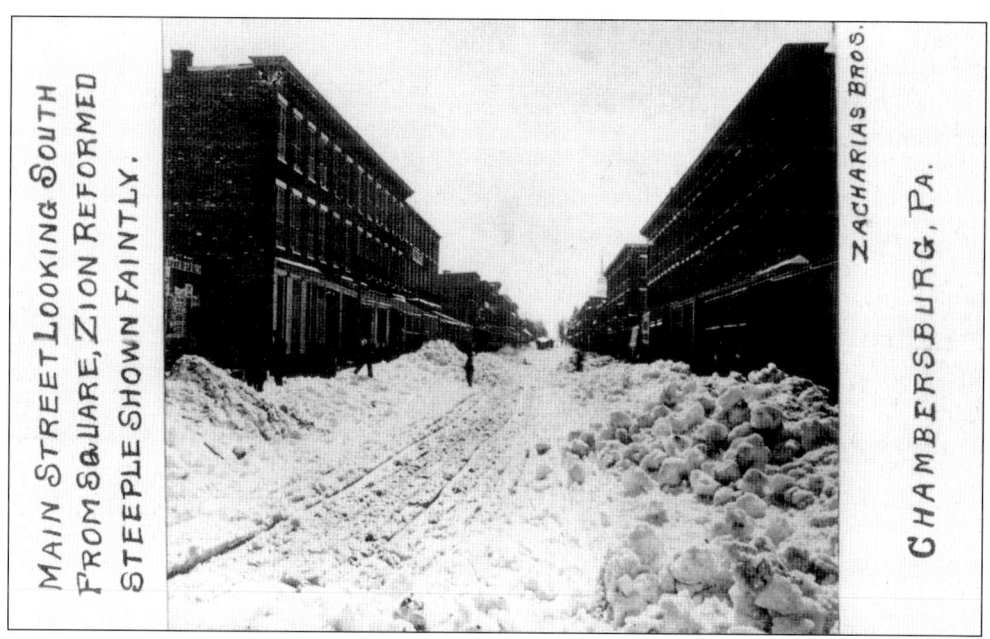

This snow scene was taken from the square looking down South Main Street in 1877. Far in the distance is the steeple of the Zion Reformed Church. This steeple is inspired by the designs of Christopher Wren.

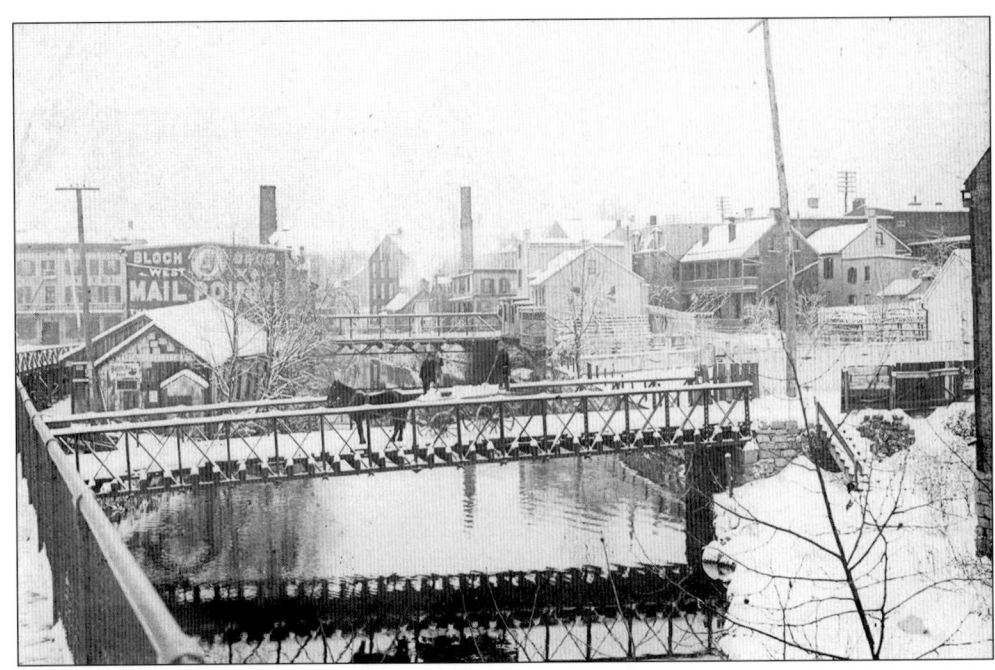

Looking north in 1904 from the Western Maryland Railroad crossing on Queen Street, two men shovel snow into the Conocogheague Creek from the old wooden Burkhart Avenue bridge.

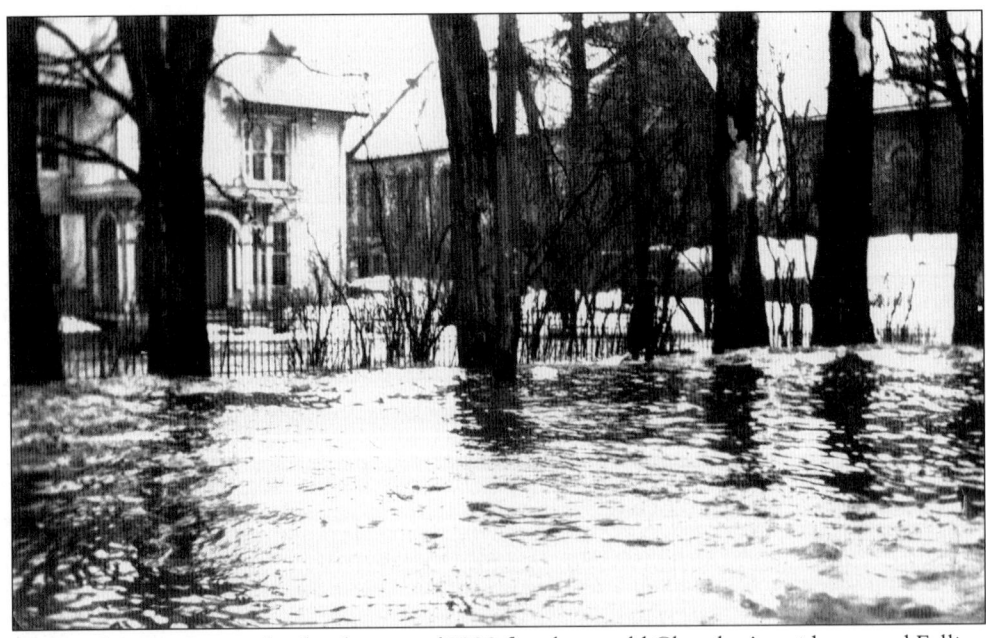

On North Main Street, the floodwaters of 1920 flow by an old Chamber's residence and Falling Spring Church.

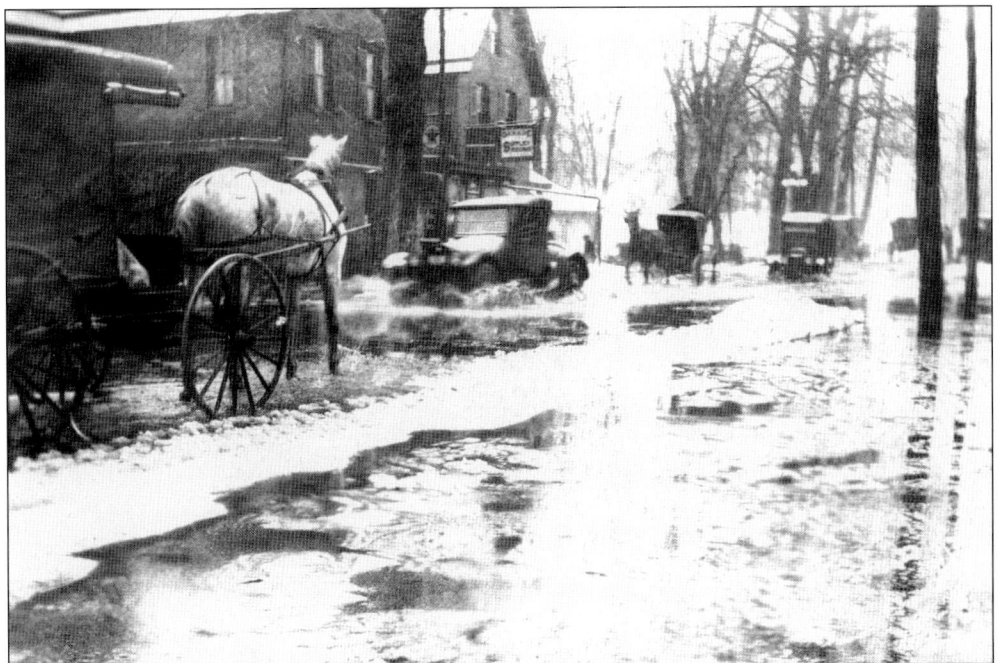

Early automobiles and horse-drawn buggies make their way through a flooded North Main Street in 1920. The scene is in front of the old post office (now Coyle Free Library), looking toward the Falling Spring.

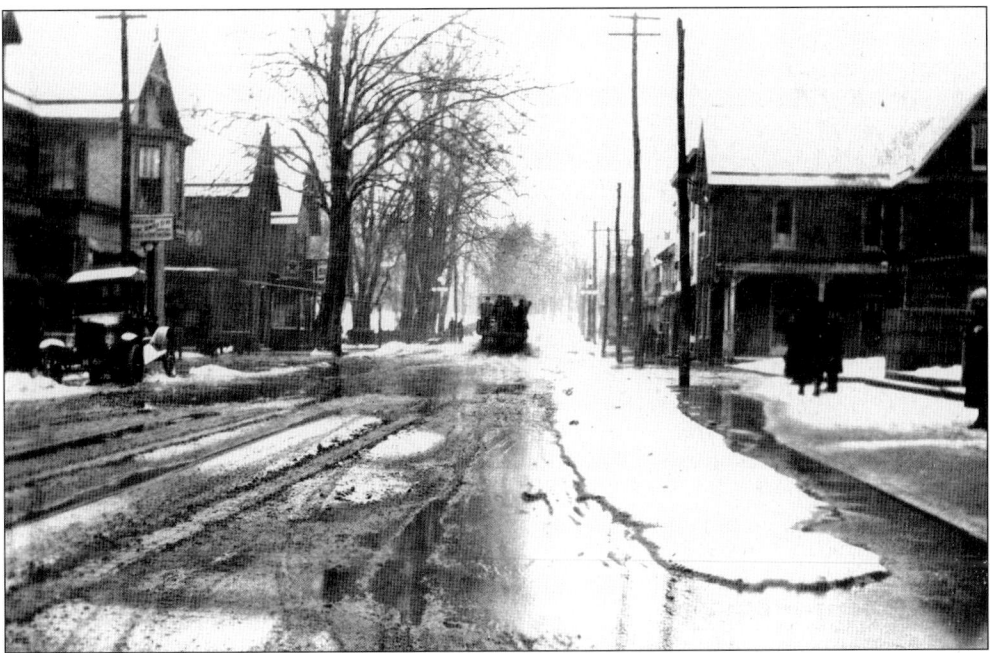

This is the waterlogged intersection of King and North Main Streets during the flood of 1920.

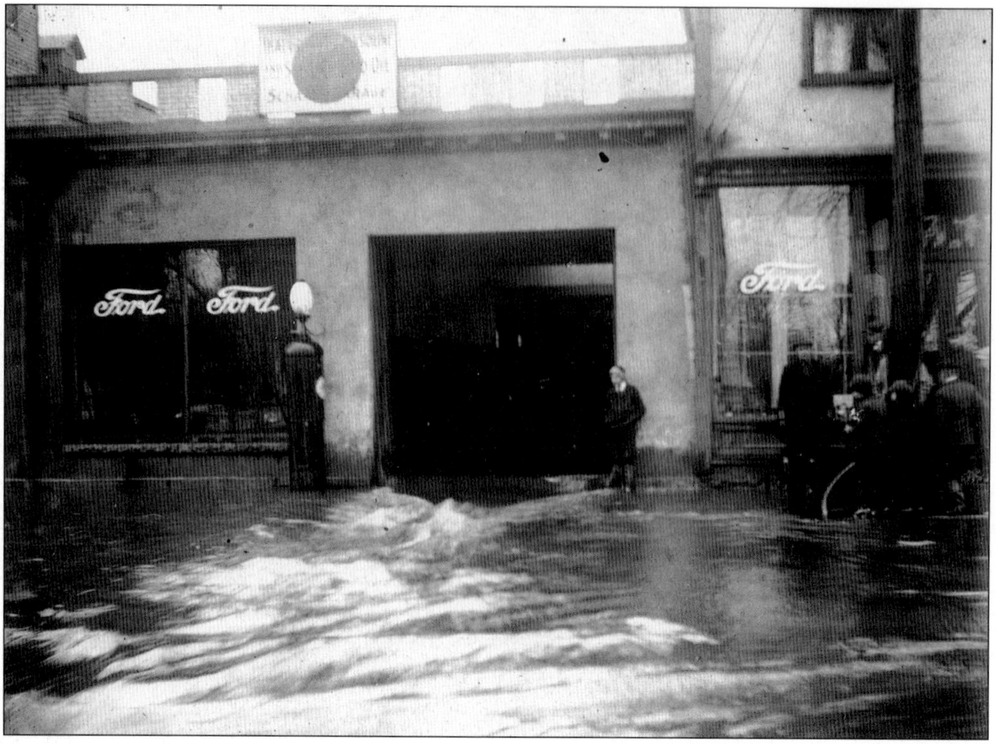

Floodwaters make their way through Schaals Ford Garage on North Main Street in 1920.

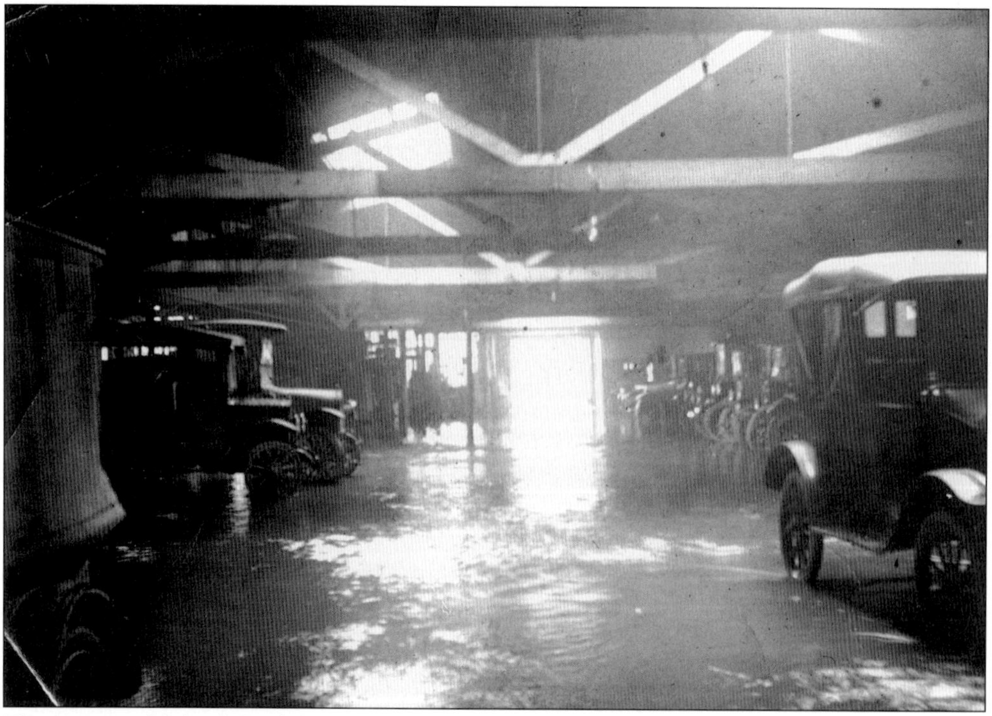

The interior of Schaals Ford Garage on North Main Street is overtaken by floodwaters in 1920.

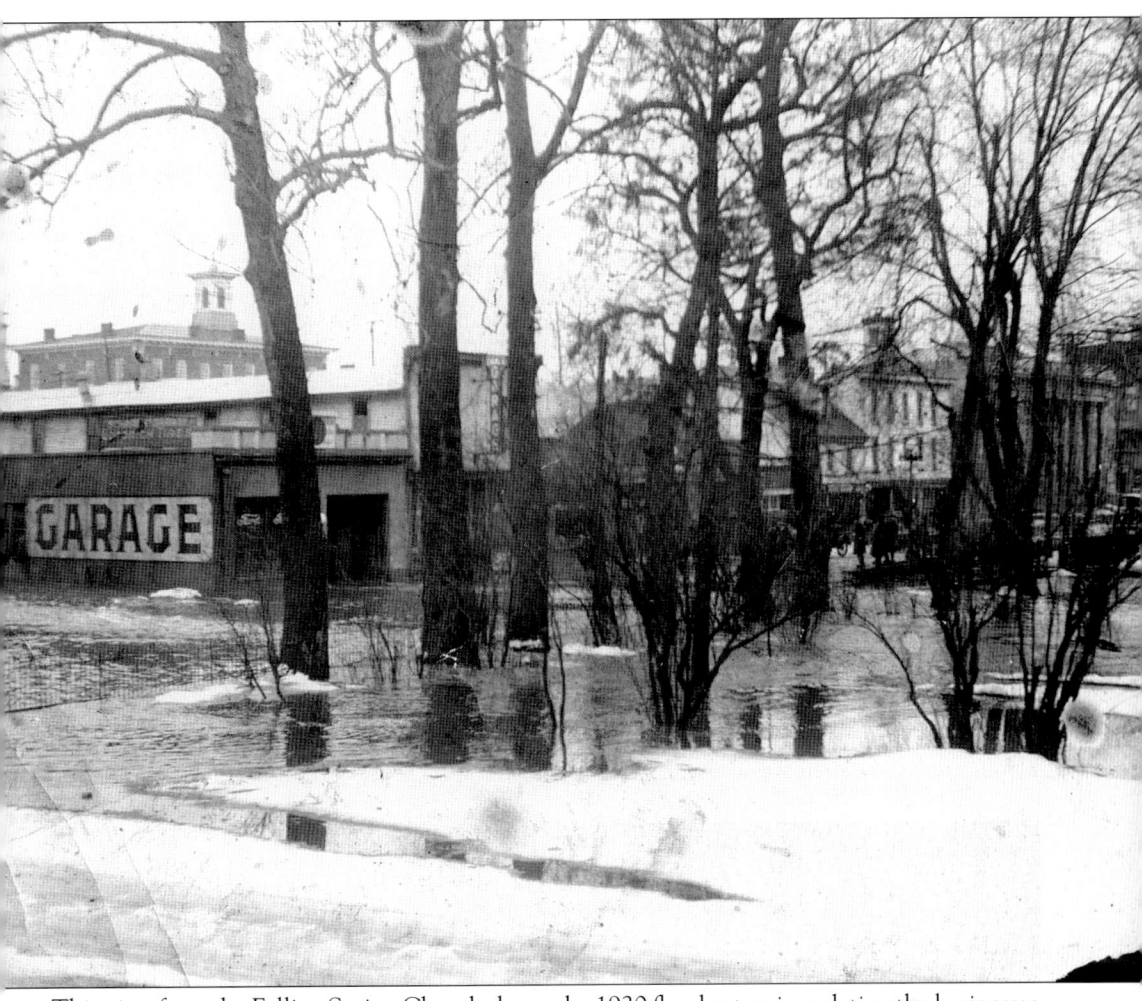

This view from the Falling Spring Church shows the 1920 floodwaters inundating the businesses along North Main Street. Notice the cupola of the King Street School in the left background.

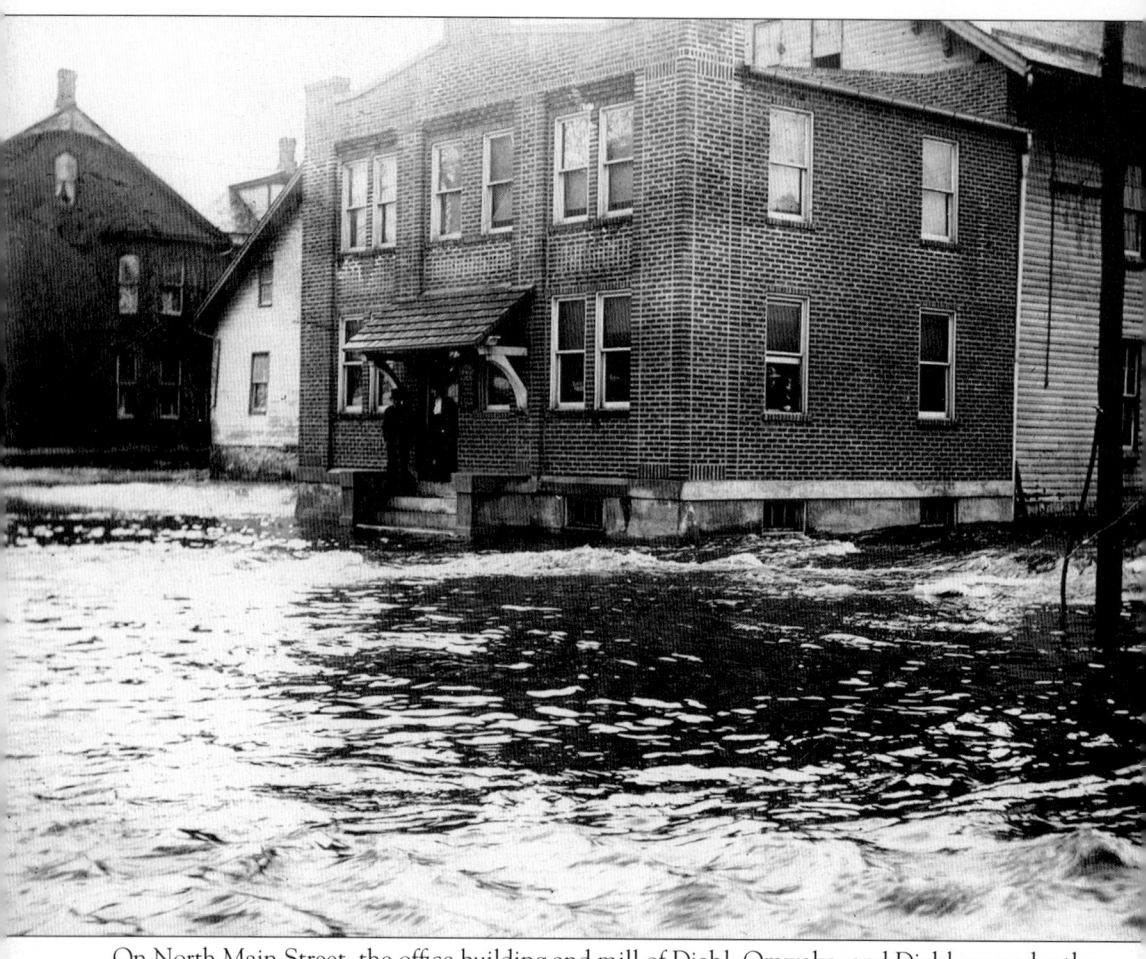

On North Main Street, the office building and mill of Diehl, Omwake, and Diehl are under the siege of floodwaters in 1920. This site was the location of Oakes and Kaufman where John Brown warehoused weapons in 1859 for his planned raid of Harper's Ferry. Brown tried to enlist the aid of Frederick Douglass when they met in the area that is now the Southgate Shopping Center. Douglass declined to participate in the plan to create a slave uprising. Brown was ultimately hung for the treasonous act of attacking a federal installation, but his actions established the differences between the North and the South as inescapable.

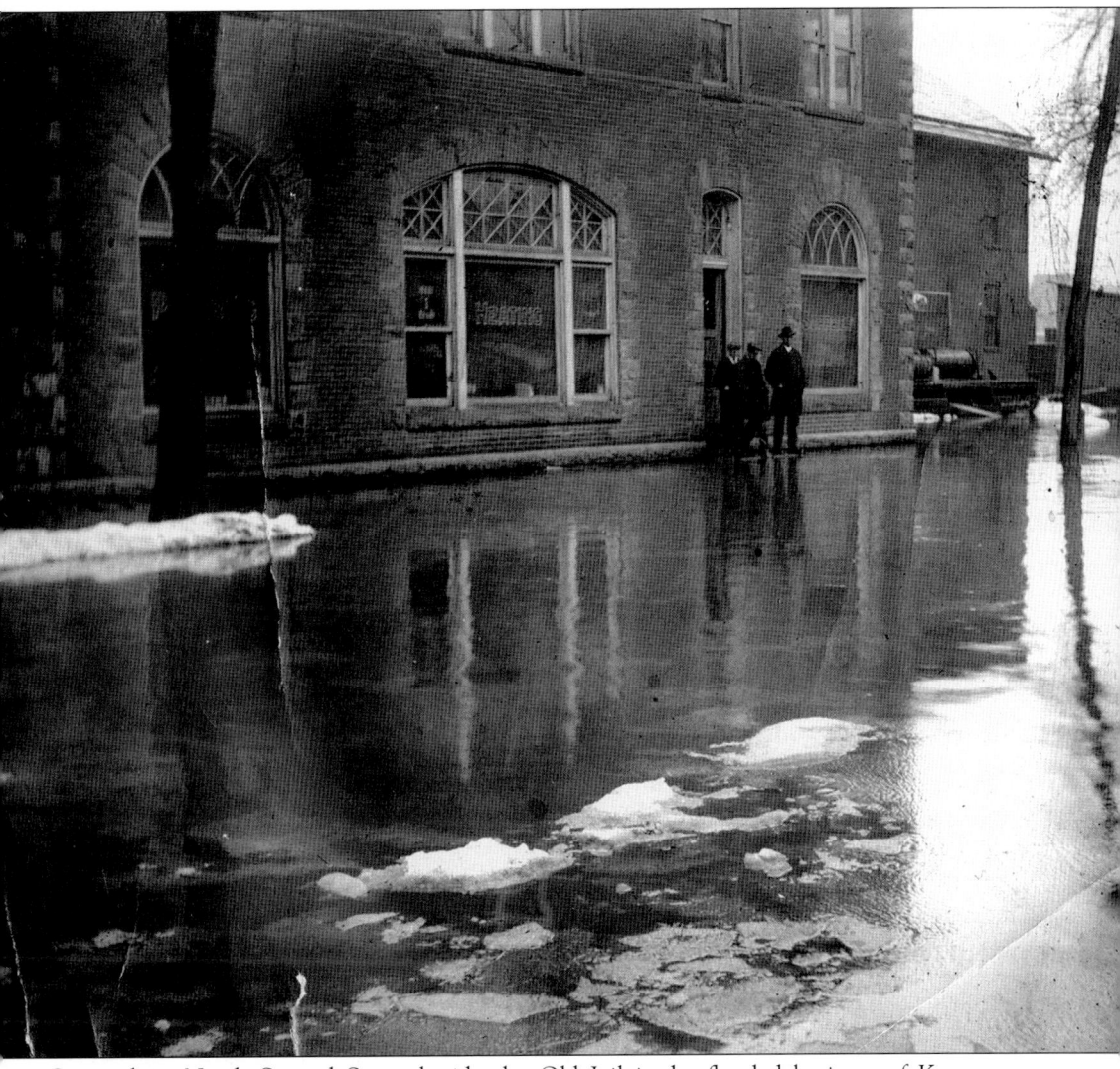
Situated on North Second Street beside the Old Jail is the flooded business of Kottcamp Plumbing and Heating in 1920.

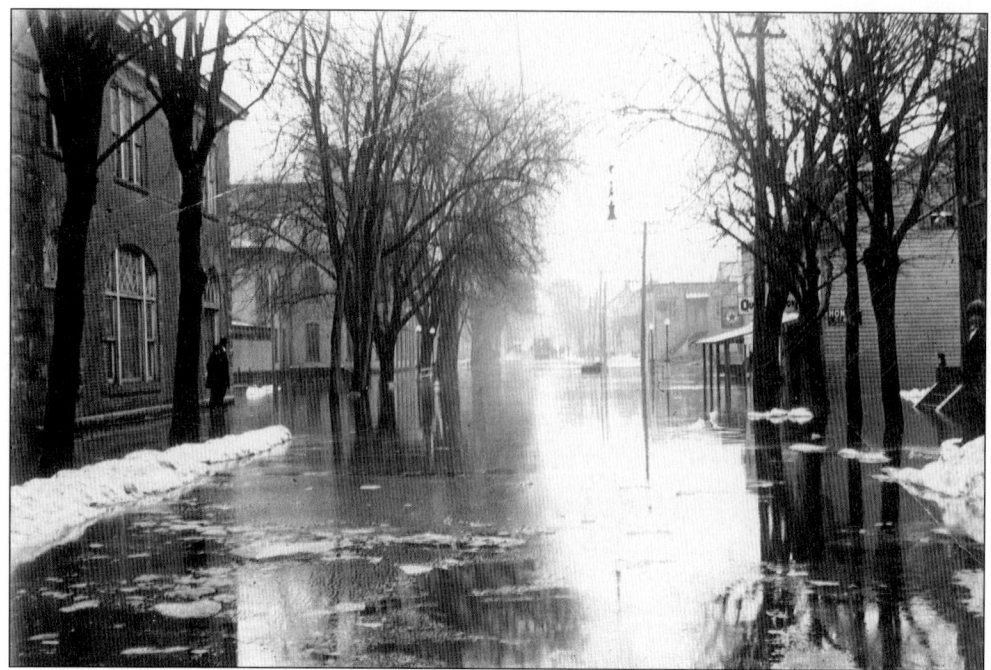

Looking north, this view shows the intersection of East King and North Second Streets and all the flooded businesses in 1920. The trolley car in the distance is at Grant Street.

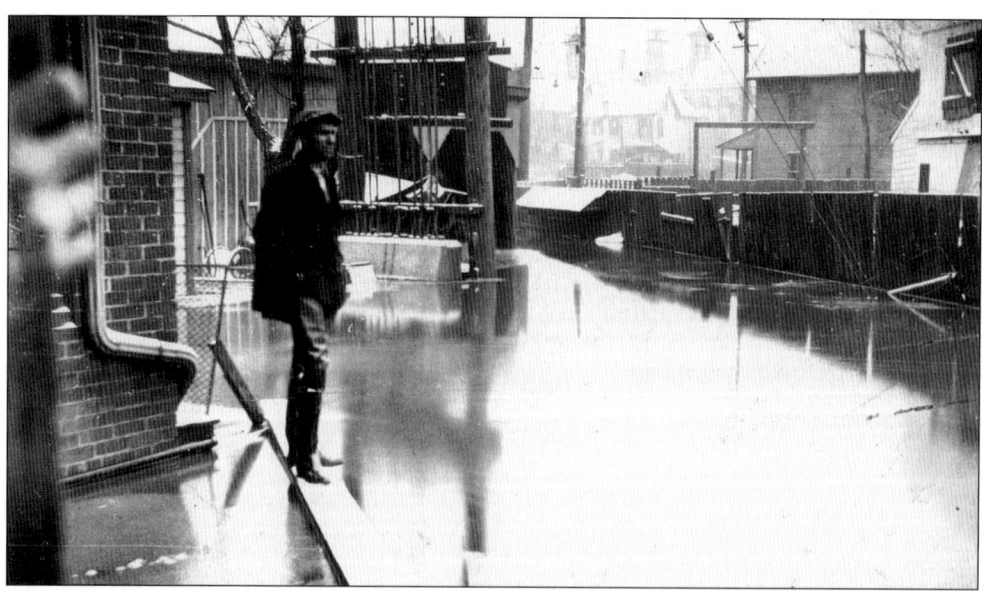

Borough employee B. F. Shaner is shown in this 1920 photograph of the flooded light plant off North Second Street.

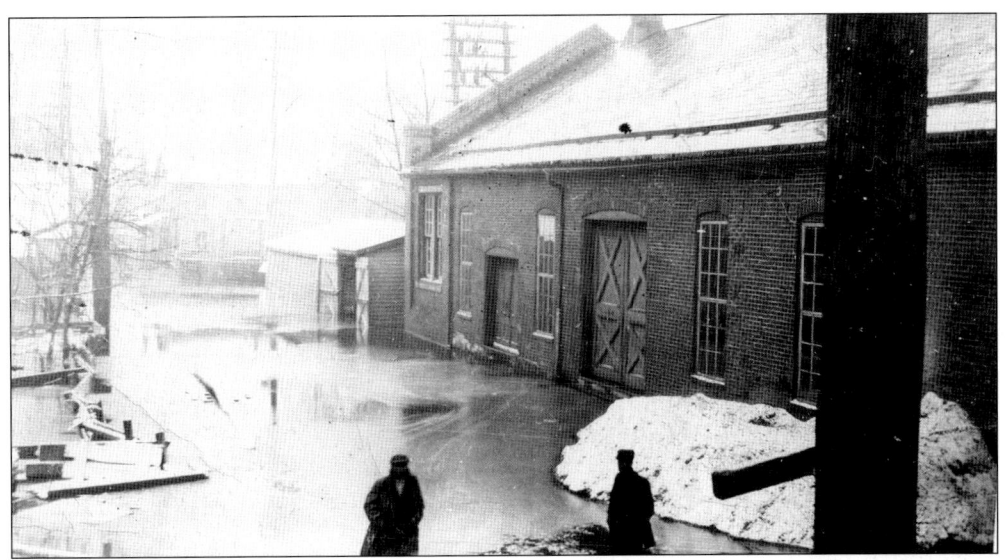

Borough light plant employee B. F. Shaner and a co-worker wade through the thigh-deep floodwaters to reach the adjacent building.

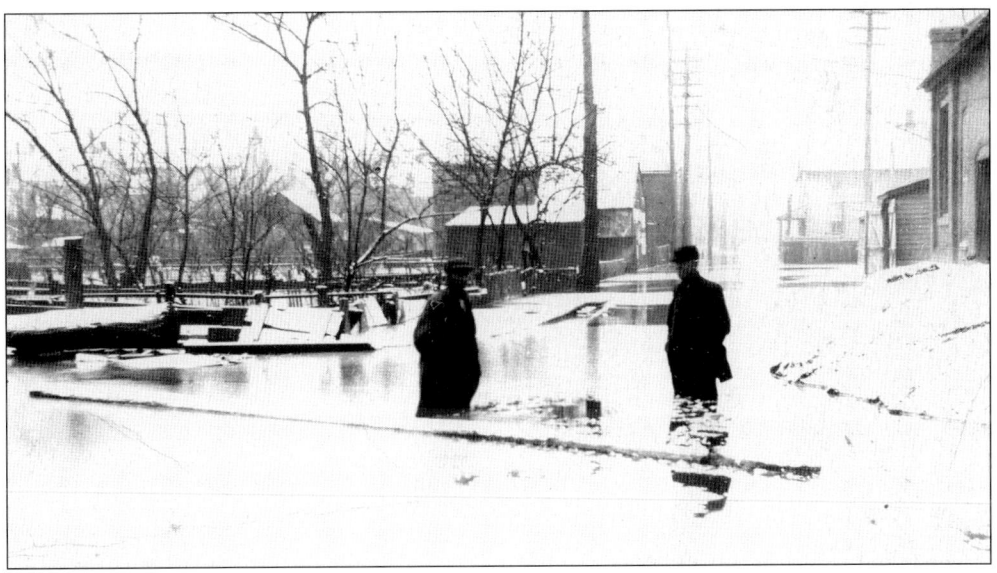

B. F. Shaner and a co-worker wade through more than two feet of floodwaters on Light Plant Avenue in 1920.

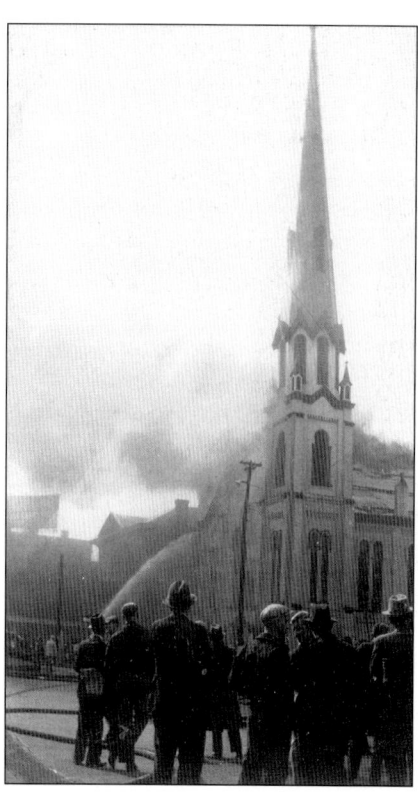

On Memorial Square in 1938, firefighters attack the very destructive fire at the 1868 Central Presbyterian Church as smoke billows from the edifice.

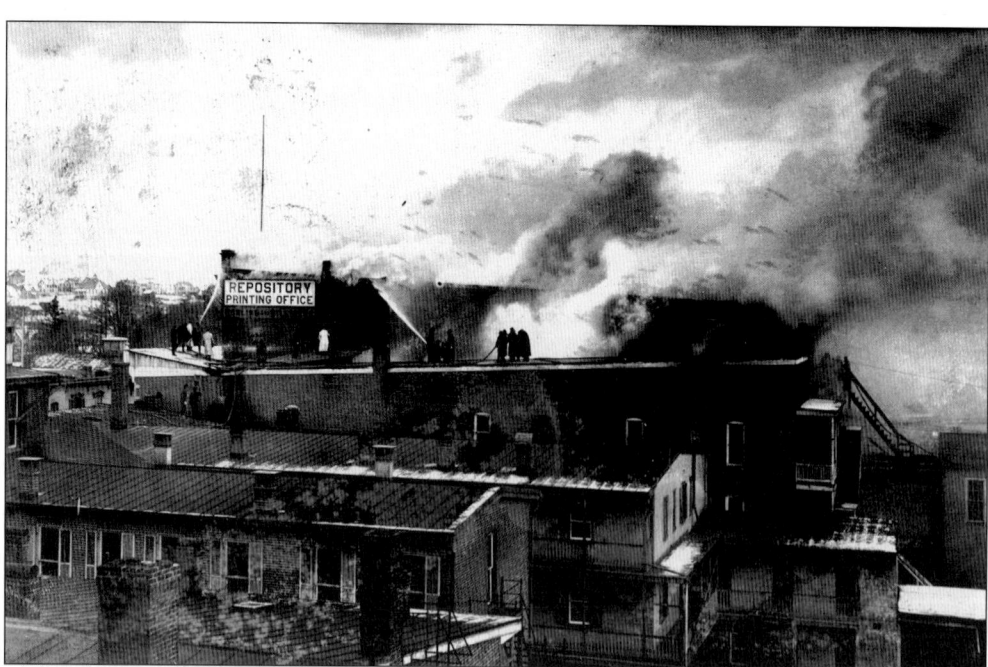

Smoke rolls out of the Repository Newspaper Building in 1909. Firefighters atop adjacent roofs try to contain the fire by throwing water onto the burning building.

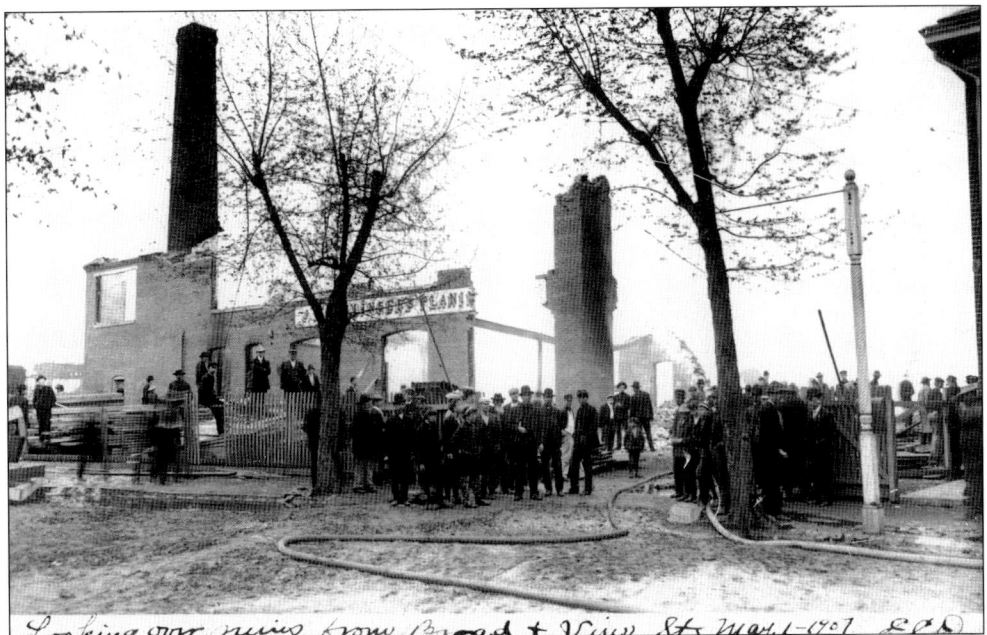

The Hollingers Planing Mill, located at 666 Broad Street, was destroyed by a massive fire on May 1, 1907. Taken at the intersection of Vine Street, this picture shows the remnants of the once prosperous business still smoldering in the background.

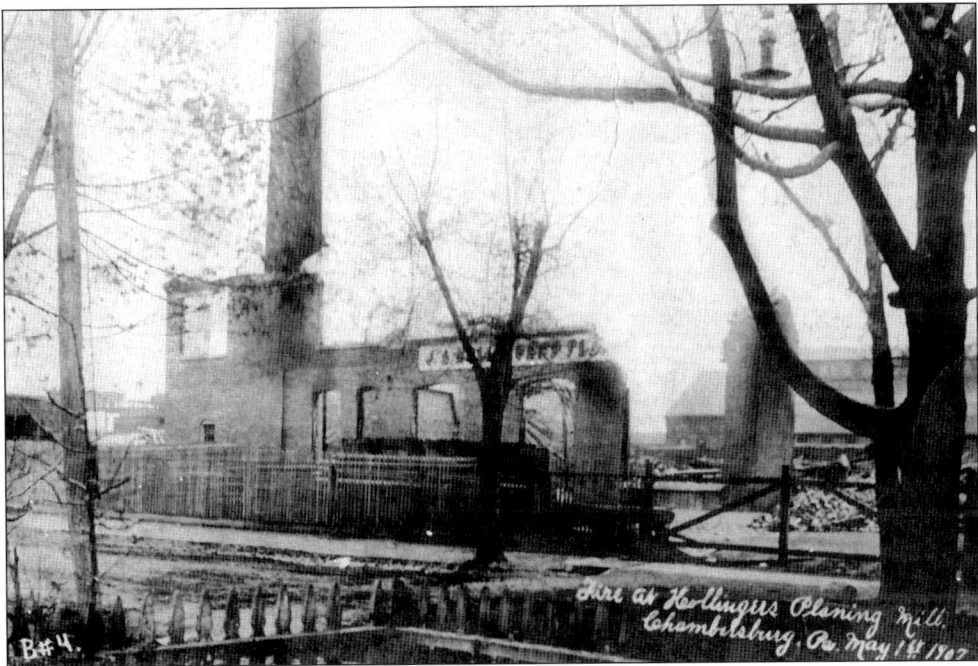

Firefighters and workers have gone. All that remains of the Hollinger Planing Mill and Lumberyard are a few scorched walls.

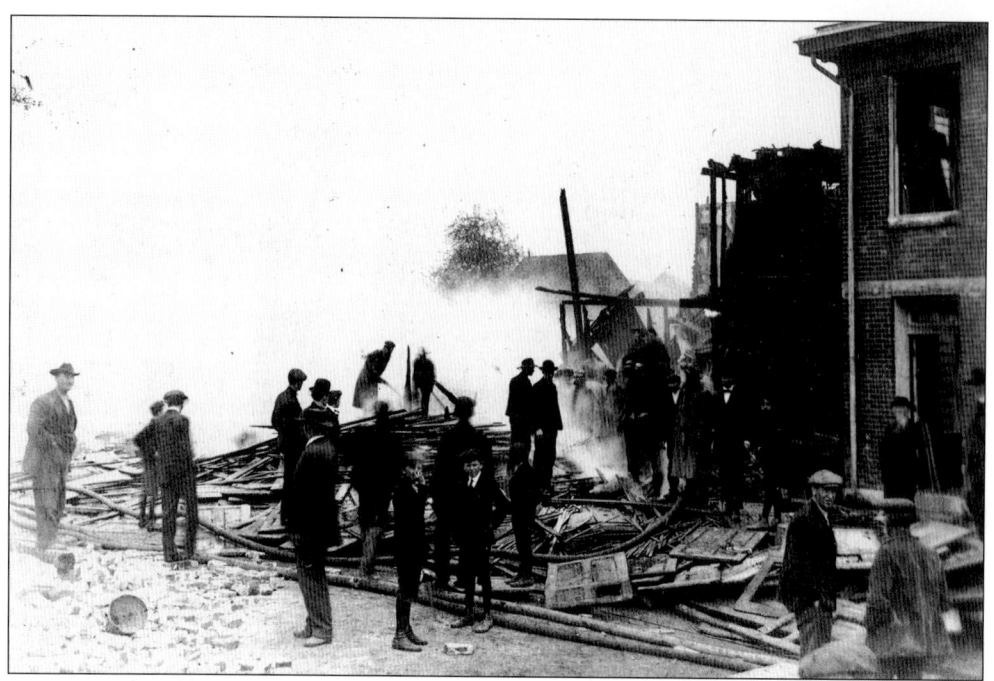
Firemen and Hollinger employees cool down the hot spots left from the fire that destroyed the planing mill and lumberyard. The walls that remain are part of the office building.

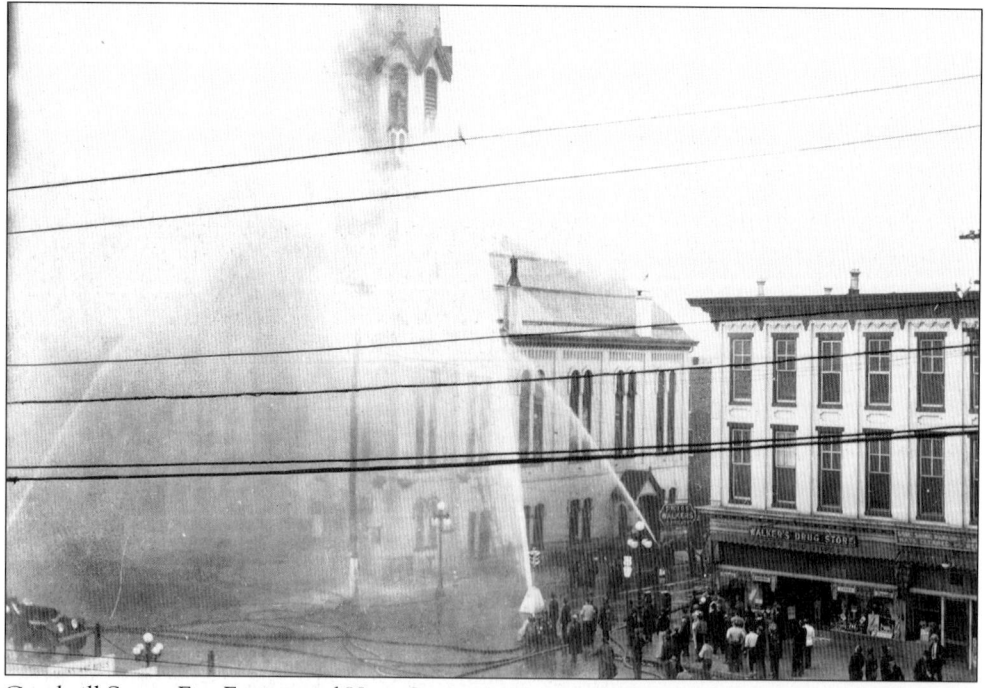
Goodwill Steam Fire Engine and Hose Company No. 3 uses the American LaFrance pumper to combat the 1938 fire at Central Presbyterian Church. The fire was a large one, and many local companies worked together to extinguish it.

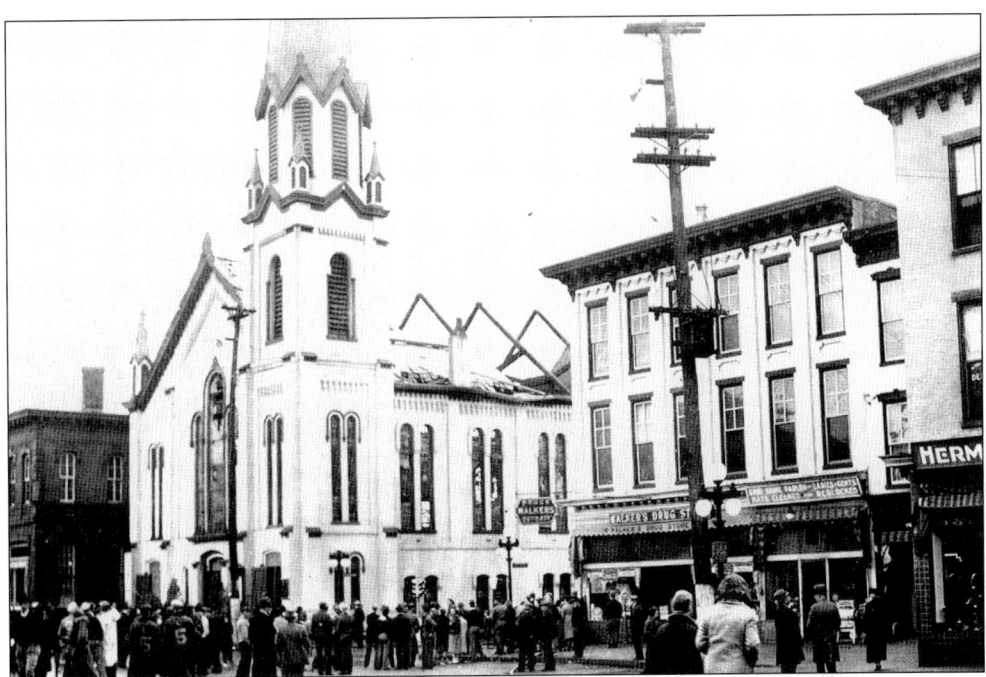

Later in the day, local citizens and church members stare in disbelief at the destruction.

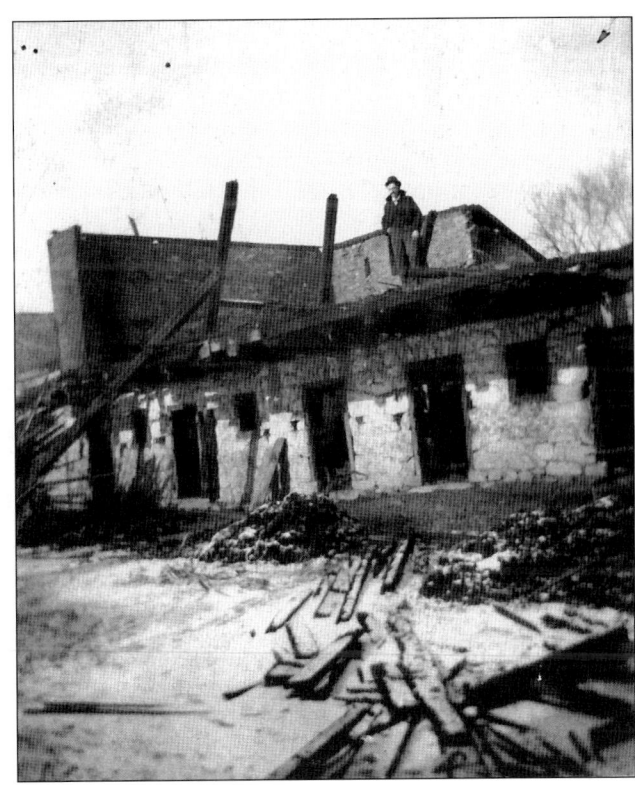

Pictured are the remains of the Linn barn after an extensive fire the on January 3, 1896. G. Fred Gibbs, chief engineer of the Chambersburg Fire Department, retired after this fire. At this same sight in 1899, Augustus Wolf built the Wolf Company.

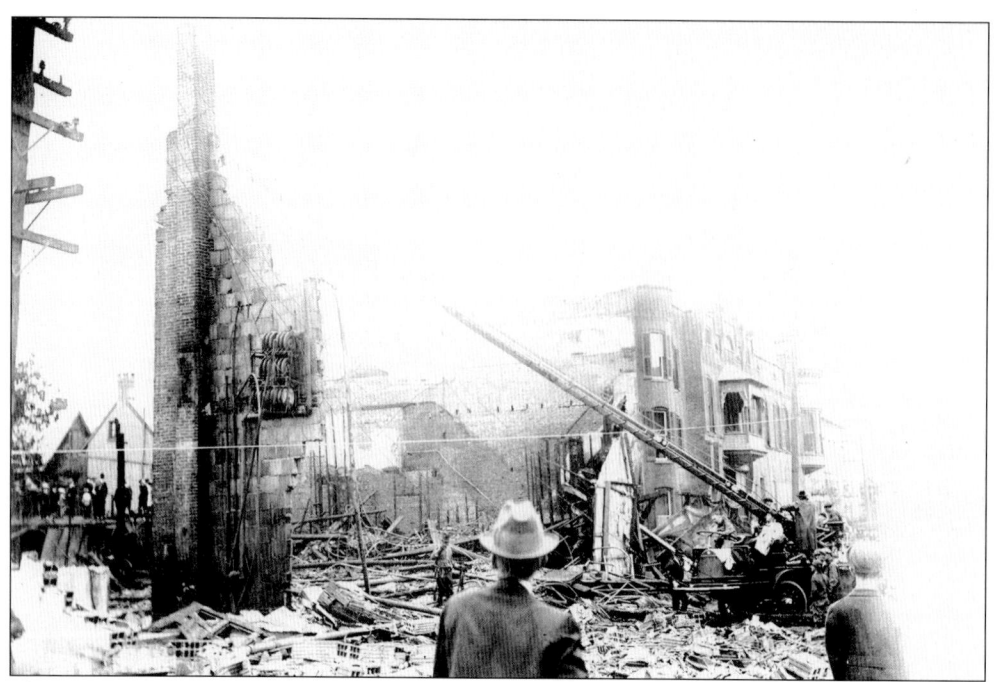

The Junior Hose and Truck Company No. 2 uses a 1917 Seagrave 65-foot ladder truck to try to battle the fire at the Orpheum Theatre on West King Street. Fire prevailed, and the Orpheum Theatre was destroyed in 1920. Today McCleary Oil Company is located at the site of the former theater.

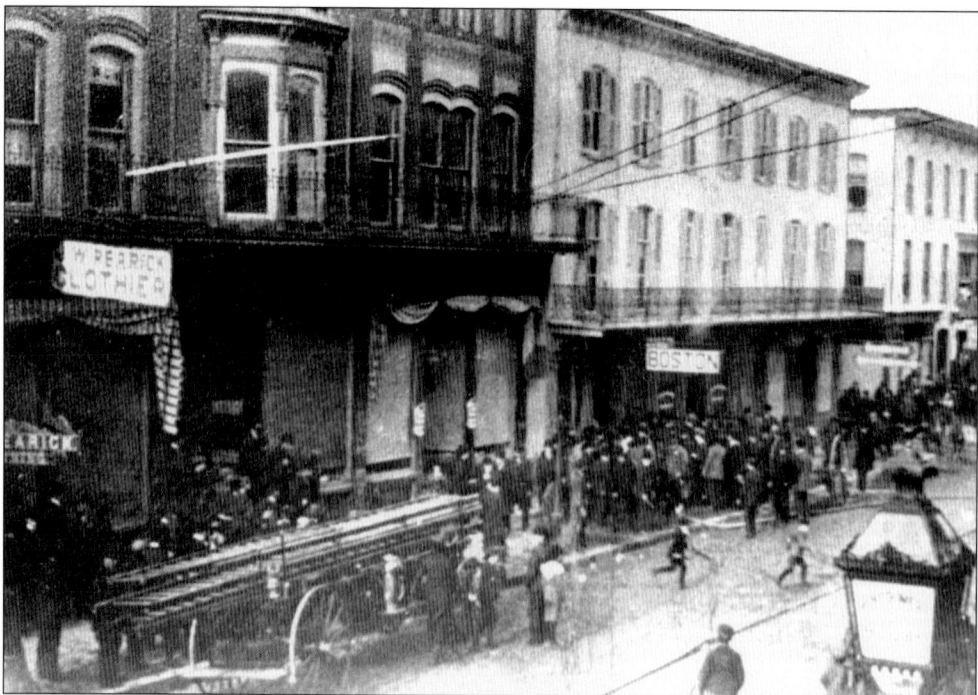

In 1878, firemen fight a blaze at the Boston House, along Main Street across from the Montgomery House. Scores of onlookers watch the efforts to suppress the fire.

Six
ANSWERING THE ALARM

Volunteer fire companies have protected lives and property in Chambersburg for more than 225 years. Following the Civil War, Chambersburg had five fire companies, with the earliest being established in 1780 and called the Friendship Company. Ironically Benjamin Franklin, the namesake of Franklin County, established the first volunteer fire company in Philadelphia. Living in Boston as a young apprentice, he was exposed to the massive fires that endangered the city. When he lived in Boston, he observed the fire clubs that were both practical and social organizations that protected only its members from fire. Franklin recognized the advantages of banding together and extended protection beyond club members to the entire community. In 1736, he organized the first volunteer company of about 30 men in Philadelphia. These volunteer organizations had only 30 to 40 participants, so Philadelphia established a number of organizations with company names like Fellowship, Hand-in-Hand, Heart-in-Heart, or Friendship—each with its own equipment and strategic location in the city. Many early American leaders served as volunteer fireman, in particular Pres. George Washington and Pres. James Buchanan, who was born in nearby Mercersburg.

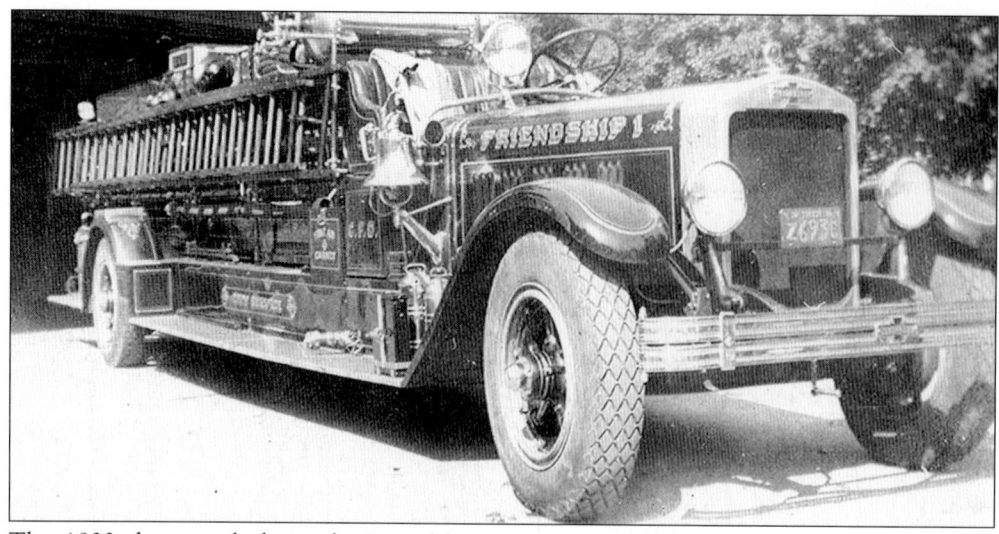

This 1932 photograph shows the Friendship Engine and Hose Company No. 1 and the 1930 American LaFrance city service fire truck in front of the old station house, located at the East Point.

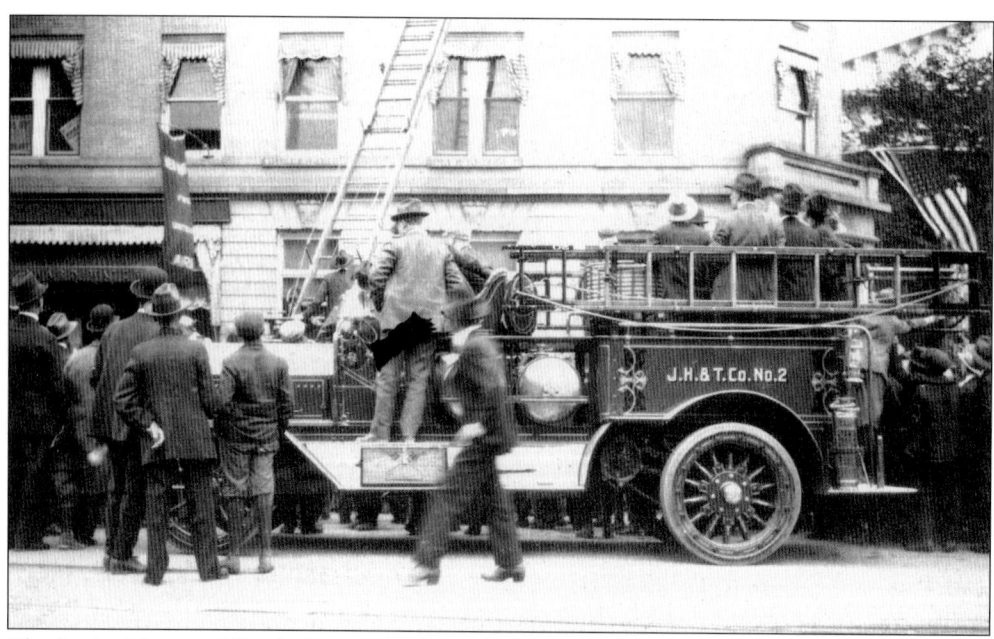

The Junior Hose and Truck Company No. 2, featuring its new 1917 chemical engine with 65-foot-long aerial ladder, performs a demonstration on the square.

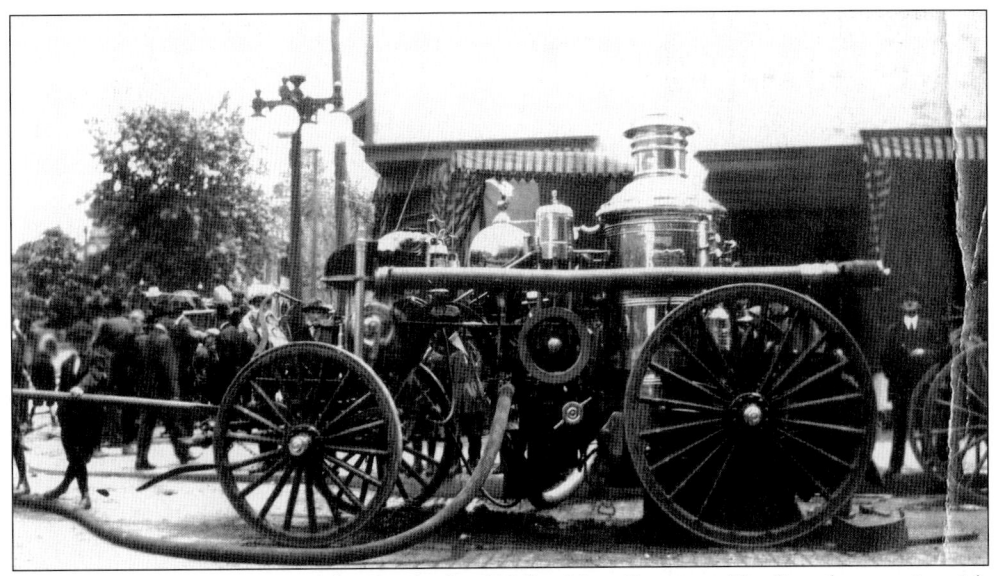

The 1903 LaFrance steamer of the Cumberland Valley Hose Company No. 5 works to extinguish a building fire at the corner of North Main and East King Streets in 1920.

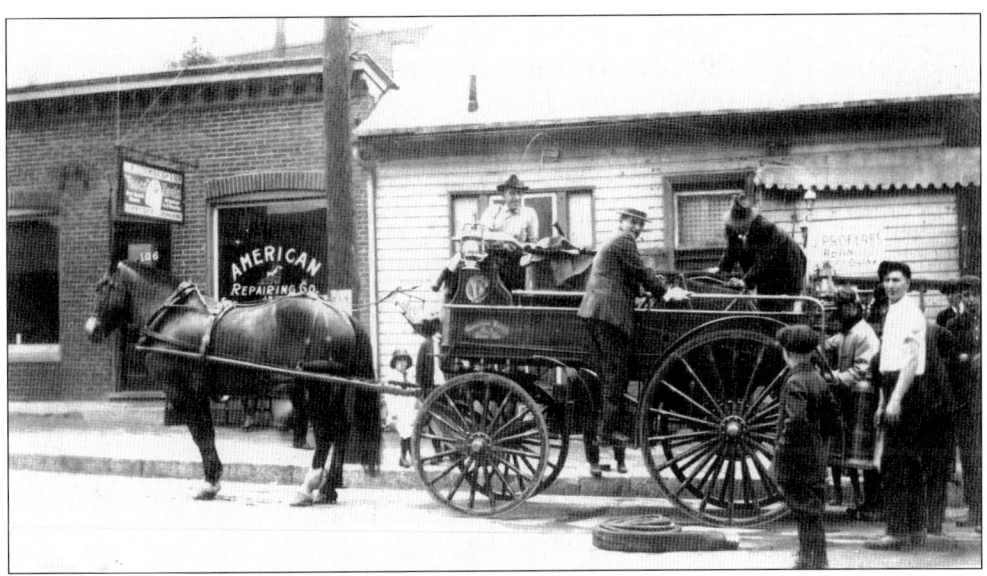

Members of the Cumberland Valley Hose Company No. 5 load the fire hose onto the 1915 hose wagon on East King Street in 1920. Pictured is John Proferes, original owner of Olympia Candy Kitchen, from 1903 to 1918, with another of his businesses in the background.

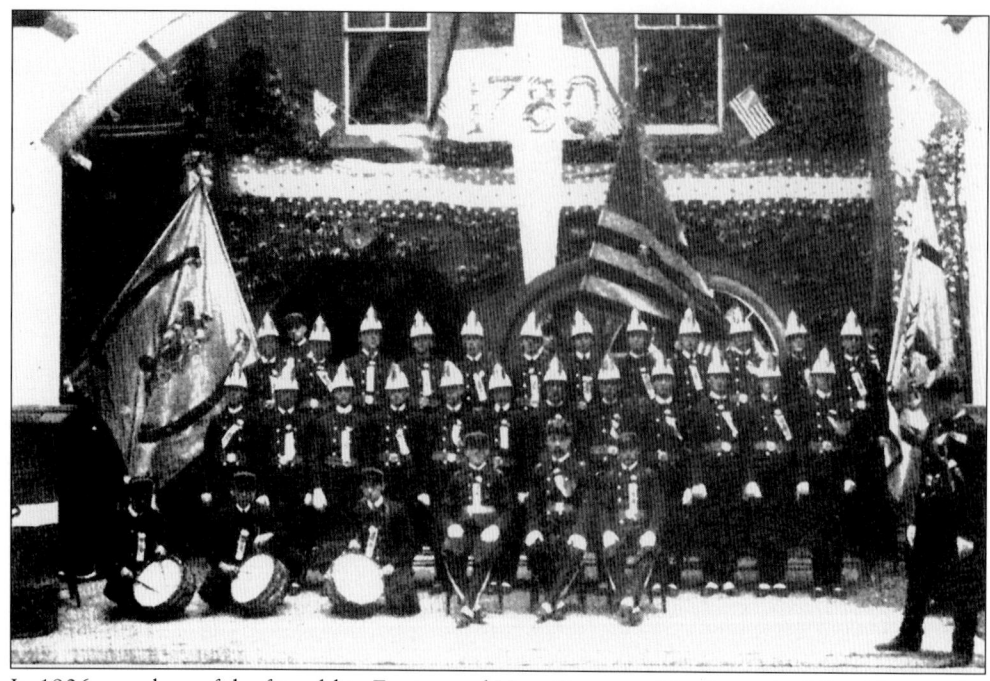
In 1906, members of the friendship Engine and Hose Company No. 1 pose in full uniform at the company's second firehouse, on South Second Street next to city hall. Organized in 1780, the fire company continues to serve the community today.

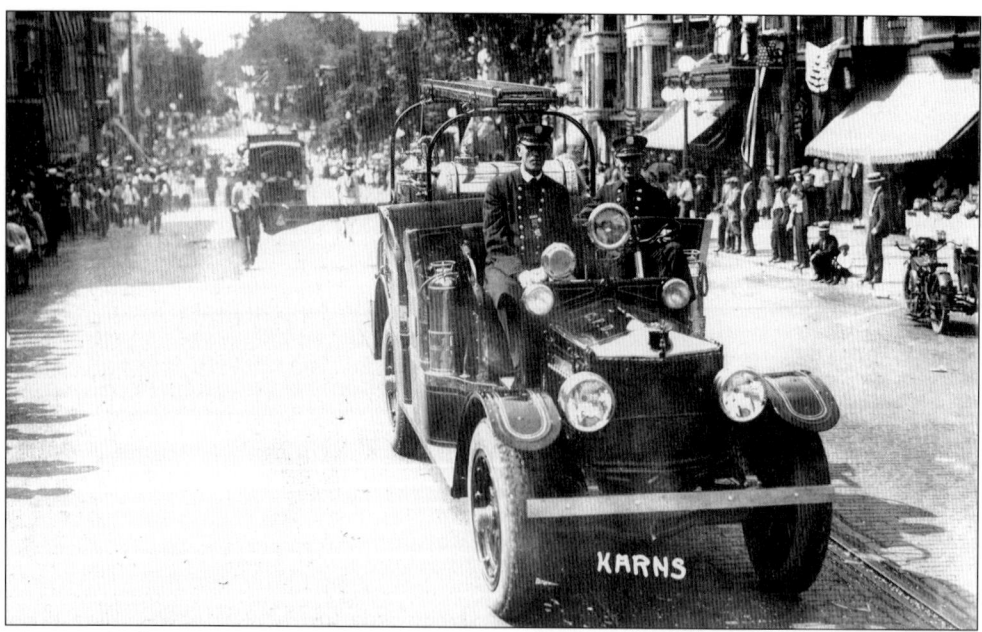
The Goodwill Steam Fire Engine and Hose Company No. 3 participates in a parade and shows off the company's new 1921 Hurlburt service truck. The truck was designed and built by H. B. McFerren, located on Third Street in Chambersburg.

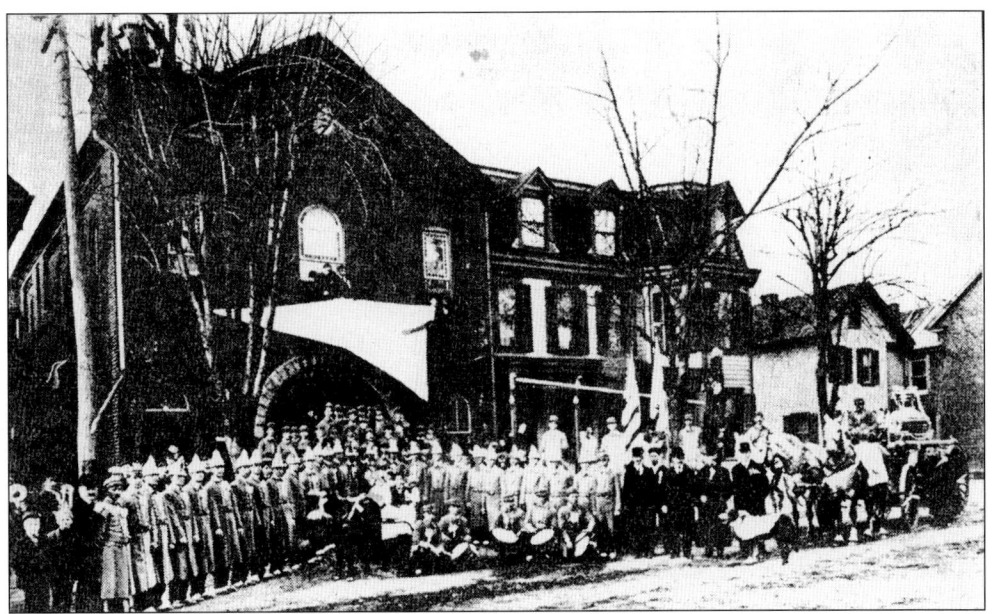

The Cumberland Valley Hose Company No. 5 stands in front of the fire station on Broad Street. The station originally had one door and later was modified for two doors to accommodate the hose wagon and steamer. This firehouse was a cooperative effort between the Cumberland Valley Railroad that constructed the building and the Chambersburg Borough that purchased the apparatus.

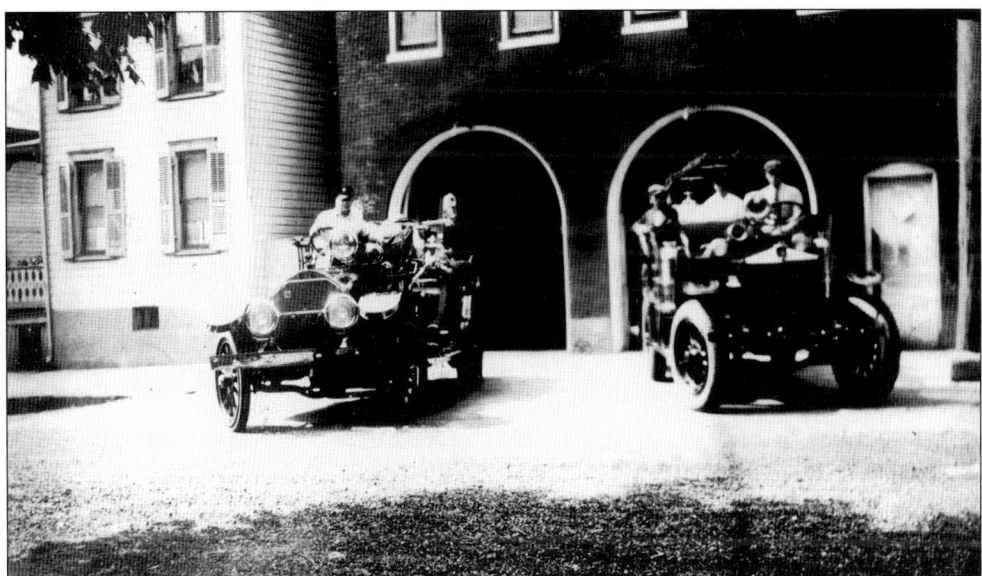

The Goodwill Fire Company proudly displays its 1920 American LaFrance pumper (left) and the 1921 Hurlburt service truck (right) at the station on East Catherine Street in 1922. The driver of the American LaFrance is Russell Kyle.

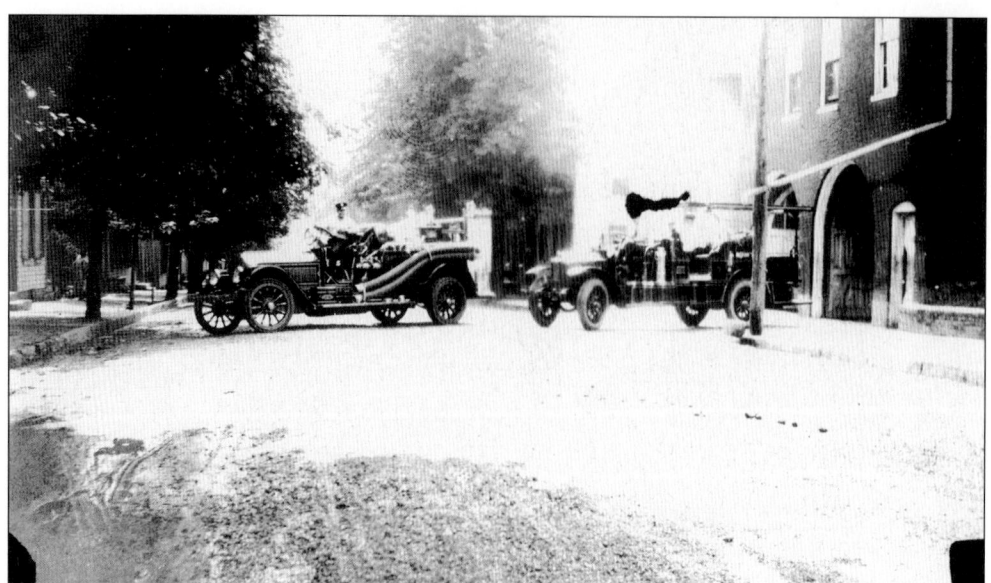
Here is a side view of the American LaFrance and Hurlburt at the East Catherine Street location of the Goodwill Fire Company. These two pieces of fire apparatus are an awesome combination.

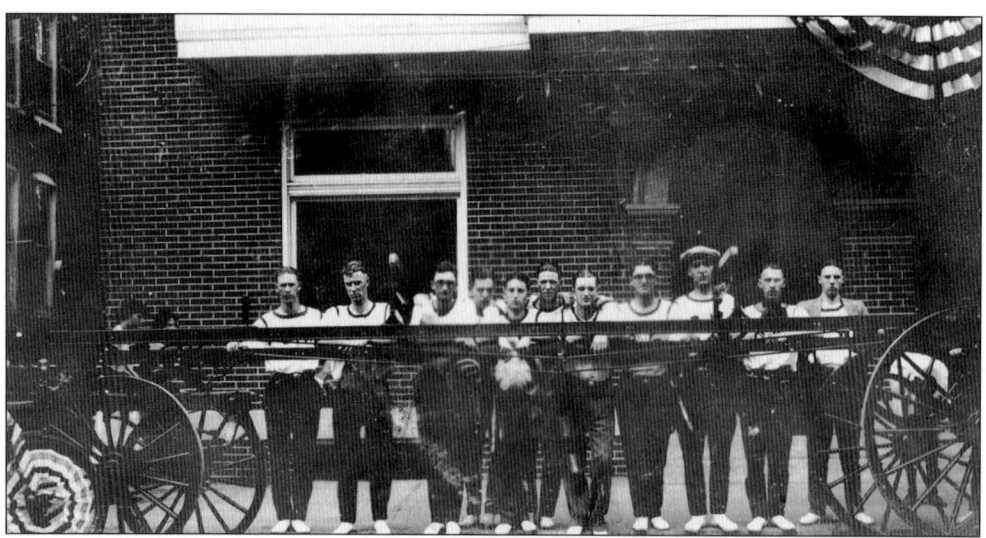
Members of the Goodwill Ladder drill team prepare for another competition in the early 1900s. The Goodwill Fire Company had a large and active membership.

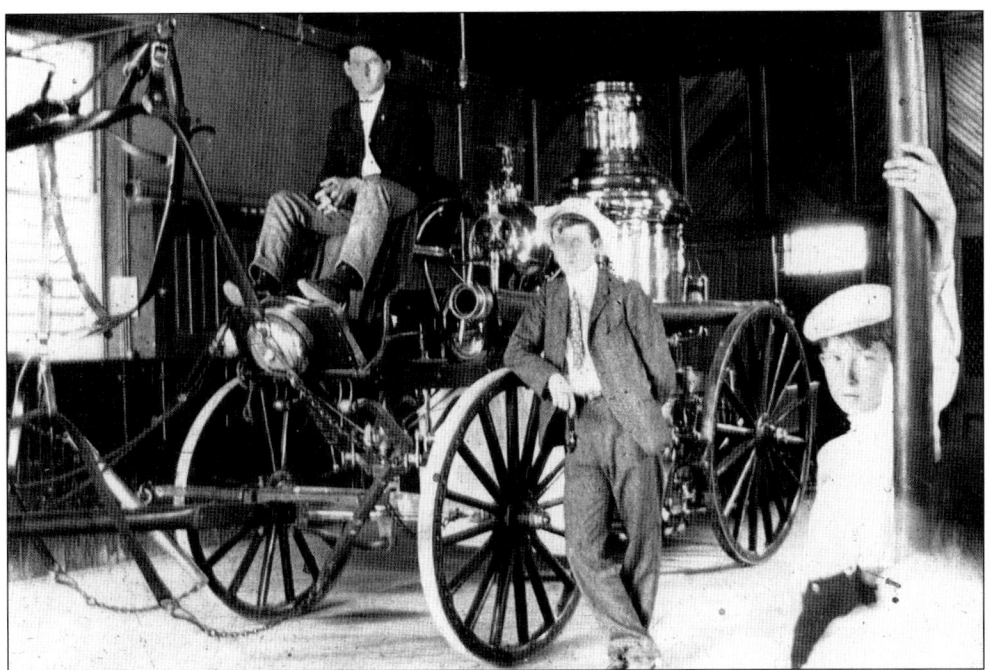

This is an interior of the Goodwill firehouse on East Catherine Street in 1892, with the new LaFrance steamer ready for action.

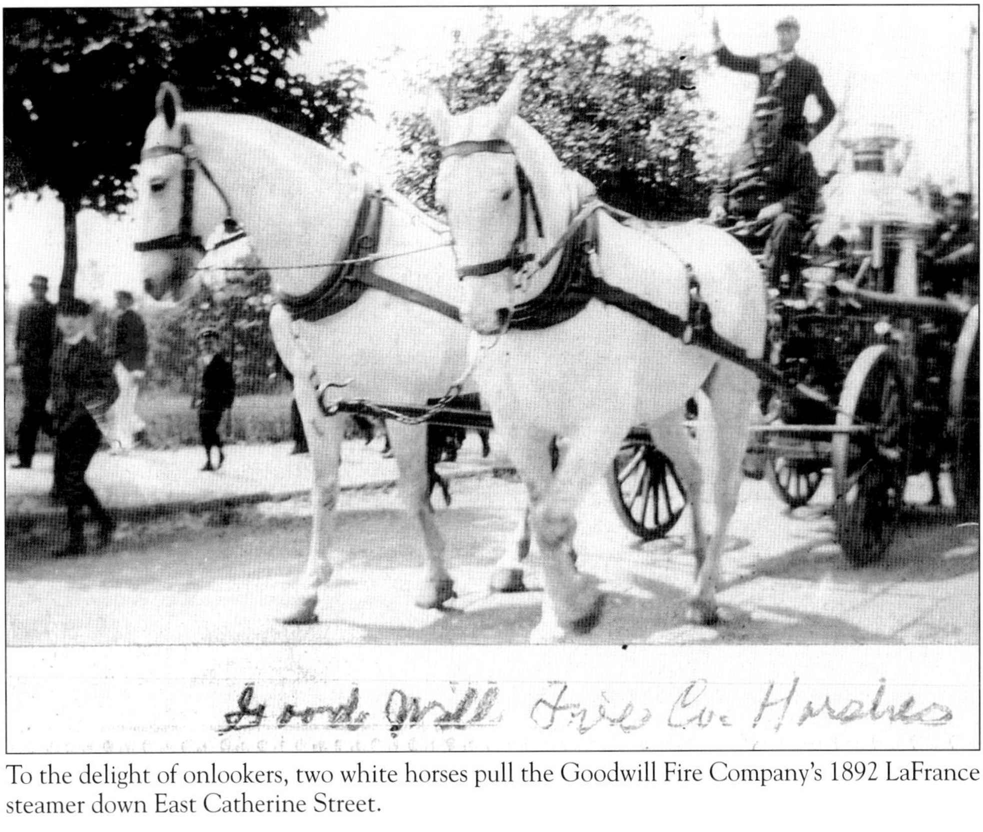

To the delight of onlookers, two white horses pull the Goodwill Fire Company's 1892 LaFrance steamer down East Catherine Street.

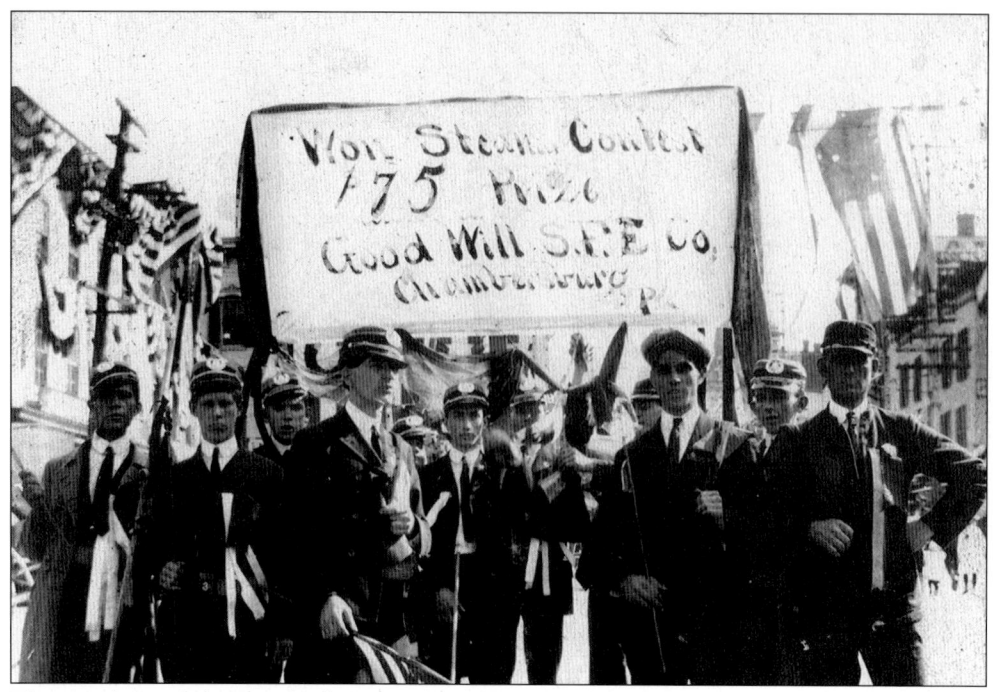

The members of the Goodwill Steam Fire Engine and Hose Company No. 3 are the proud winners in the steam fire engine contest. They received $75—an ample amount of prize money in the early 1900s.

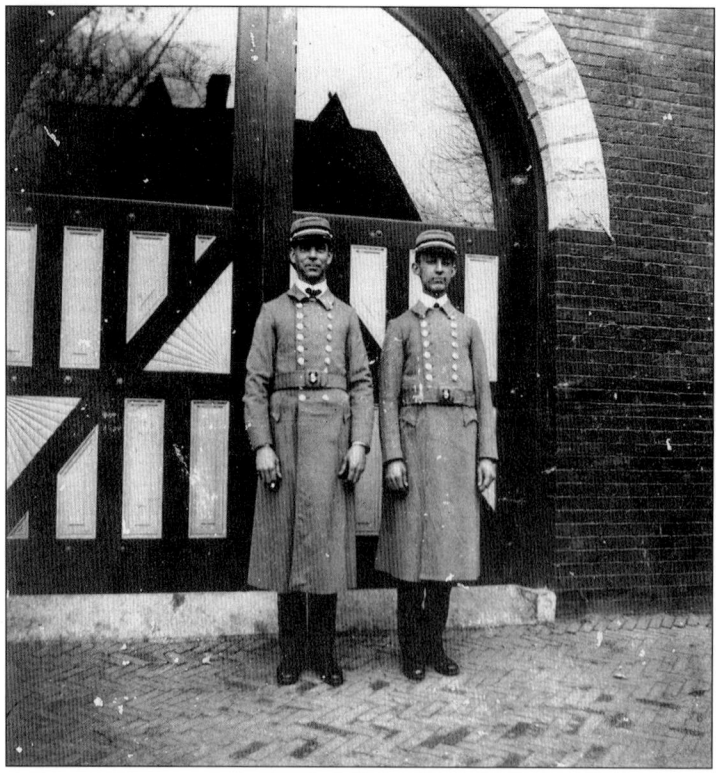

Getting ready for a parade, two members of the Cumberland Valley Hose Company No. 5 wear the uniforms of the day. This picture was taken on Broad Street.

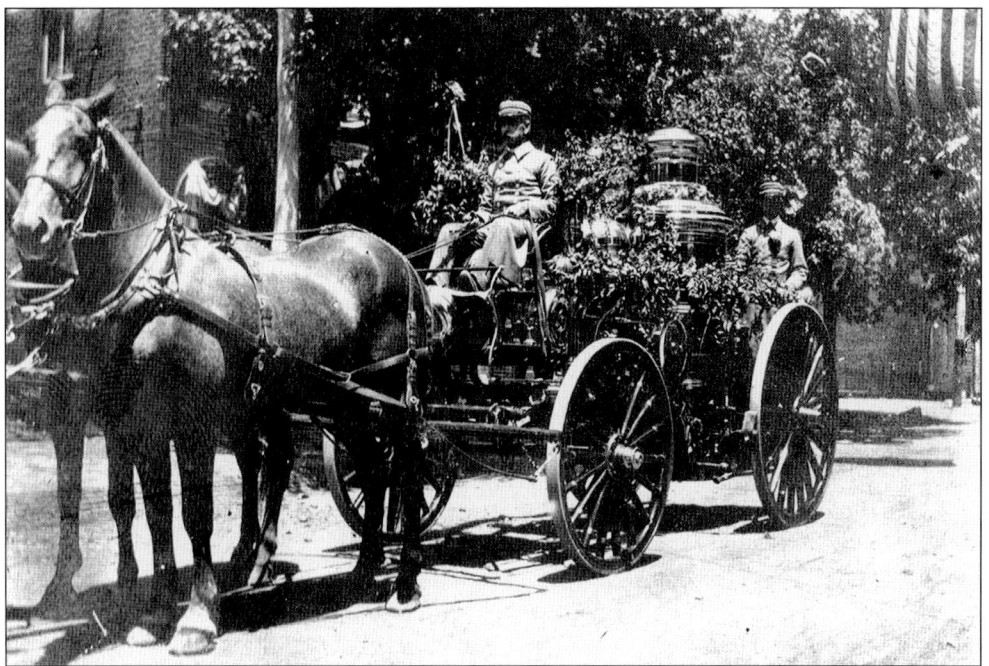

The Cumberland Valley Hose Company No. 5 has decorated its 1903 LaFrance steamer for a parade. The photograph was taken on Broad Street near North Second Street.

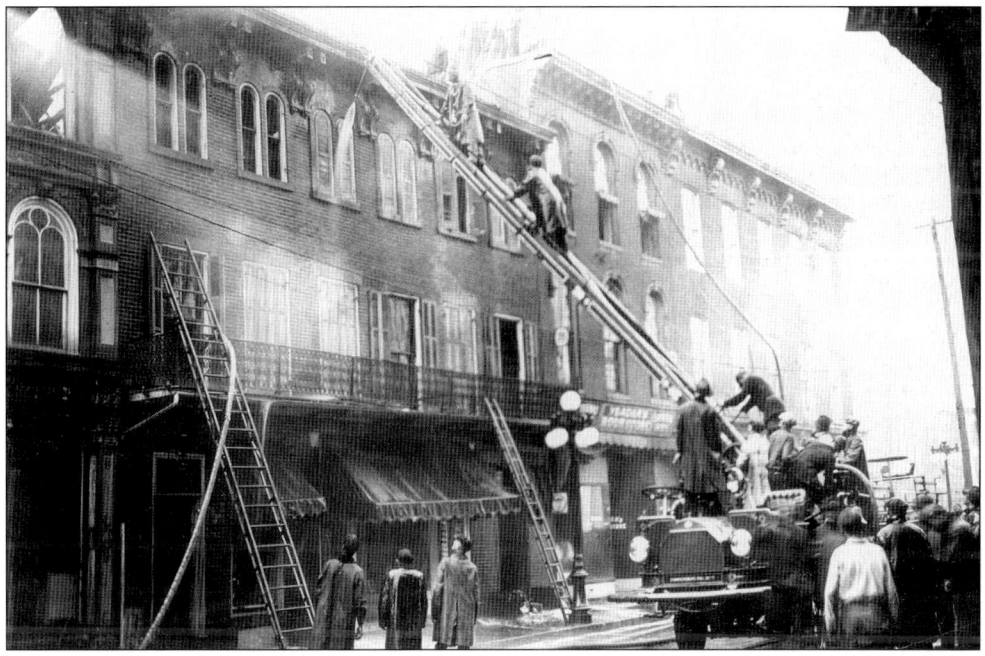

The Junior Hose and Truck Company No. 2 operates its Seagrave ladder truck at P. Nicklas on South Main Street in 1920. Many firefighters fought the very destructive fire, which caused significant damage to adjacent buildings. Barely visible behind the smoke is the Central Presbyterian Church steeple.

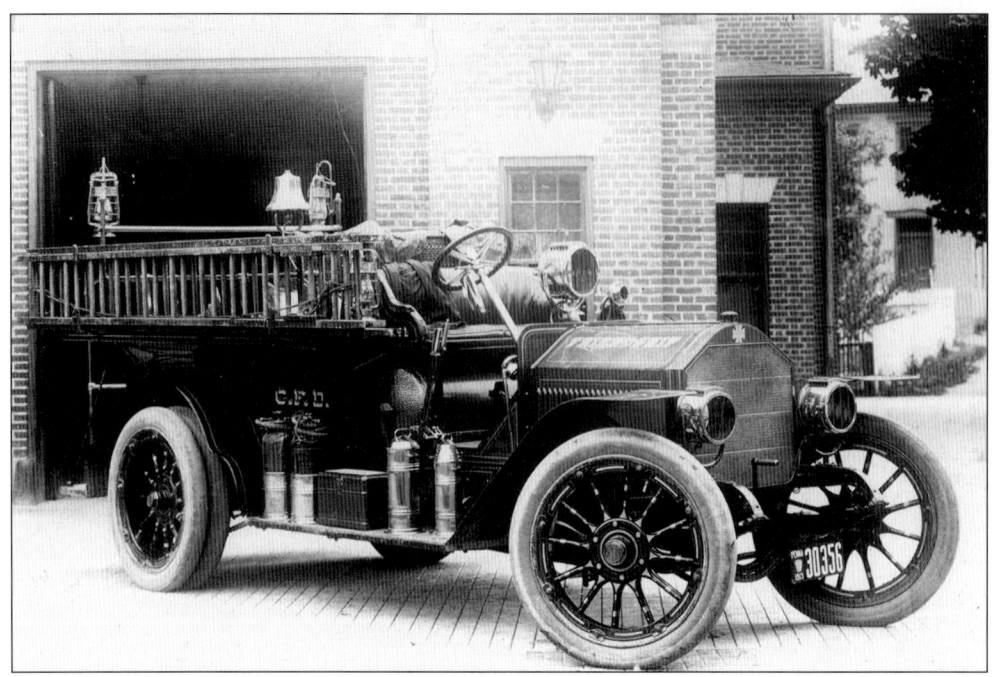

The Friendship Engine and Hose Company's 1911 American LaFrance chemical engine is ready to answer the alarm in 1913. This view was taken from Lincoln Way East next to the station.

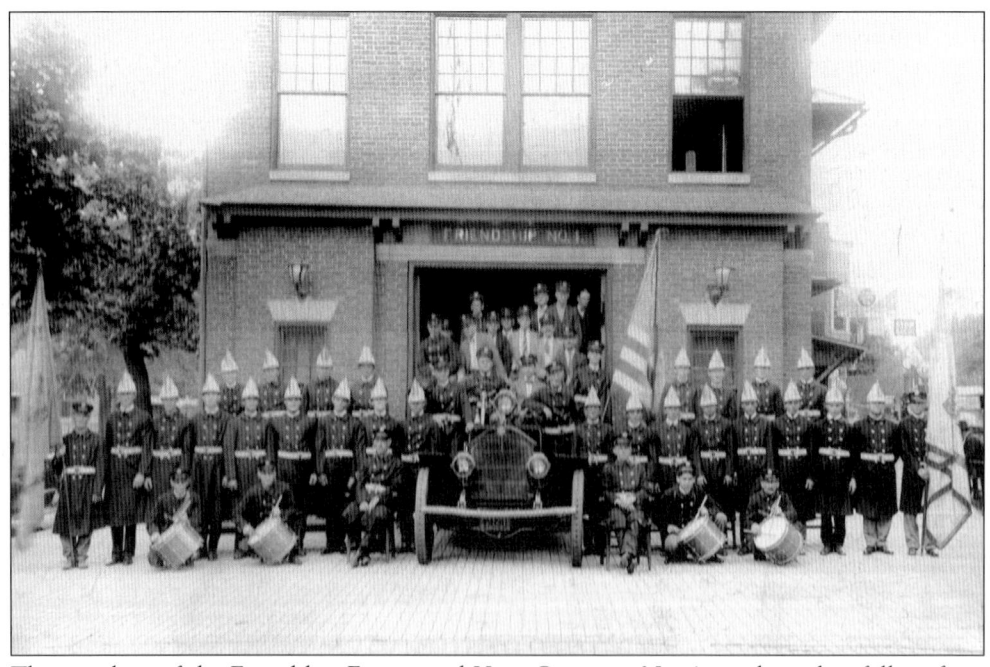

The members of the Friendship Engine and Hose Company No. 1 are dressed in full uniform and stand with the company's new 1911 American LaFrance chemical engine at the East Point station. Visible through the open window on the second floor is the brass pole that the firemen slid down.

Seven
BUSINESS AND INDUSTRY

Excellent location has always been an advantage of operating a business in Chambersburg. Founder Benjamin Chambers recognized the confluence of the Conococheague Creek and the Falling Spring as a unique place to situate a gristmill. In the first half of the 19th century, Chambersburg—the eastern terminus on the turnpike to Bedford—was an outstanding location for lodging and dining establishments. The Franklin, Montgomery, and Golden Lamb Hotels were popular accommodations for travelers.

Years later, at the beginning of the 20th century, the waterpower that attracted Chambers drew more business. A variety of mills and woolen factories located their operations along the Conococheague and the Falling Spring. The Cumberland Valley Railroad was also a strong employer in the early part of the 20th century.

The oldest continuing business in Chambersburg is the T. B. Woods Company, established here in 1857 as a producer of wood-burning stoves. The business evolved to its present-day product line in 1900, when it began to manufacture power transmission products. In the early years of the 1900s, small business developed, as merchants established stores in downtown Chambersburg. Ludwig's Jewelers opened in 1877. Olympia Candy Kitchen opened in 1903. Harmon's Furniture Store opened in 1906. All are alive and well in Chambersburg today.

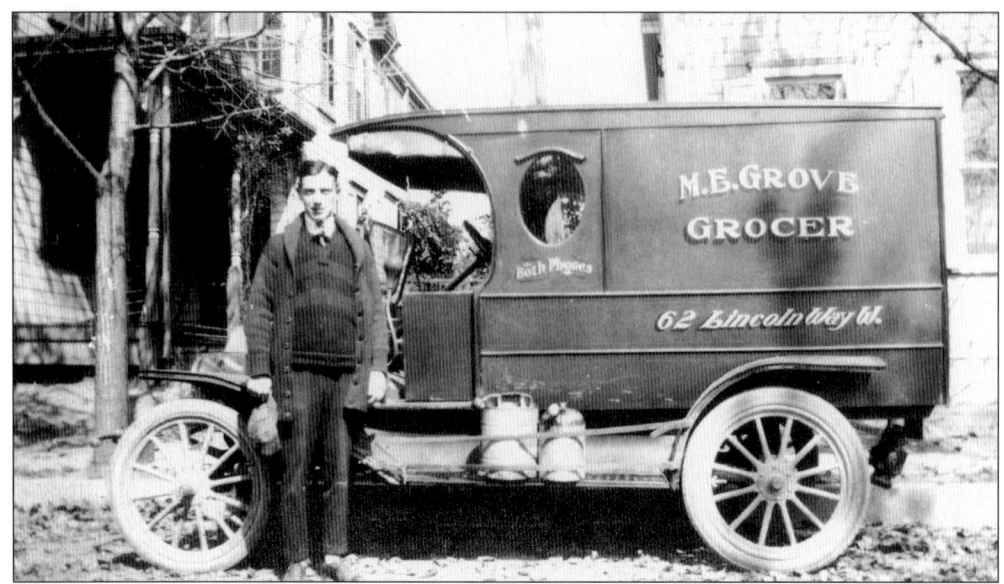

Using an early Ford delivery truck, grocer M. E. Grove makes a delivery on German Street in 1914. His store was located at 62 Lincoln Way West. German Street was renamed Liberty Street during World War I.

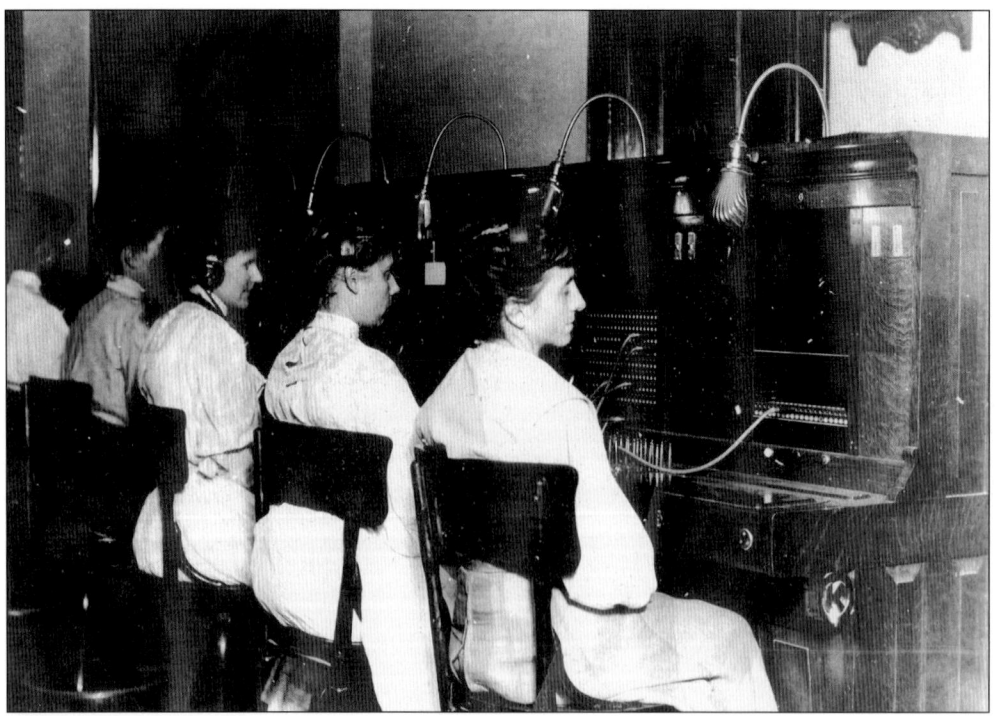

These young ladies working for the Cumberland Valley Phone Company await incoming calls in the early 1900s.

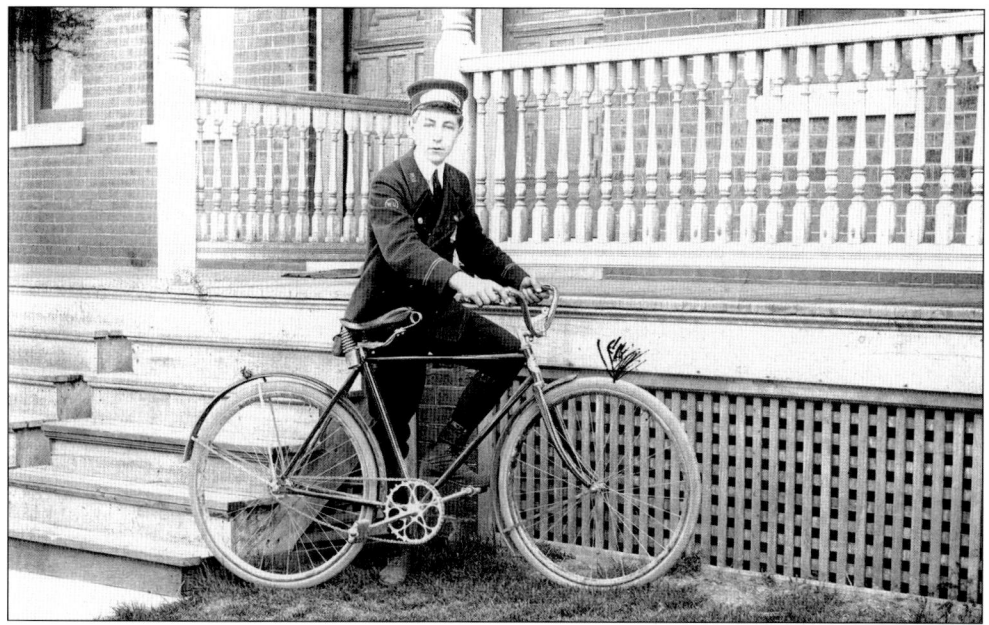

The young man has just made a delivery for Western Union to a residence on South Second Street in 1910.

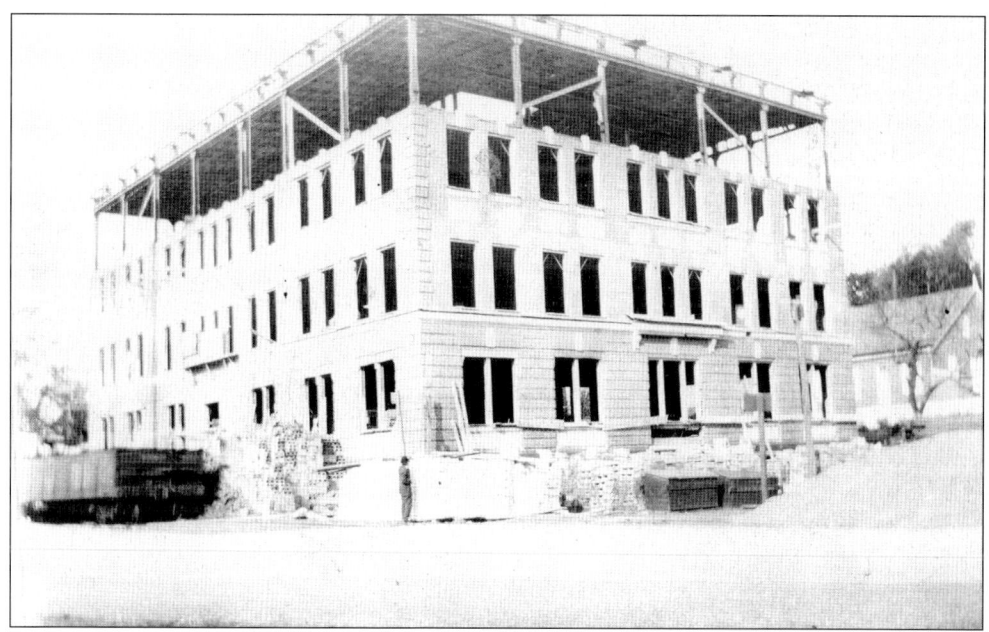

Pictured is the Cumberland Valley Railroad administration building under construction in 1914. Today this building is known as the Professional Arts Building.

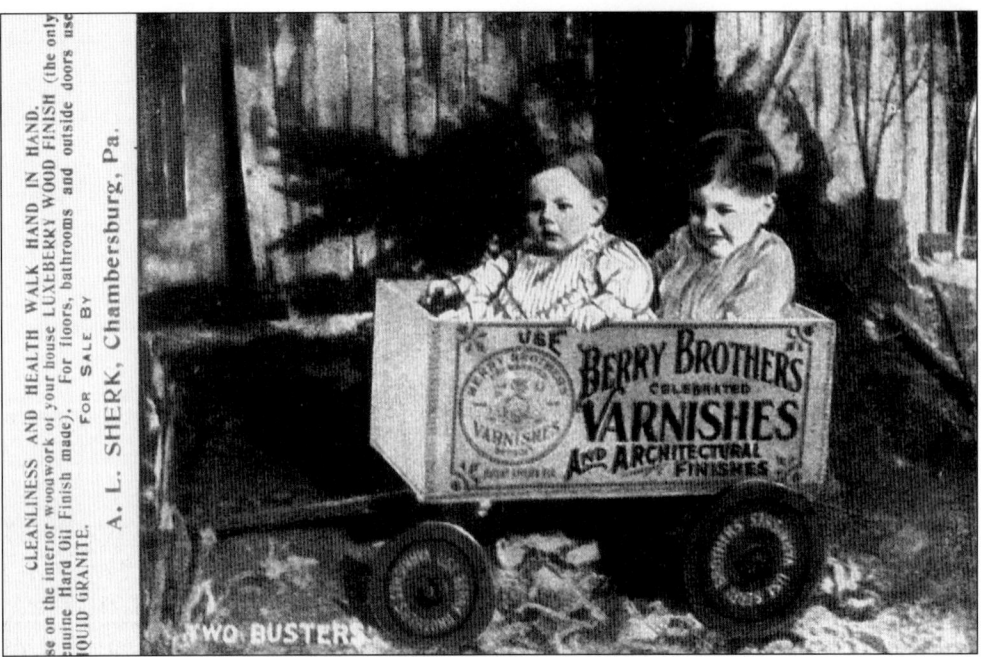

Shown is a 1905 advertisement postcard from A. L. Sherk, a hardware store located at 100 South Main Street.

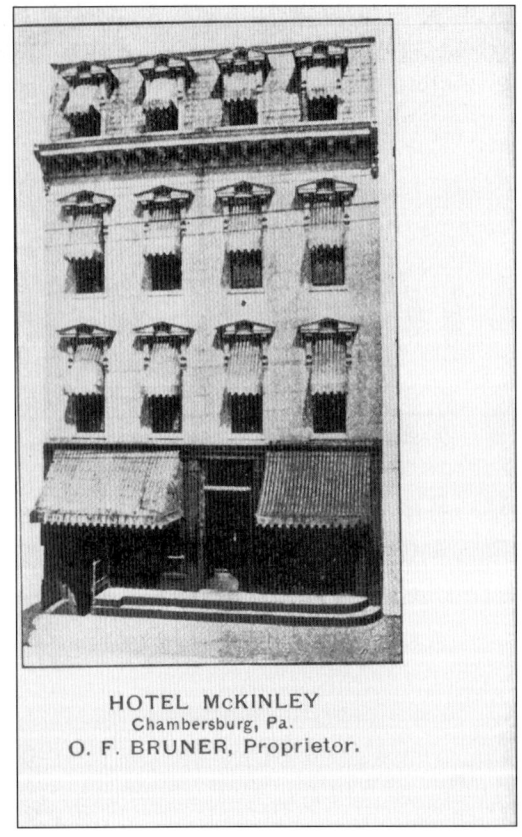

Here is a 1905 advertisement postcard of the Hotel McKinley, a popular attraction located on North Main Street.

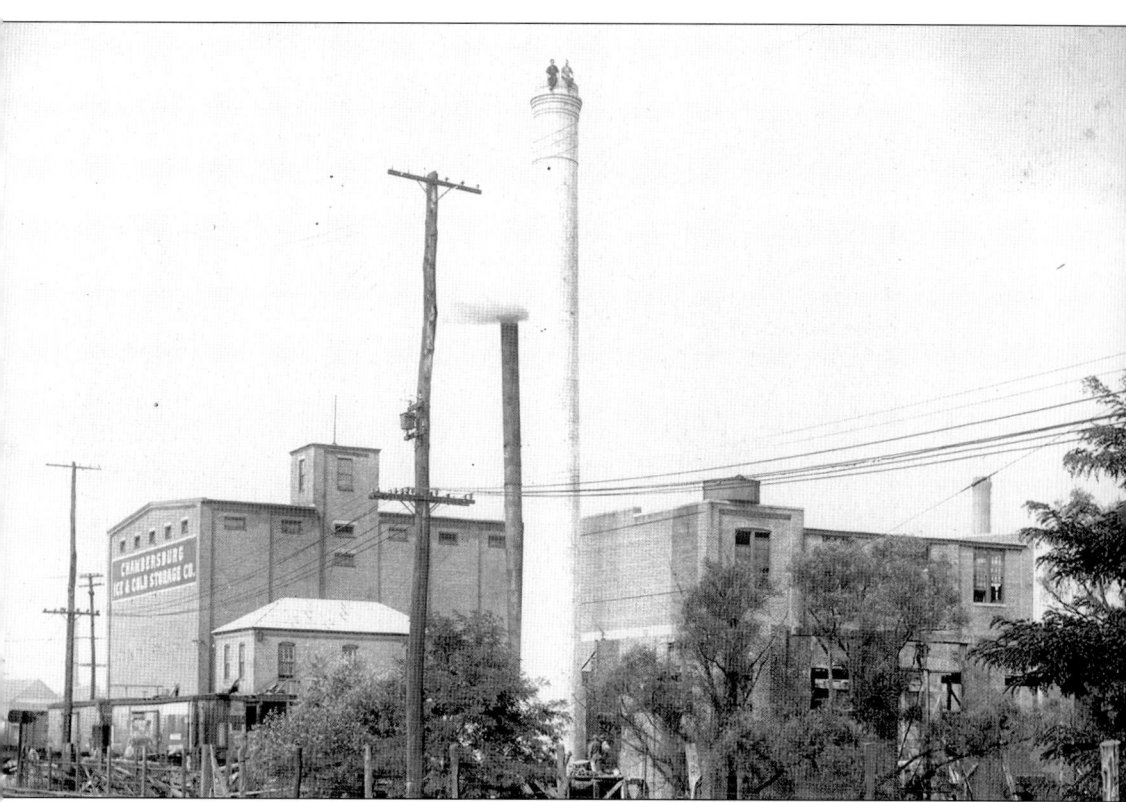

Enjoying the view in 1910, two men stand high atop the towering smokestack of the Chambersburg Ice and Cold Storage Company, on the corner of Kennedy and Grant Streets. The picture was taken from South Third Street at the Cumberland Valley Railroad Station.

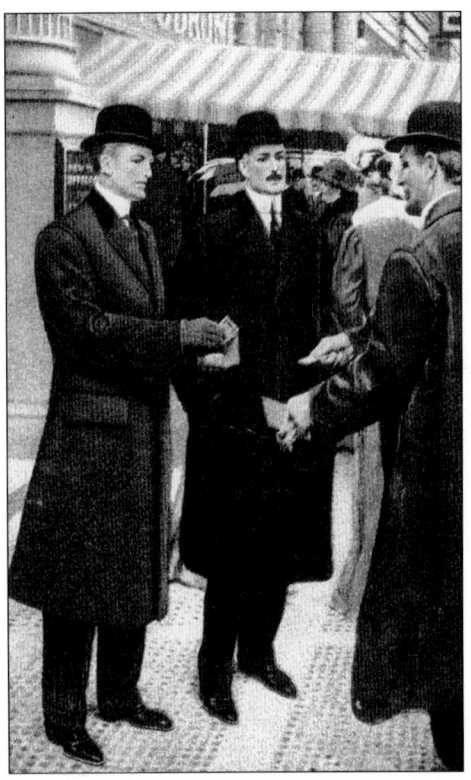

This 1909 advertisement postcard depicts well-dressed gentlemen in New York, spreading the word that similar garments may be purchased at L. G. Lyon Clothing Store in Chambersburg. Still in business today, the store is located at the corner of South Main and West Queen Streets.

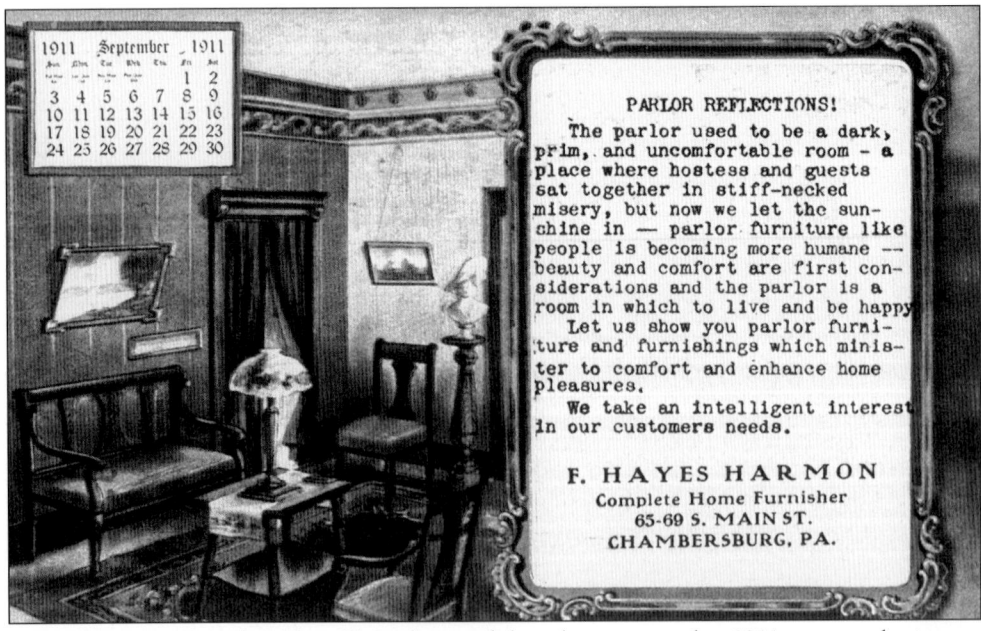

F. Hays Harmon, Complete Home Furnisher, used this advertising card in 1911 to attract business.

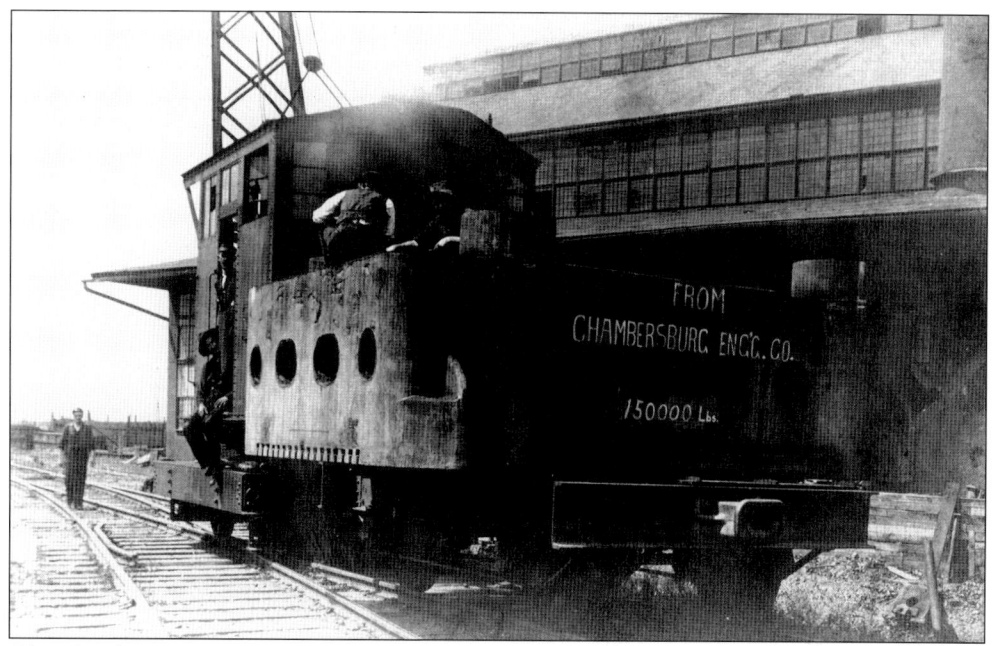

Chambersburg Engineering, a worldwide producer of drop-forging equipment, began its industrial operation in Chambersburg. This 1907 picture shows the crane and casting at the Chambersburg Engineering company; the weight of the casting is 150,000 pounds. The business was located on South Main Street, Derbyshire Avenue, and Wayne Avenue. Chambersburg Engineering operated for over 100 years, but with the technological changes to machine tooling, it closed in 2001.

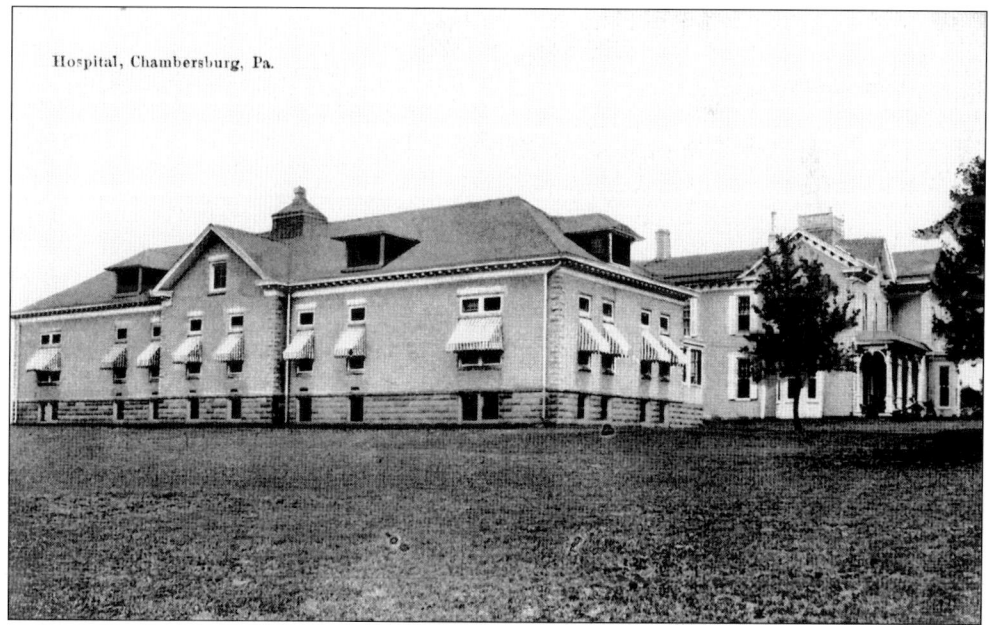

The old Chambersburg Hospital, located on Lincoln Way East, and was removed many years ago to expand for new facilities. The health care service industry has grown and provides a significant number of jobs to Chambersburg and Franklin County residents.

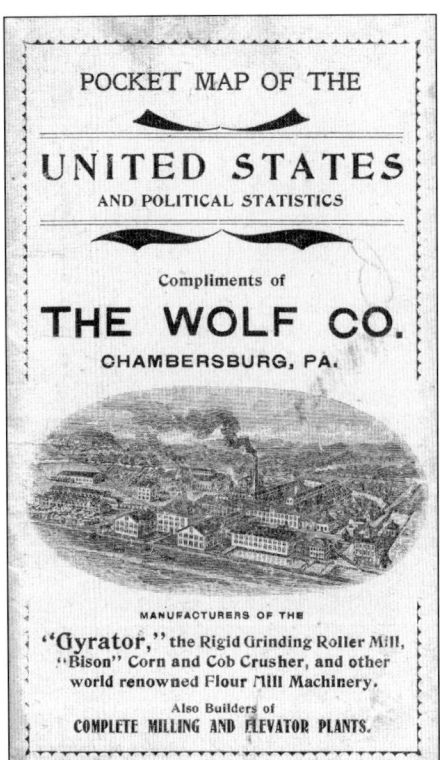

In the early part of the 1900s, the Wolf Company was one of the world's largest manufacturers and purveyors of milling equipment. In addition, the company manufactured artificial stone used in building and created Wolf's Lake Park. Today neither the businesses nor the pleasure park exist.

This early-1900s brochure was used by the Wolf Company to market fine milling equipment.

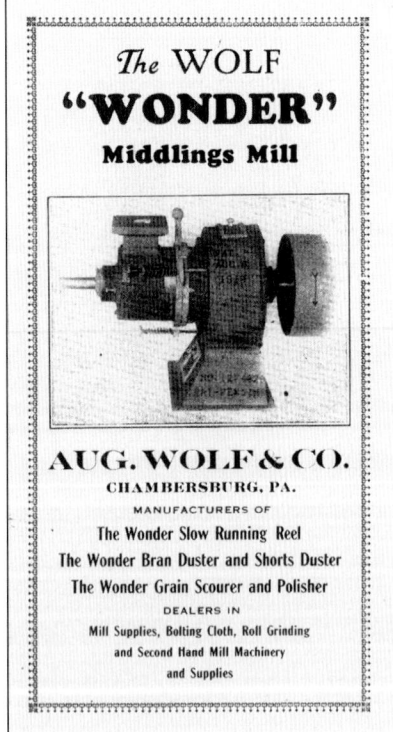

This advertisement card promotes the writings of Joseph R. Winters. Winters was of African American and Native American descent. Active in the Underground Railroad, he was not only an author but also an inventor of fire apparatus, patenting the scissor ladder with a rescue basket. He lived to be 100 years old and is buried in the Mount Lebanon Cemetery on Lincoln Way West.

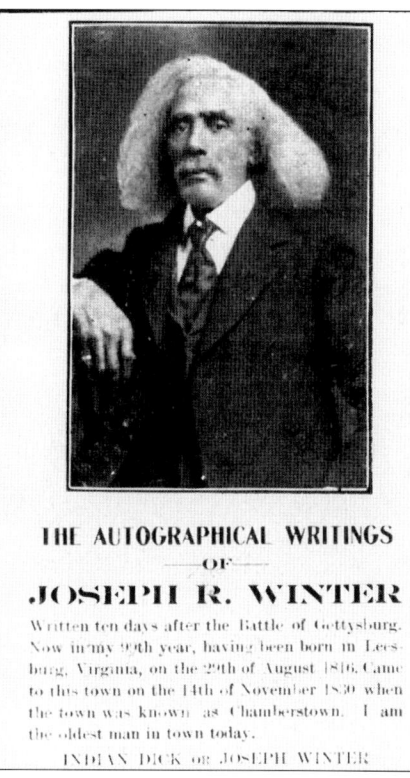

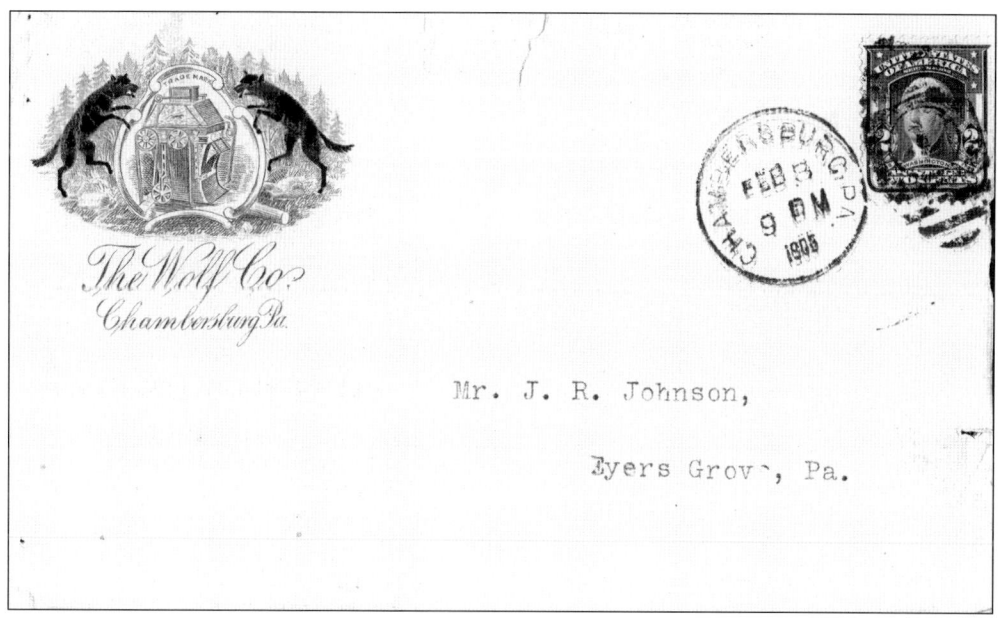

This piece of Wolf Company stationery is postmarked in 1905 and displays the company logo in the left corner.

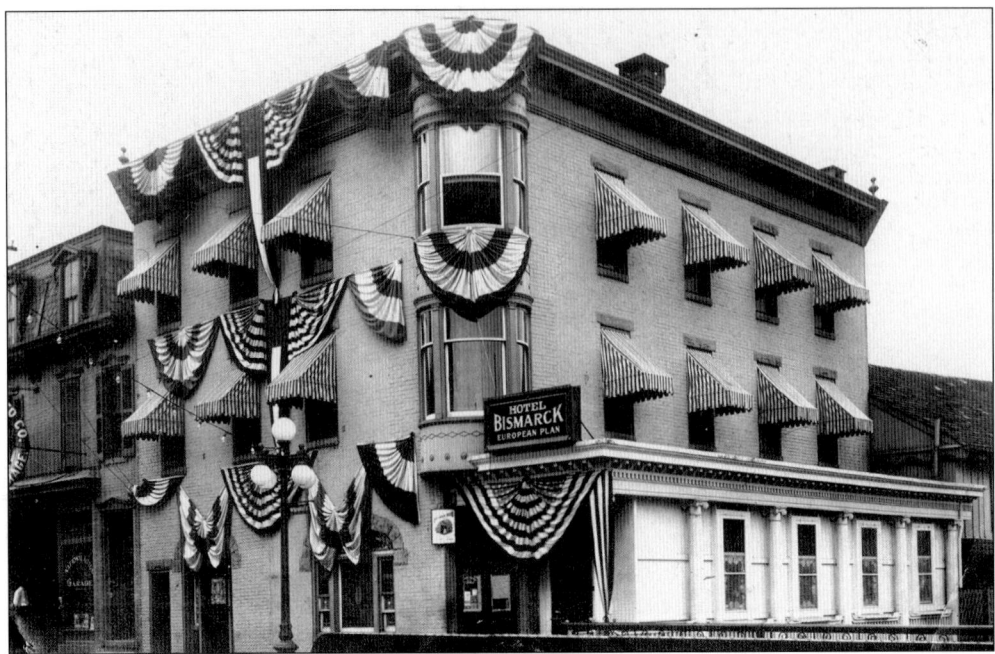

Hotel Bismarck is decorated for Old Home Week of 1914. During World War I, it was renamed Hotel Lincoln. Situated along Lincoln Way West, it now serves as an apartment building.

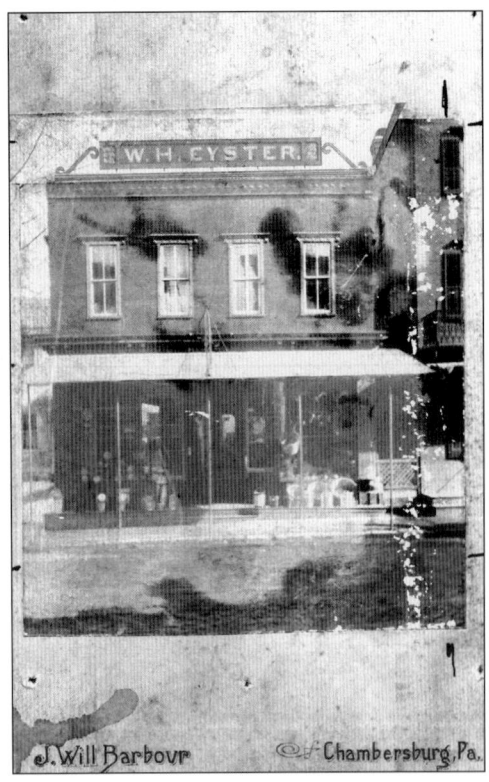

J. Will Barbour photographed the storefront of W. H. Eyster on North Main Street in the late 1890s.

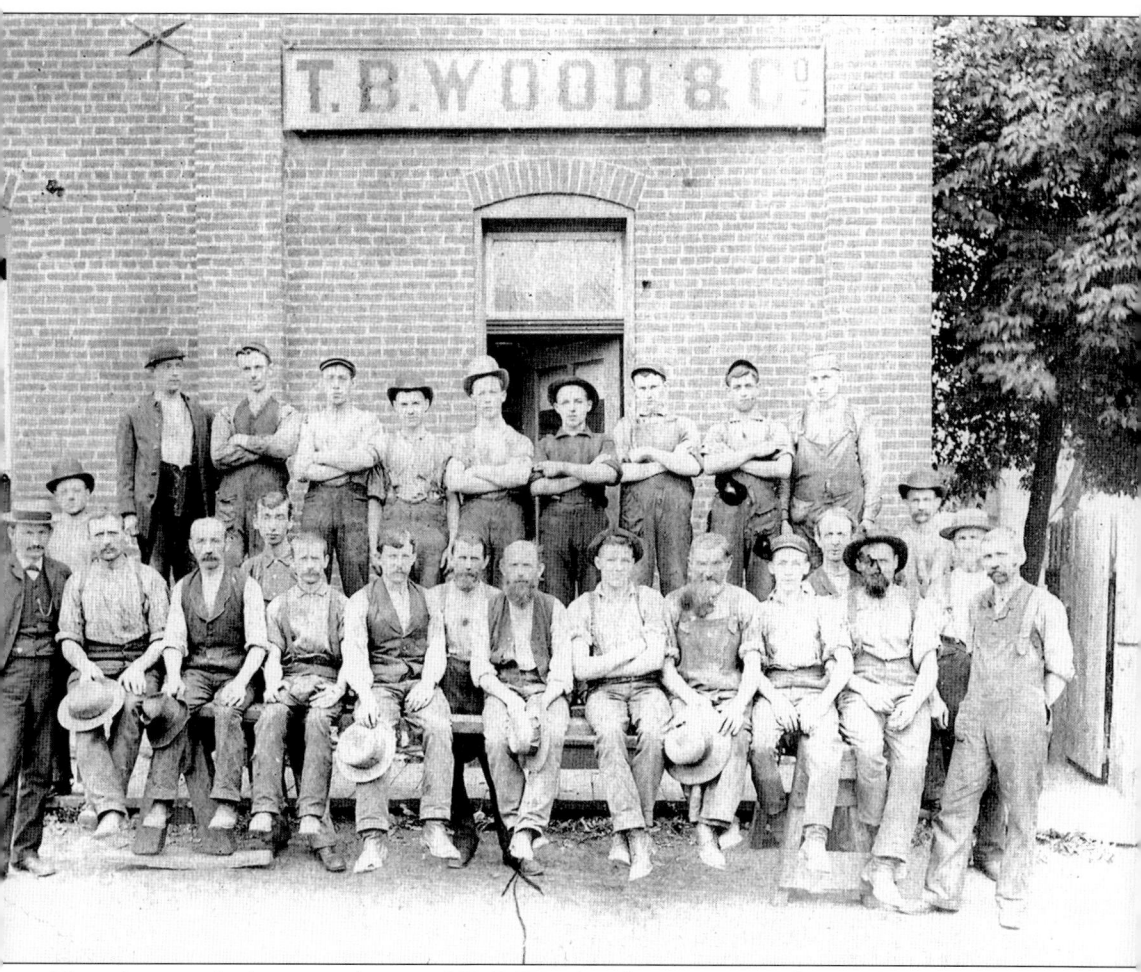

This photograph shows employees of T. B Wood and Company at the North Third Street business next to the Cumberland Valley Railroad Station in the 1880s. The business is currently located on North Fifth Avenue.

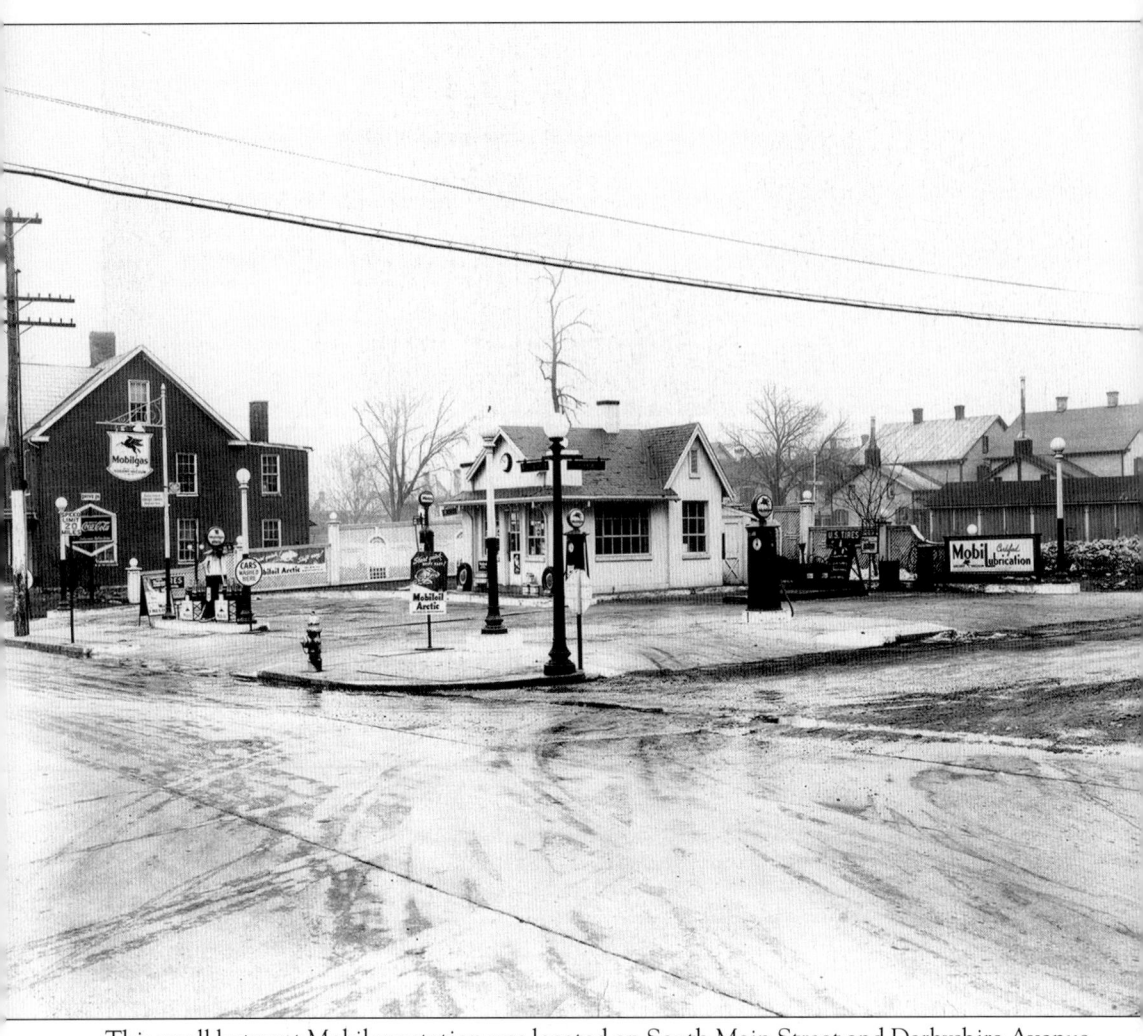
This small but neat Mobil gas station was located on South Main Street and Derbyshire Avenue in the 1930s.

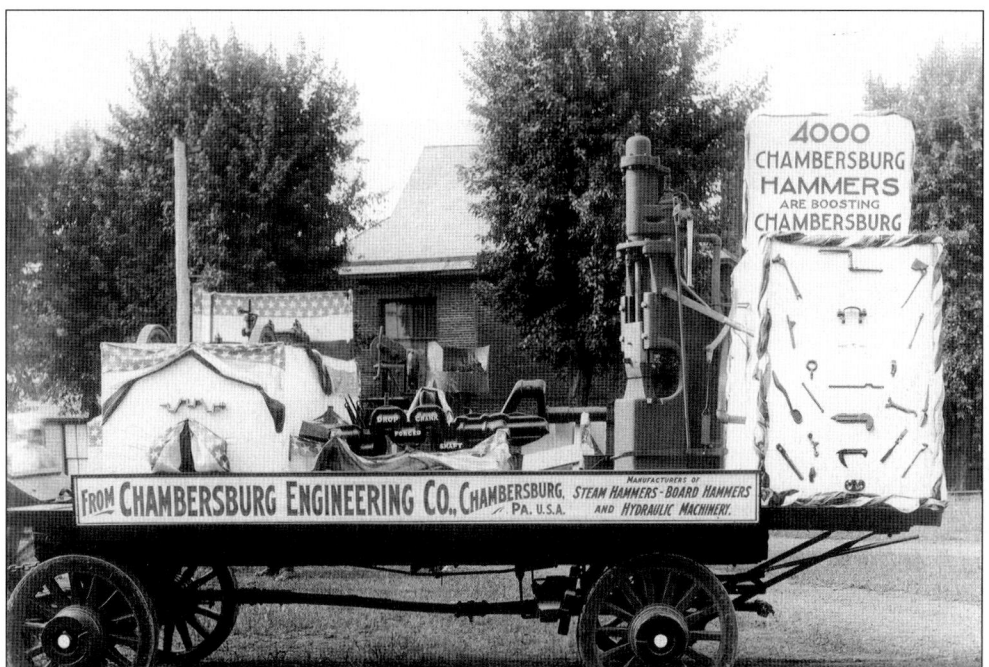

The Chambersburg Engineering Company shows some of the tools made by its skilled employees on this promotional wagon. It publicizes that more than 4,000 Chambersburg hammers are promoting the town.

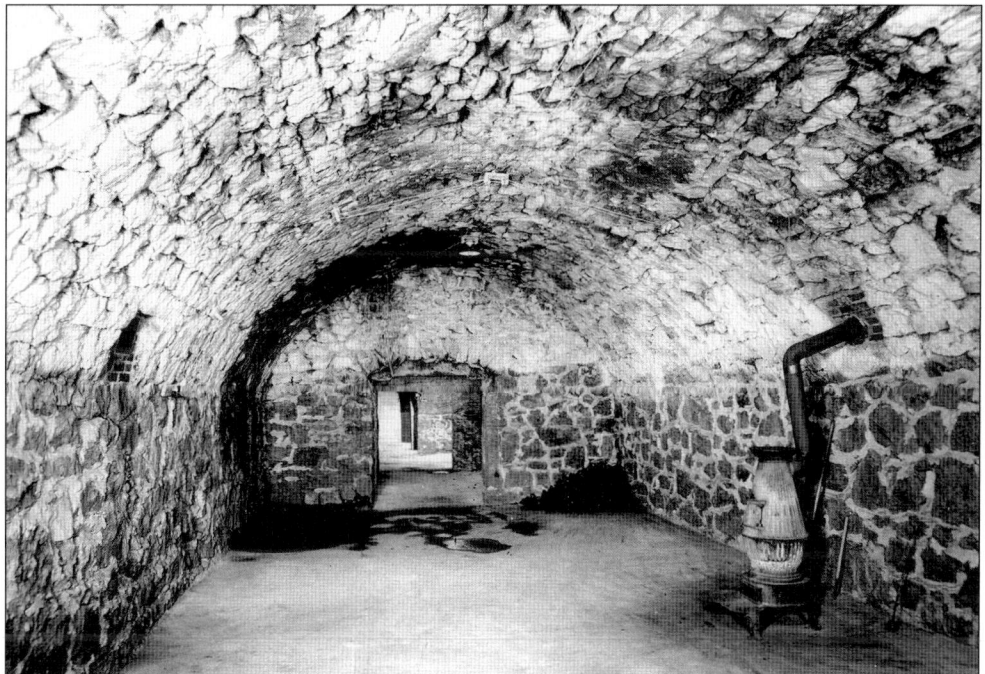

This modified cave, located beneath the shopper's parking lot just off of Burkhart Avenue, was used as an ale vat room in the Ludwig Brewery operation. The stone arch structure, built in 1854, was 12 feet by 46 feet by 19 feet. It was converted to an air raid shelter during World War II.

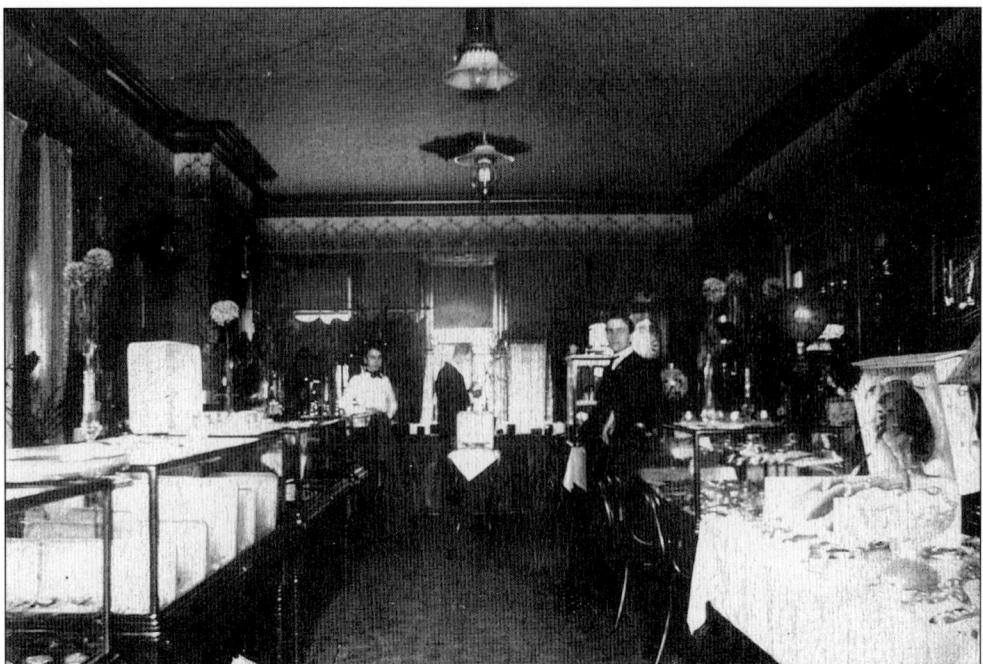

A 1902 photograph of the interior of Ludwig's Jewelers shows, from left to right, William Ludwig, George Ludwig, and Walter Ludwig.

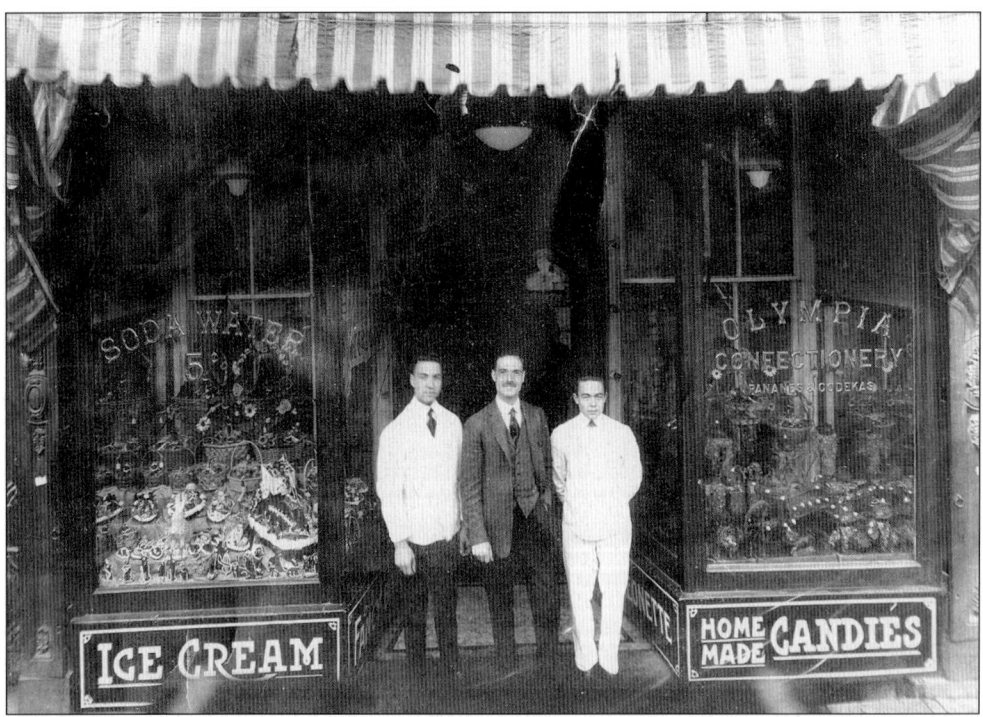

This c. 1920 photograph shows Olympia Candy Kitchen on South Main Street after brothers George Pananes (left) and James Pananes (center) purchased the shop from Jon Proferas. Displayed are hand-decorated Easter eggs; the largest, on the left, weighed seven pounds.

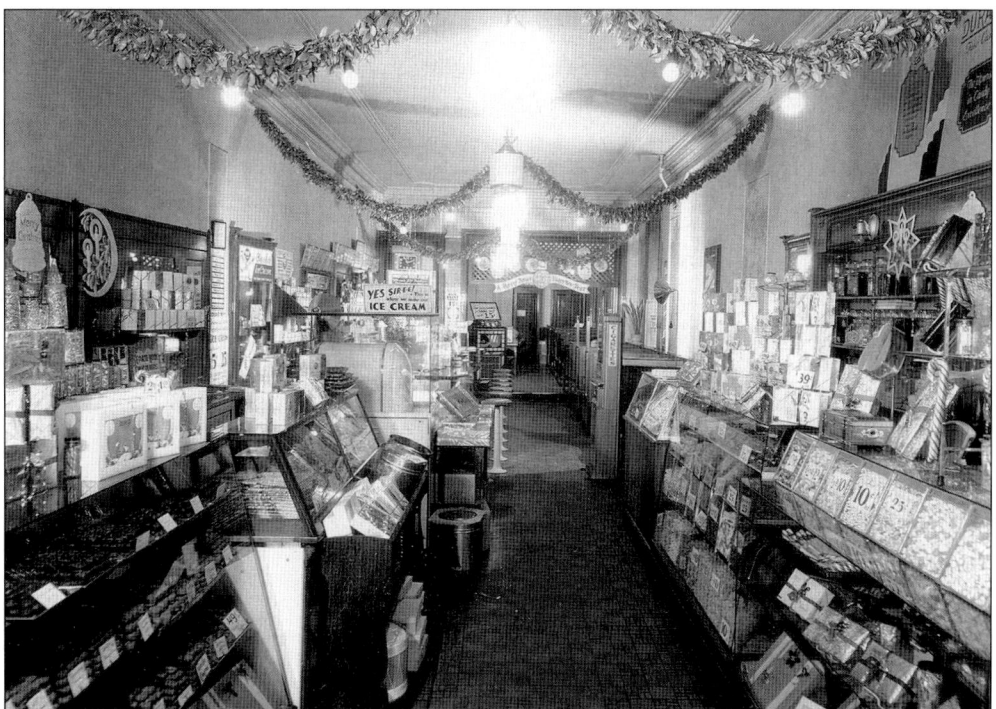

This 1930s interior view of Olympia Candy Kitchen shows wall-to-wall candy and Christmas decorations. The candy case on the right advertises taffy for 10¢ for a half pound.

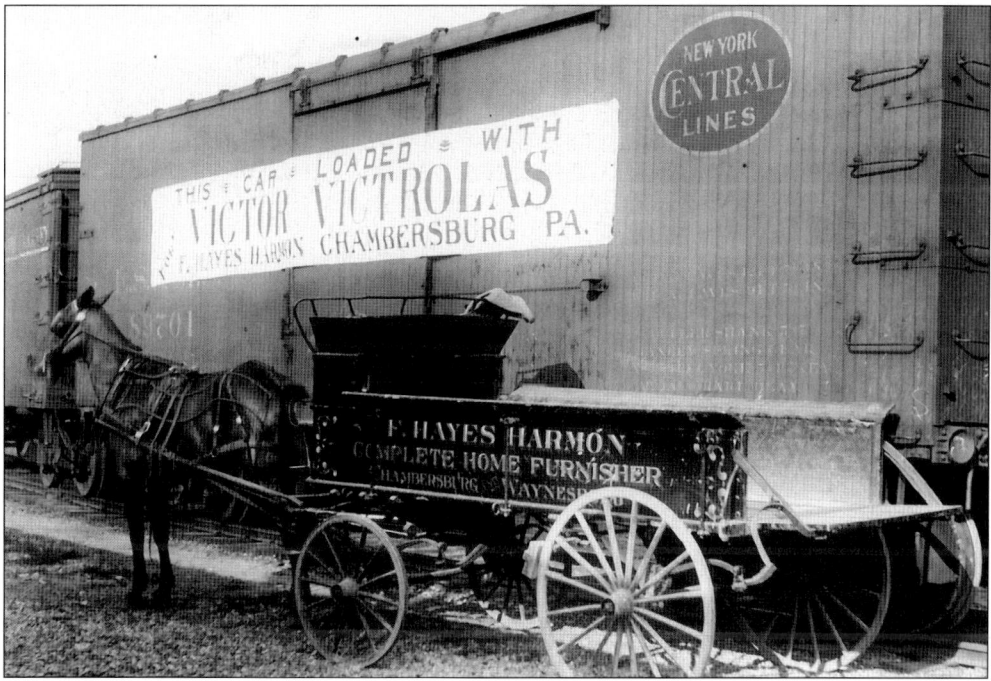

Harmon's Furniture, established by F. Hayes Harmon in 1906, is ready to receive a shipment of Victrolas, transported to Chambersburg via rail car. Harmon's wagon shows two locations, one in Chambersburg and one in Waynesboro.

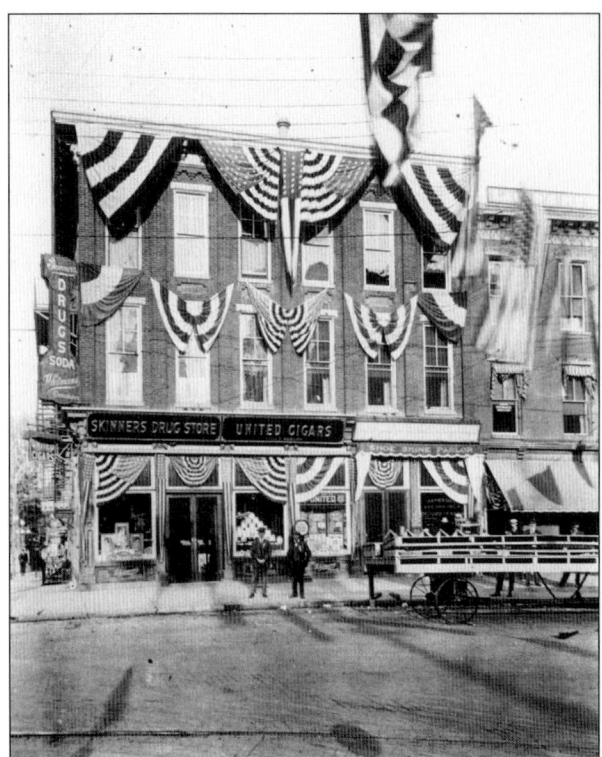

Skinner's Drugstore, established in 1898, occupied the northwest corner of Memorial Square along popular Route 30. The predecessor of Walker's Drugstore, Skinner's was well-known for United Cigars, Whitman's Chocolates, and the Rexall store.

Shown is the tobacco humidor in Bob's Smoke and Gift Shop, owned by J. Robert Cromie, at 27 North Main Street.

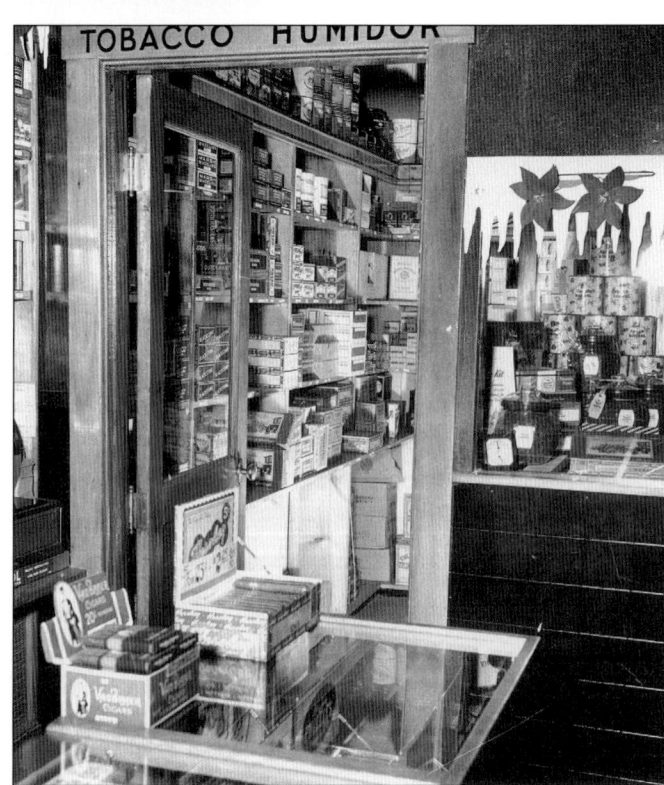

Eight
Advertisements of the Old Queen City

Lively and vibrant trade cards were a popular form of advertising in the late 1800s and early 1900s. Chambersburg merchants gave trade cards to promote their business and product lines. Some were stock cards, and others were customized originals designed especially for the business. Hoping for a future sale, traveling salesmen also used trade cards to advertise. As a pastime, many people collected the colorful cards.

The earliest trade cards date back to 17th-century London, where merchants used them to promote their business and show the way to their shop. Trade cards found their way to Colonial America and remained popular until mass communication with the U.S. postcard was realized as a marketing tool. The first baseball cards were actually trade cards.

The trade cards that follow date from the late 1860s to the early 1900s. No matter what their size, shape, color, or style, the cards' purpose remained the same, to draw customers in and make a sale.

C. SNELL. L. BRANDT.

Union Hotel!

SOUTH MAIN STREET,
CHAMBERSBURG, PA.,

SNELL & BRANDT, PROPRIETORS.

Ample Accommodations for Guests,

GOOD STABLING ATTACHED.

TERMS REASONABLE.

An advertisement of the Union Hotel on South Main Street promises good accommodations for not just the guests but also their horses.

JNO. G. WINGERT

Cigars, Tobacco & Candy

Pool Parlor in Rear

90 WEST MARKET STREET
CHAMBERSBURG, PA.
OPPOSITE W. M. R. R. DEPOT.

J. G. Wingert, located across from the Western Maryland Railroad depot, advertises tobacco, candy, and a pool parlor.

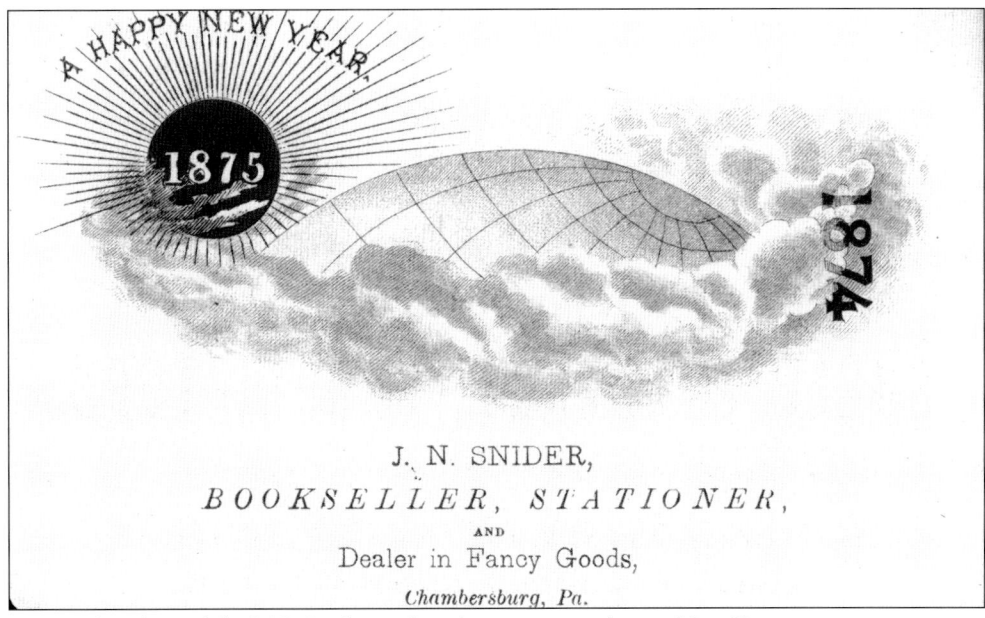

An 1875 trade card for J. N. Snider wishes the recipient a happy New Year.

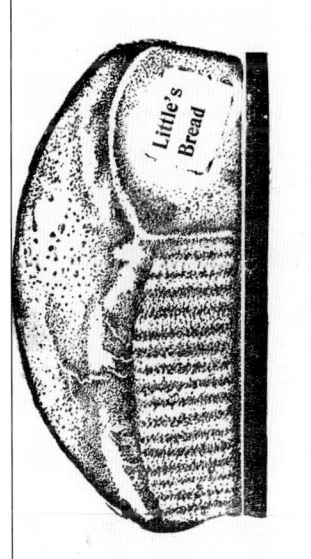

C. B. Little, located at 533 South Main Street, offers bread at 4¢ a loaf and is even willing to deliver.

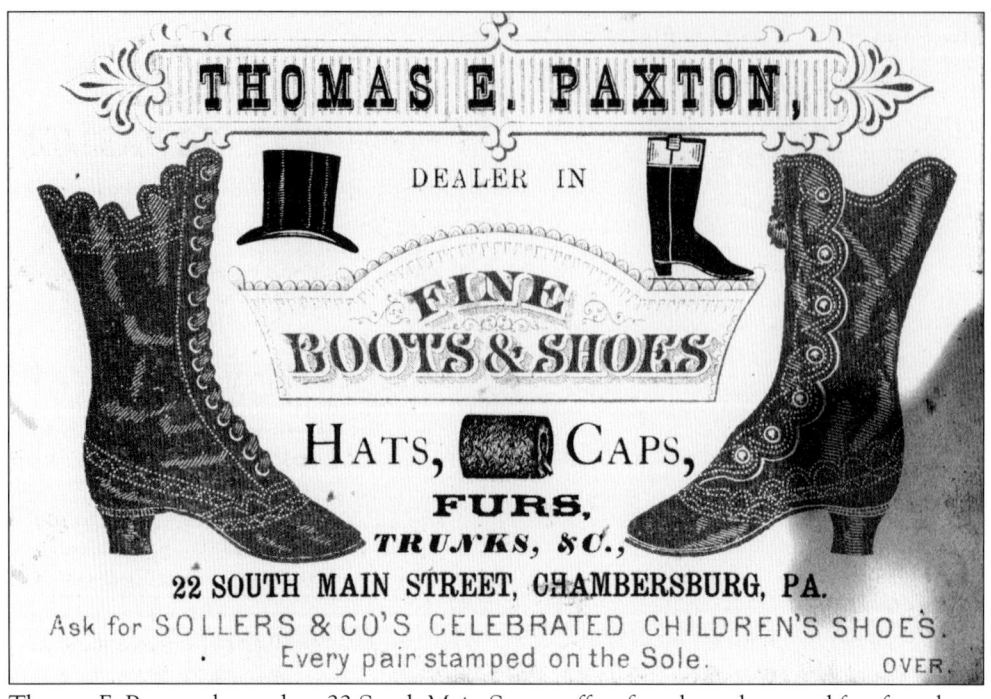

Thomas E. Paxton, located on 22 South Main Street, offers fine shoes, hats, and furs for sale.

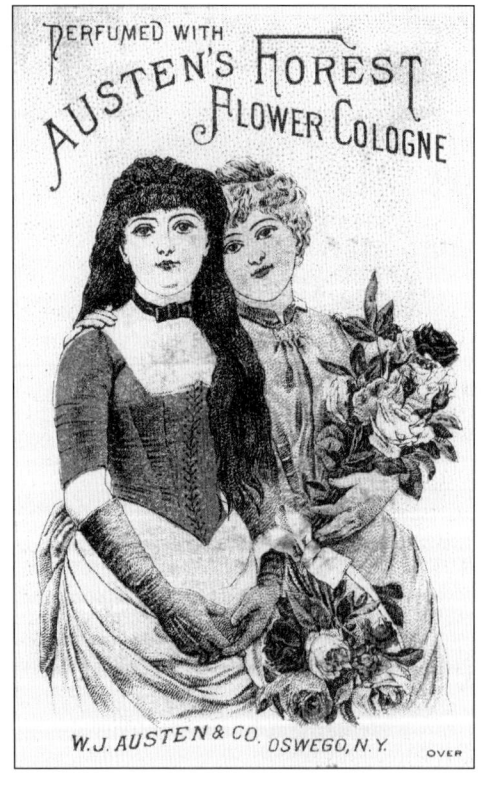

This trading card is imprinted with a promotion of Austen Forest flower cologne.

This is the reverse side of the Austen Forest flower cologne trading card. It promotes a new shaving parlor on North Main Street, opposite the Montgomery House, where many of its customers probably stayed.

F. T. SEIPPLE,

HAS REMOVED TO HIS

NEW SHAVING PARLOR,

Opposite the Montgomery House,

N. Main St., CHAMBERSBURG, Pa.

Where you will find polite and gentlemanly artists who will give you an Easy Shave and a Neat Hair Cut.

Forest Flower Cologne!

The Richest and most Fashionable Perfume Known.

Its Permanence and Delicacy of Odor have won for it the

FRONT RANK.

Accept no Other! SEE OUR NAME BLOWN IN BOTTLE!
For sale by all Druggists and Fancy Goods Dealers.
Price 15, 25 and 50 Cents. · Large Size, One Dollar.

MANUFACTURED BY

W. J. AUSTEN & CO., · OSWEGO, N. Y.

NEW YORK OFFICE,

106 DUANE STREET.

J. N. SNIDER,

CHAMBERSBURG, PA.,

Bookseller, Stationer & Bookbinder.

DEALER IN

SCHOOL AND MISCELLANEOUS BOOKS,

Blank Books and Staple Stationery.

Also dealer in Berlin Zephyrs, Cashmere Yarns and Germantown Wool, Working Canvas, Zephyr Slipper Patterns, and Fancy Goods generally. Old Books, Music and Periodicals bound to order. Paper ruled to pattern.

BLANK BOOKS MADE TO ORDER.

Agency for Mme. Demorest's Reliable Patterns.

This advertisement card features the exclusive goods of J. N. Snider.

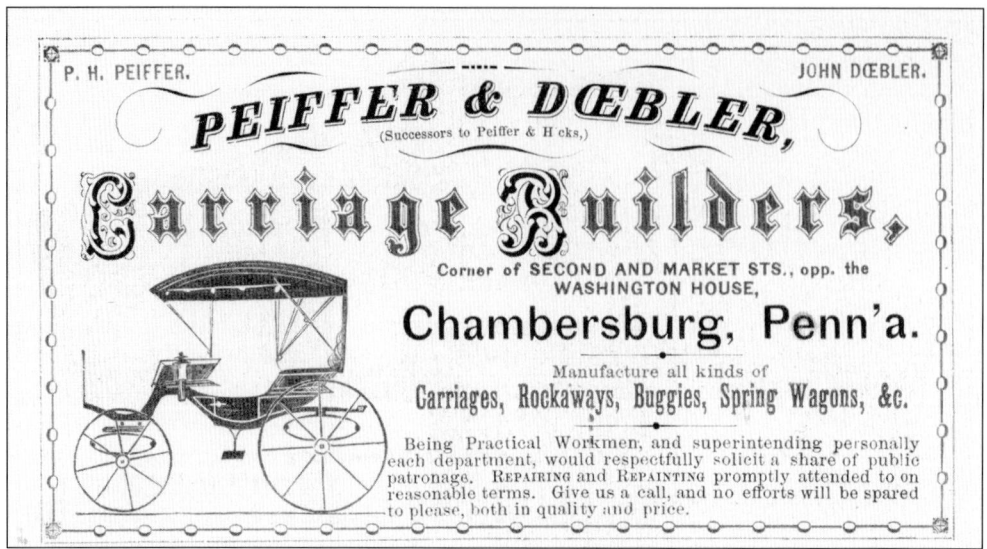

Peiffer and Doebler Carriage Builders, located at Second and Market Streets across from the Washington House, not only manufactured carriages of various sorts but also repaired and repainted them.

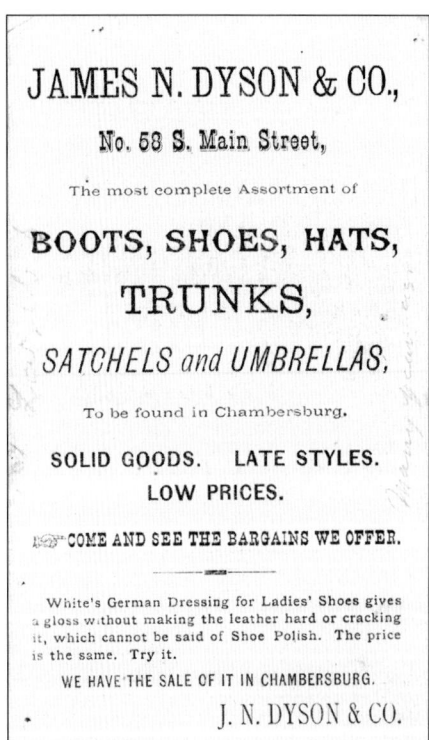

Dyson's Shoe and Hat Store card touts solid and stylish goods with low prices. The store was located at 58 South Main Street.

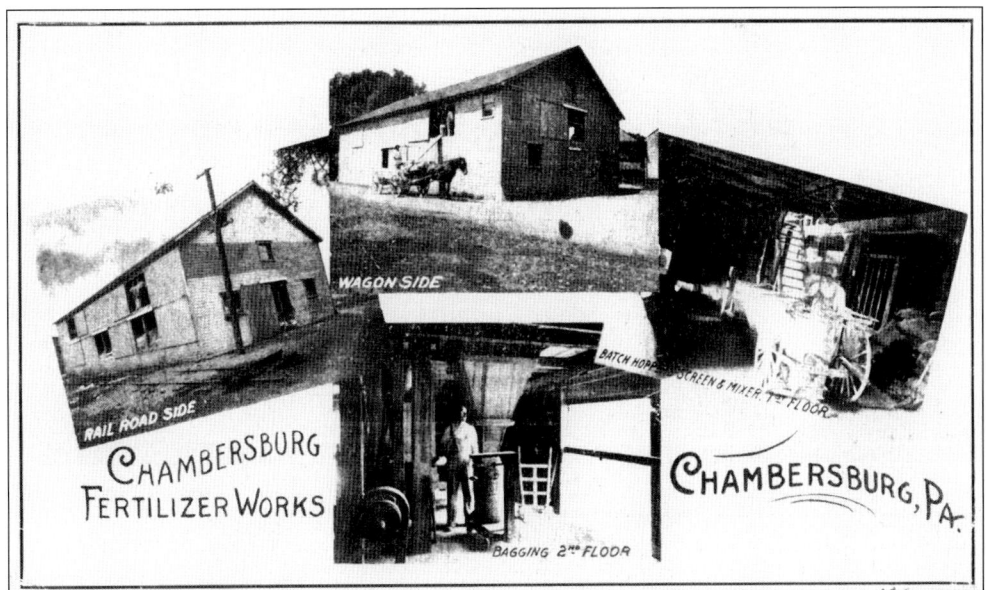

This card promotes the Chambersburg Fertilizer Works.

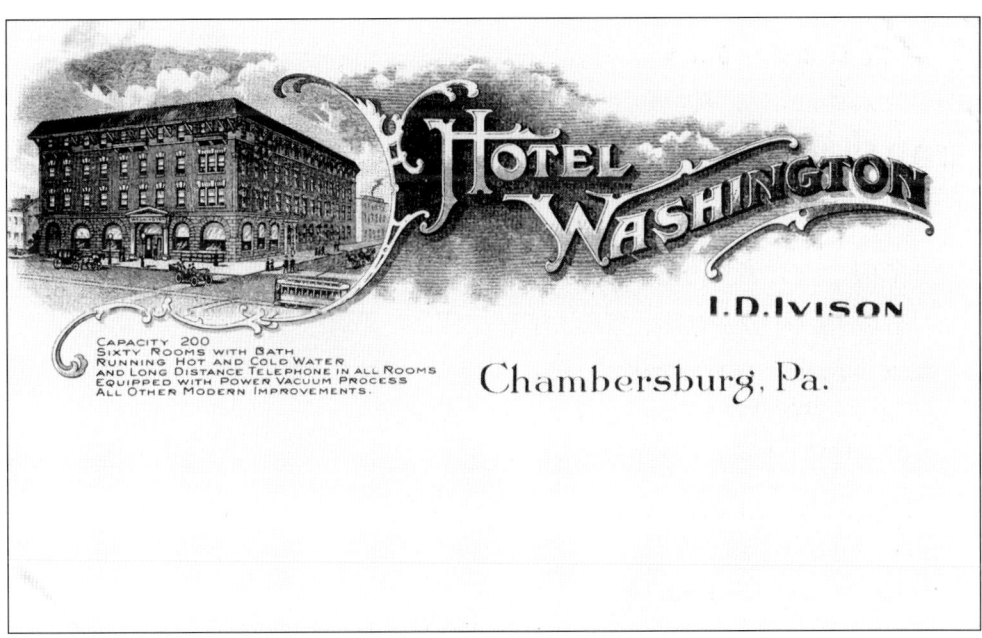

Hotel Washington advertised a capacity of 200, a total of 60 rooms, baths with hot and cold running water, and long-distance telephone service in each room.

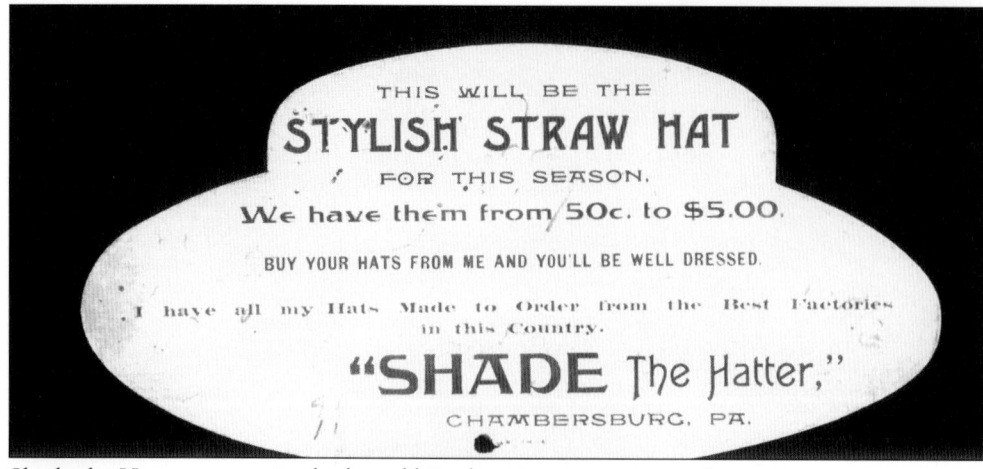

Shade the Hatter appropriately shaped his advertisement as a straw hat.

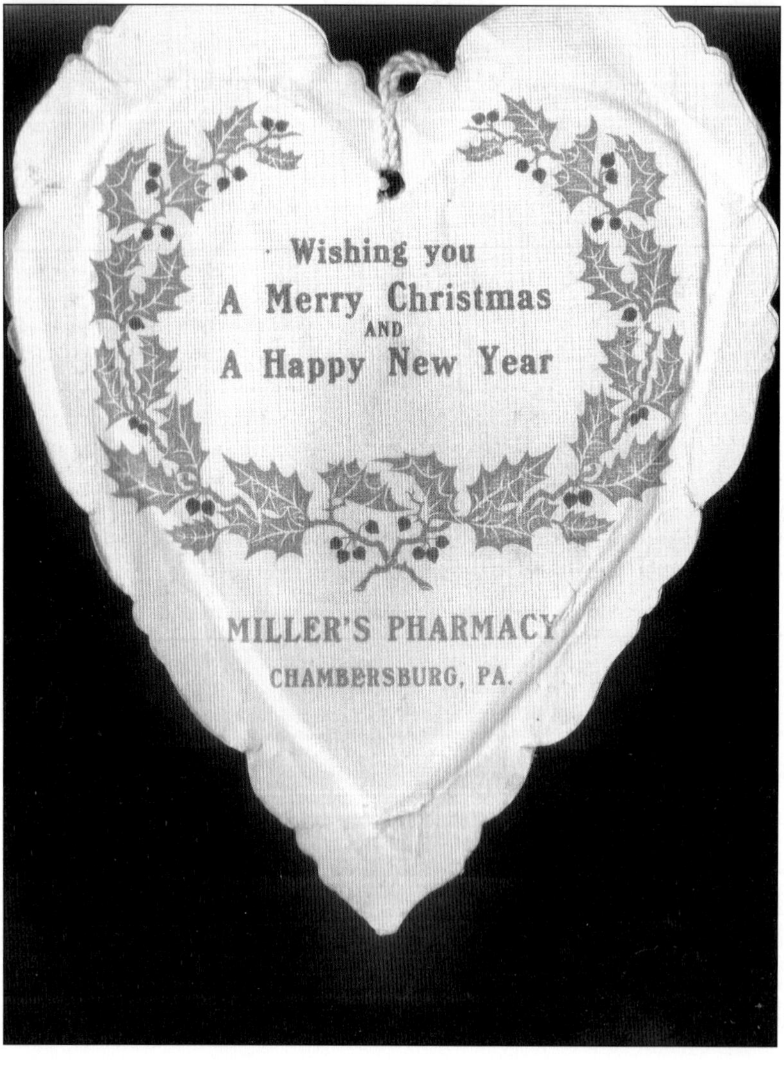

With this promotion, Miller's Pharmacy, located on the Diamond, sends wishes for a merry Christmas and a happy New Year.

Nine
STREETSCAPES

By the beginning of the 20th century, Chambersburg had grown to nearly 14,000 people. Nestled in a verdant valley, its natural beauty was attractive to home seekers. It also offered a choice of churches, fine schools, libraries, theaters, and a variety of membership organizations. With strong transportation facilities, the availability of good fire protection, and its own electric, water, and gas companies, Chambersburg also developed a solid reputation as a worthwhile location for business and industry. Such a prosperous and pleasant atmosphere prompted the Franklin Repository to describe Chambersburg as "the Queen City of the Cumberland Valley" in its 1909 special industrial edition.

The images in this final chapter show Chambersburg alive and excited with people and activity; the special beauty of its buildings, its fountains, and its square; and the quiet peacefulness of an earlier era. These times are passed but not gone, simply secured in streetscapes that celebrate Chambersburg as "the Queen City of the Cumberland Valley."

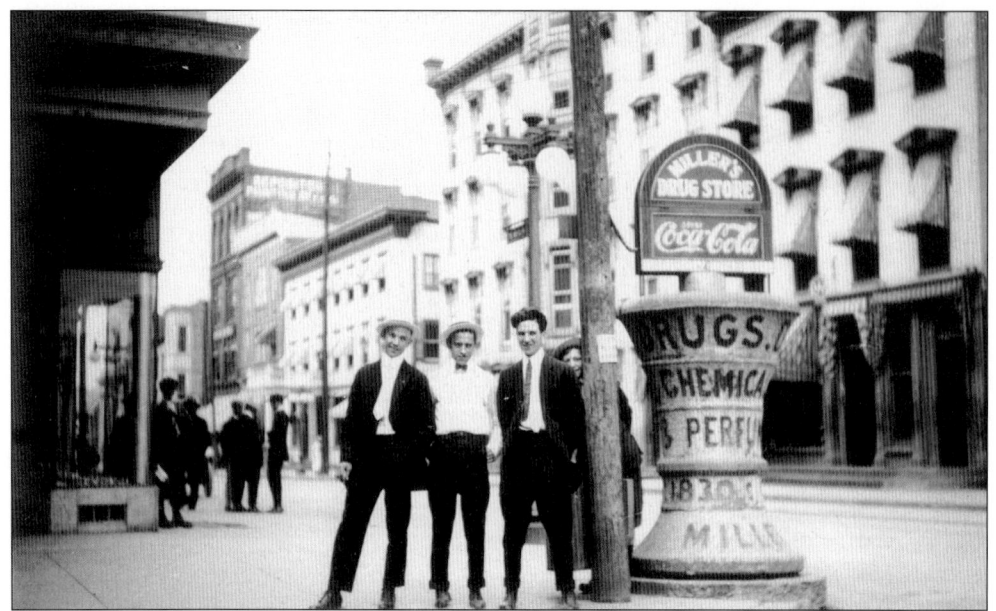

In January 1917, four young lads, out for a good time on North Main Street, stand beside the mortar and pestle at Miller's Drugstore.

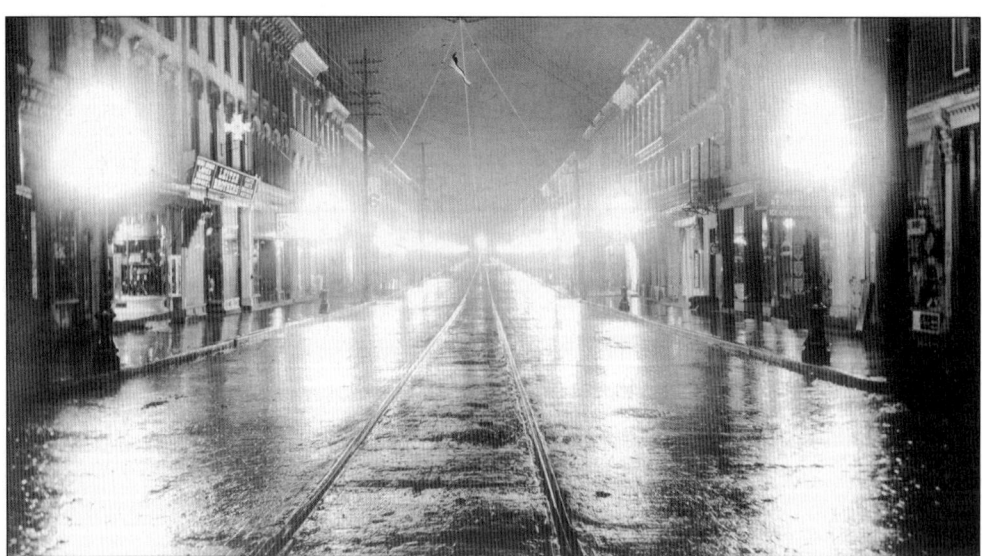

Silence is golden. This peaceful street scene was taken from the square looking down South Main Street at 10:00 p.m. during Old Home Week of 1914.

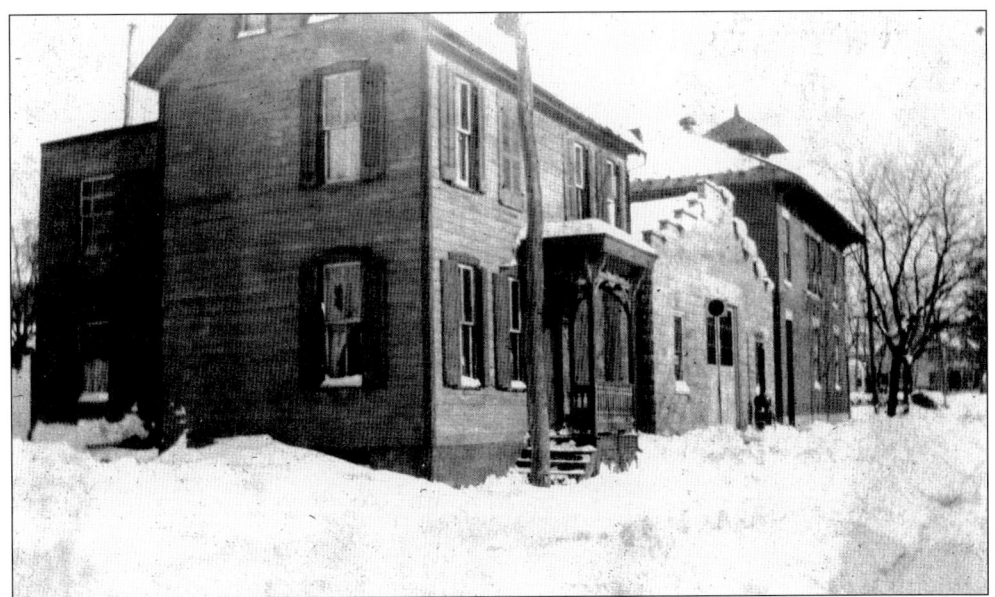

This old home was located on East Queen Street at the East Point until it was torn down in 1919. Later the new structure built on this site housed some notable businesses, including Thompsons motorcycle shop, Marotte's Barbershop, and Chick's Tavern.

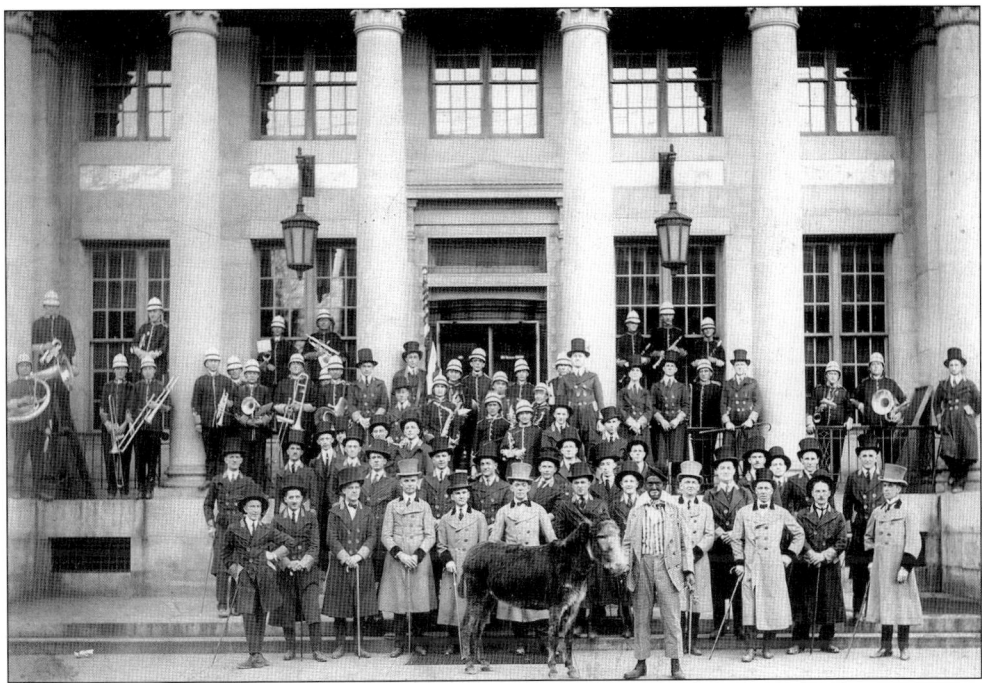

The Knights of Pythias Minstrels assemble on the steps of the Chambersburg Post Office, North Main and King Streets, after performing at the Rosedale Theatre on March 6–7, 1922. The post office building eventually became the Coyle Free Library.

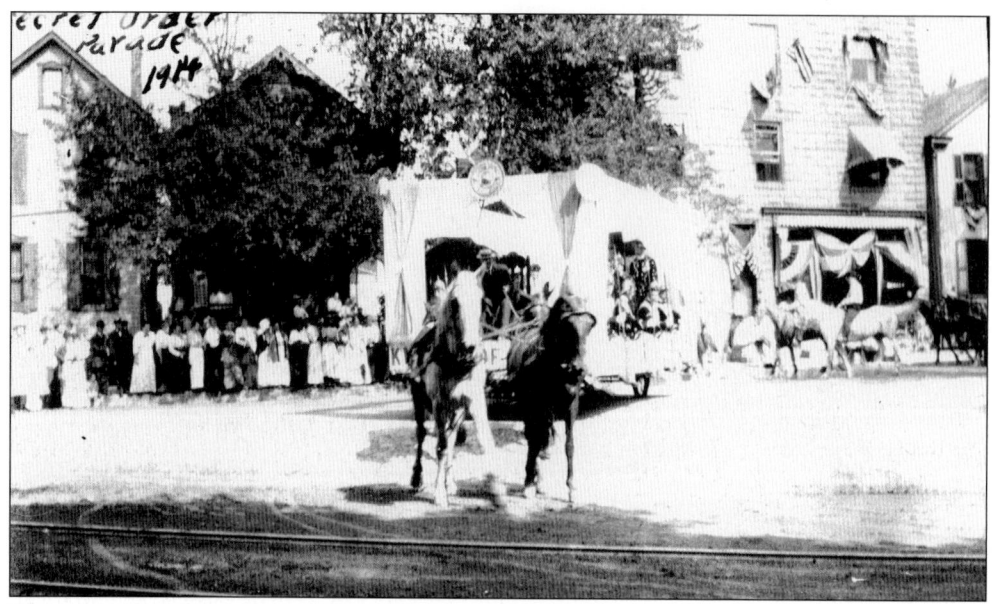

The Secret Order Parade passes the decorated grocery store of A. M. Funk on Second Street and turns onto Philadelphia Avenue during Old Home Week of 1914.

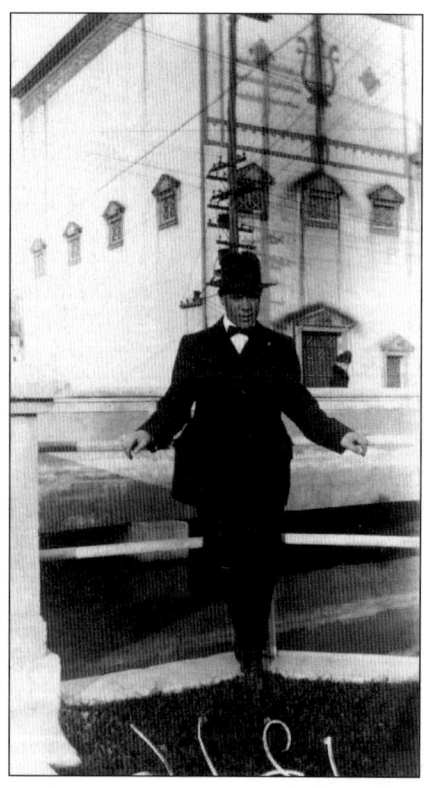

This young man is at the Falling Spring on West King Street across from the Orpheum Theatre in 1919.

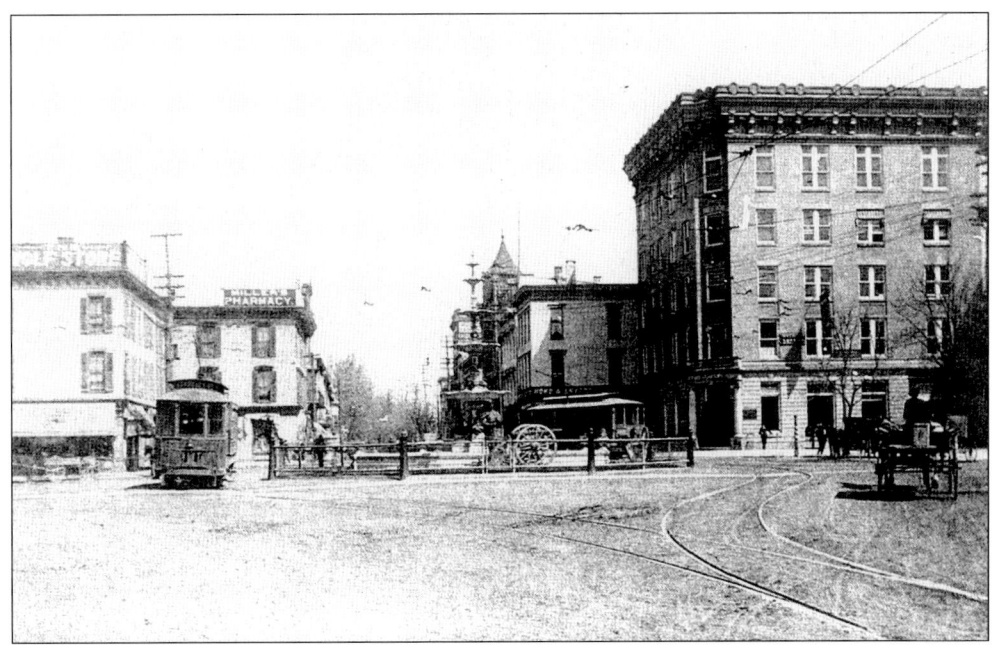

A Chambersburg and Gettysburg electric trolley car makes its way through the square in 1910.

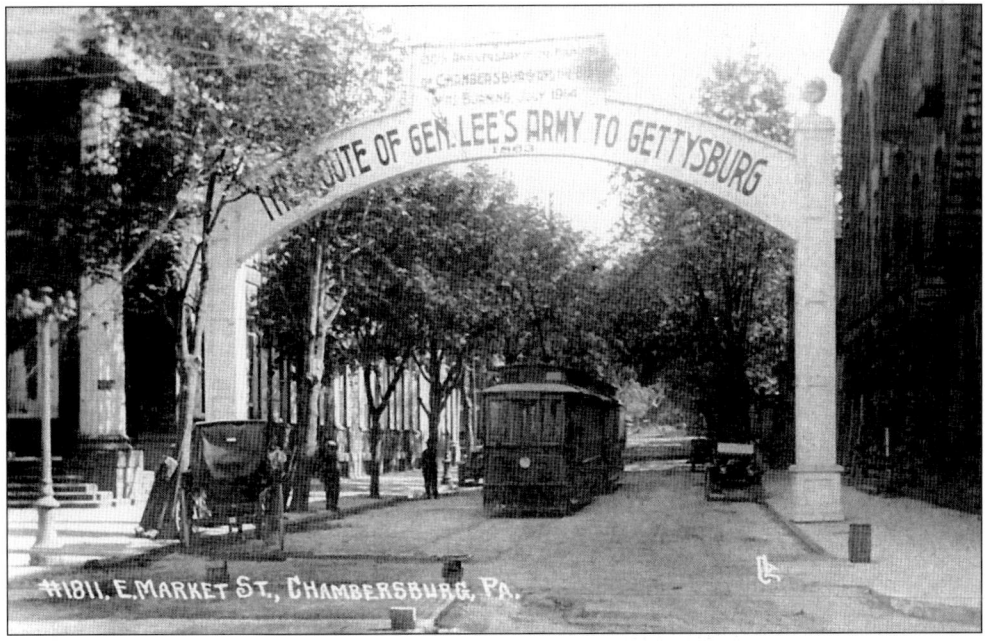

A Chambersburg and Gettysburg trolley car makes its stop on East Market Street (Lincoln Way East) at the arch in 1914. The distinctive pillars of Franklin County Courthouse appear in the fringe on the left. The old Valley National Bank building is also slightly visible.

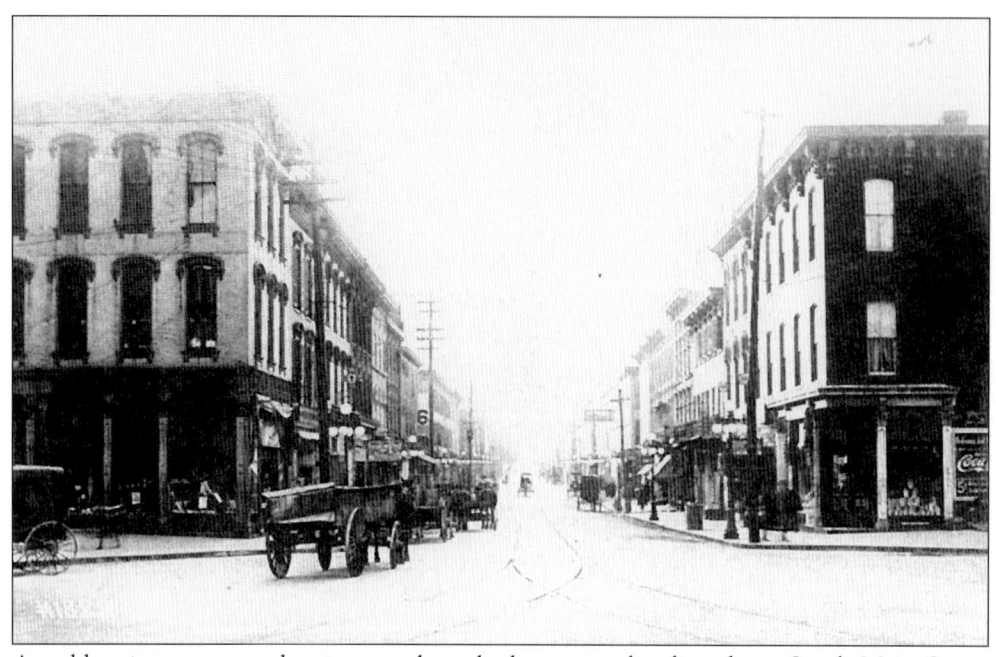

An old spring wagon makes its way through the square, heading down South Main Street in 1909.

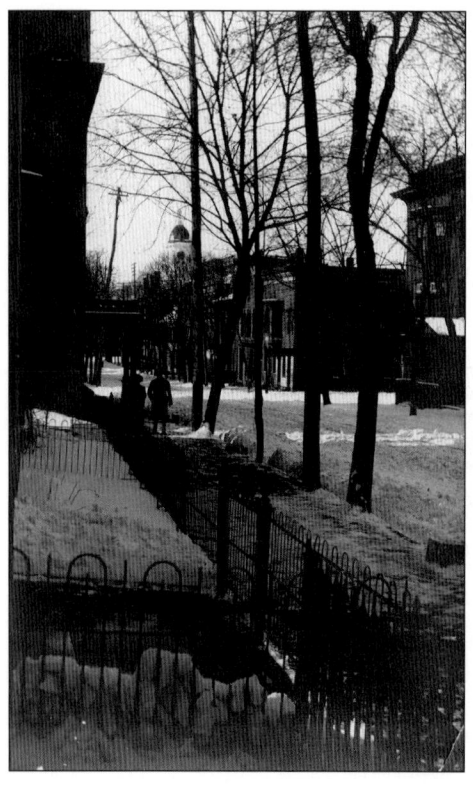

This view was taken beside the Washington House and looks down Lincoln Way East on a snowy day in 1911.

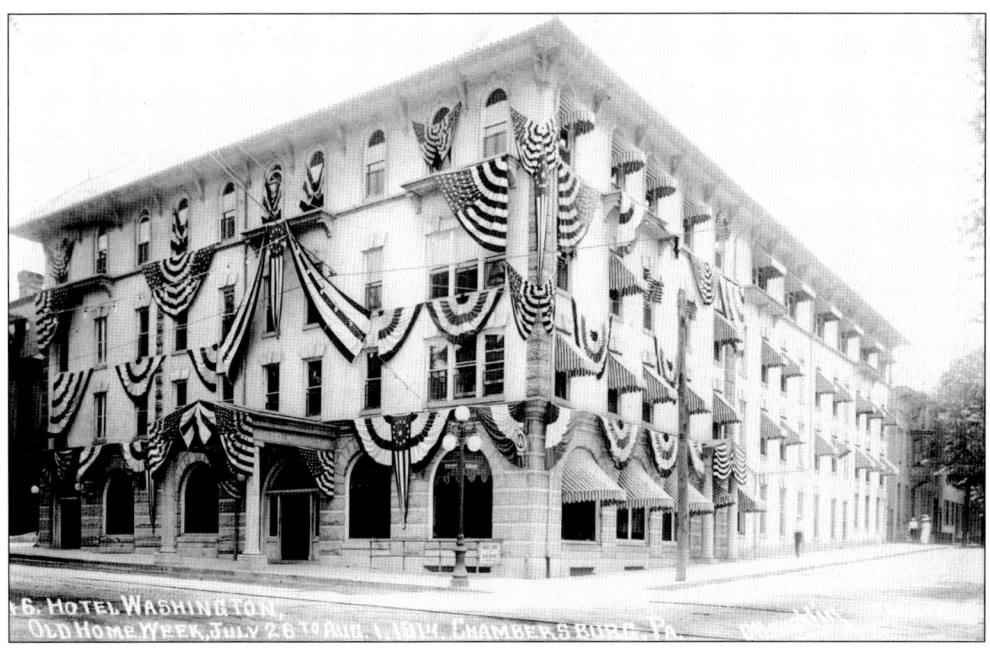

The old Washington Hotel, located at the corner of Lincoln Way East and South Second Street, is finely decorated for the Old Home Week activities held from July 26 to August 1, 1914. Known for its excellent cuisine, the Washington House attracted a number of famous people, including Mary Pickford, Douglass Fairbanks, Jimmy Stewart, Babe Ruth, Enrico Carusso, and Basil Rathbone.

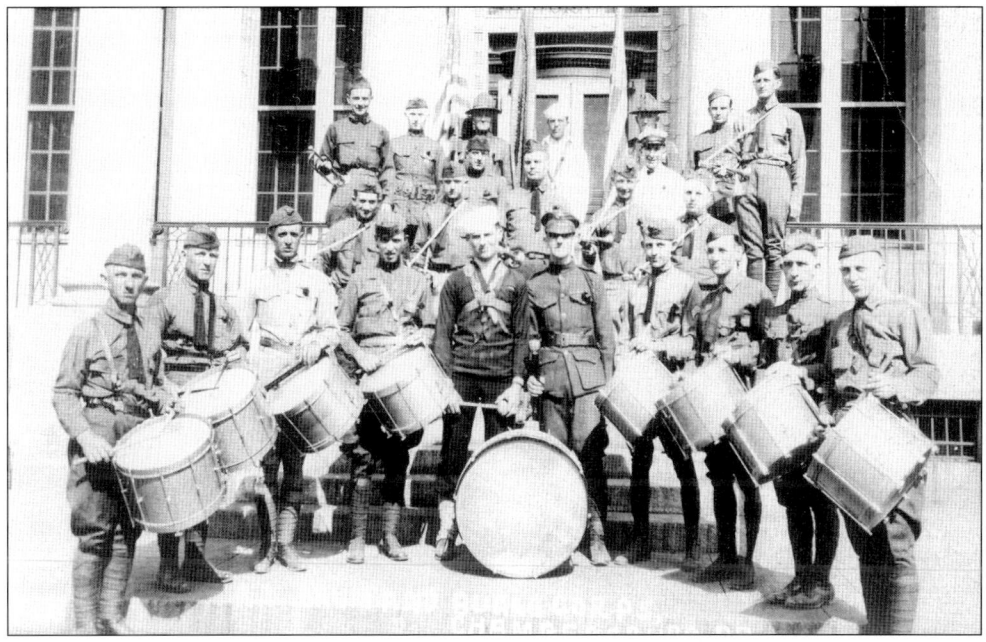

The American Legion Drum and Bugle Corps is ready to strike up a tune in front of the old post office on North Main Street.

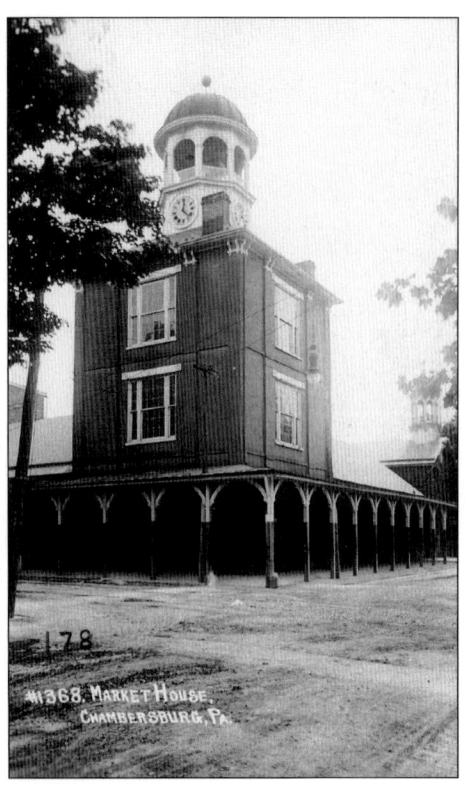

This 1907 photograph shows the Old Market House, built in 1830 at the corner of East Queen and South Second Streets. The clock in the cupola was added in 1832. In 1930, the borough started opening offices in the Old Market House and, by 1945, fully occupied the building.

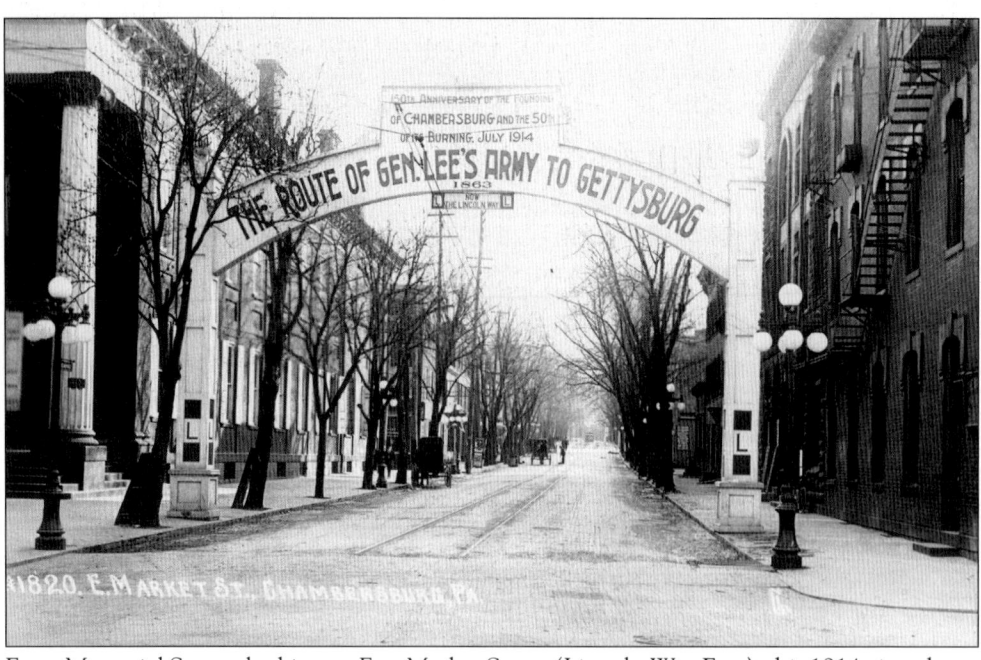

From Memorial Square looking up East Market Street (Lincoln Way East), this 1914 view shows the great arch, commemorating the 50th anniversary of the burning of Chambersburg.

J. N. Snider Book and Stationery Store stands next to the Valley National Bank on the square in 1914.

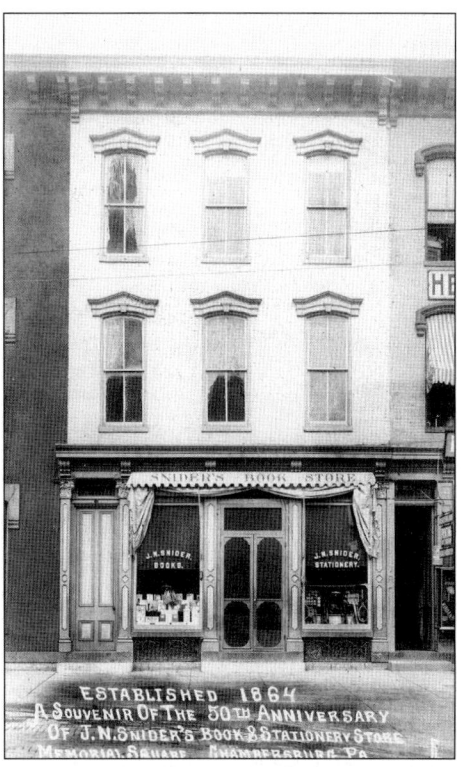

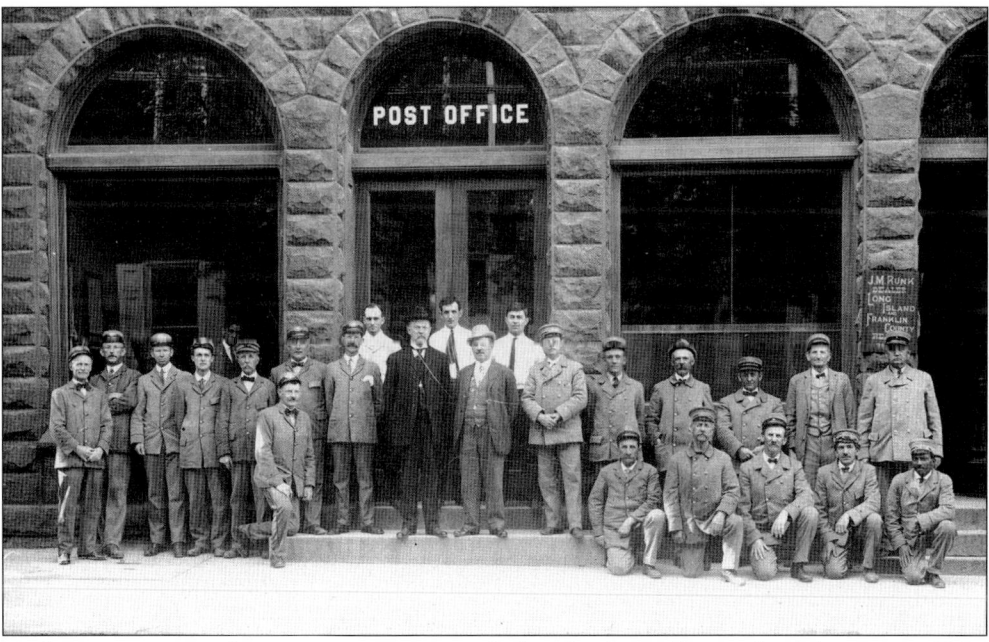

Mail carriers receive last-minute instructions before heading off to make deliveries in 1908. They are at the old post office building, on Lincoln Way East, adjacent to the future site of the Valley National Bank.

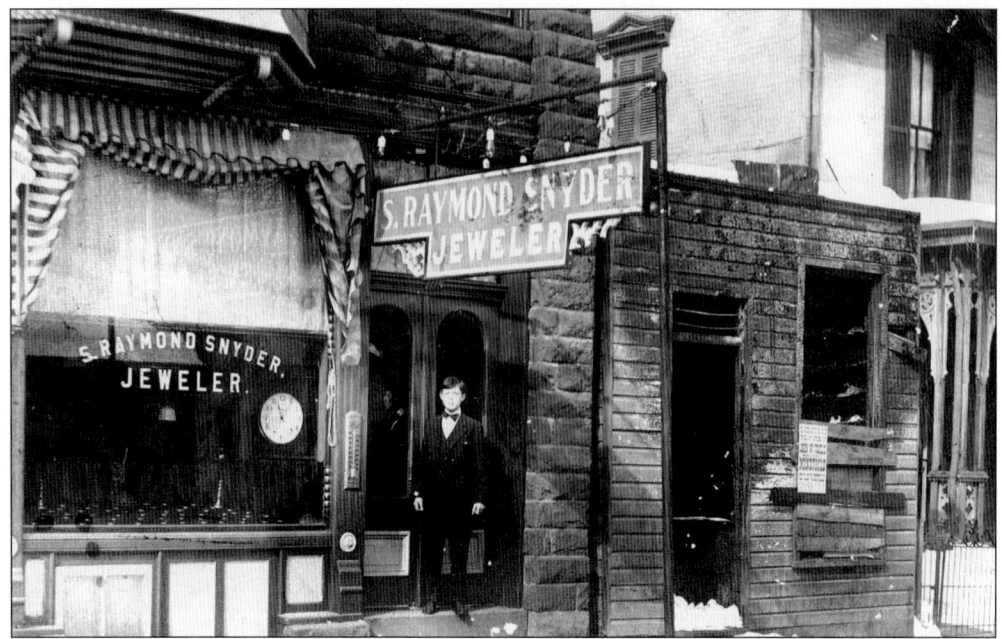

The S. Raymond Snyder jewelry store stands on North Main Street in 1908.

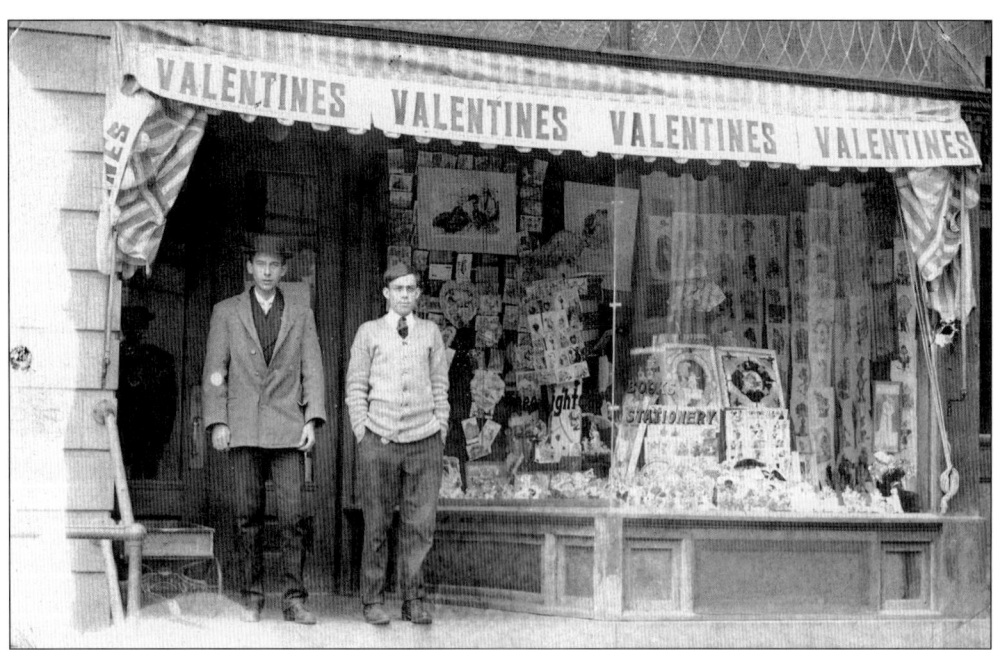

The display window of the book and stationery business of Theo Lightcap is attractively decorated for Valentine's Day 1908. The shop was located in the Chambersburg Trust Company building on the square.

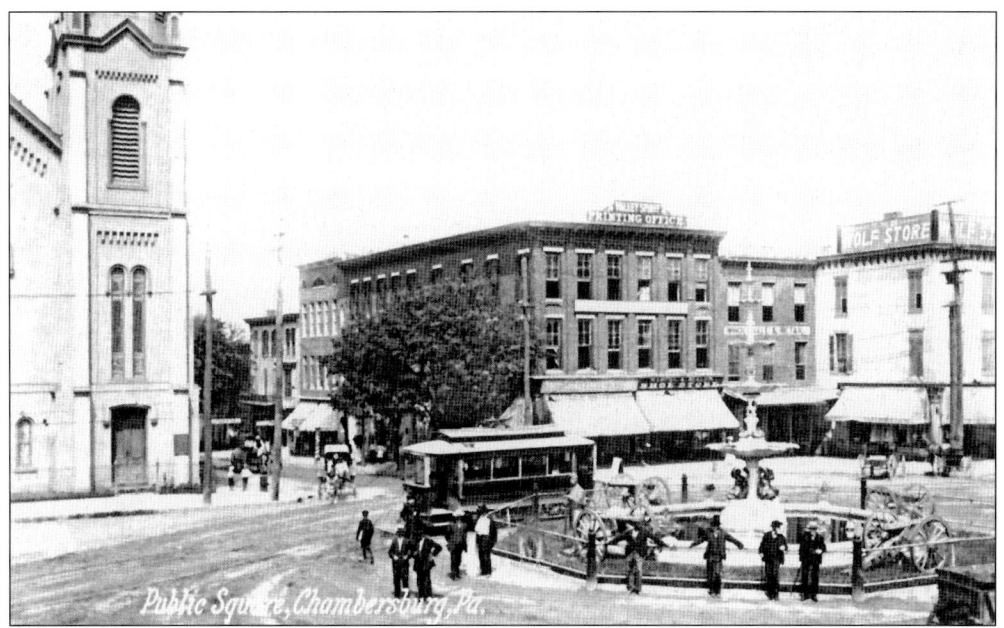

In 1909, some citizens relax on Memorial Square as a trolley car passes behind the fountain.

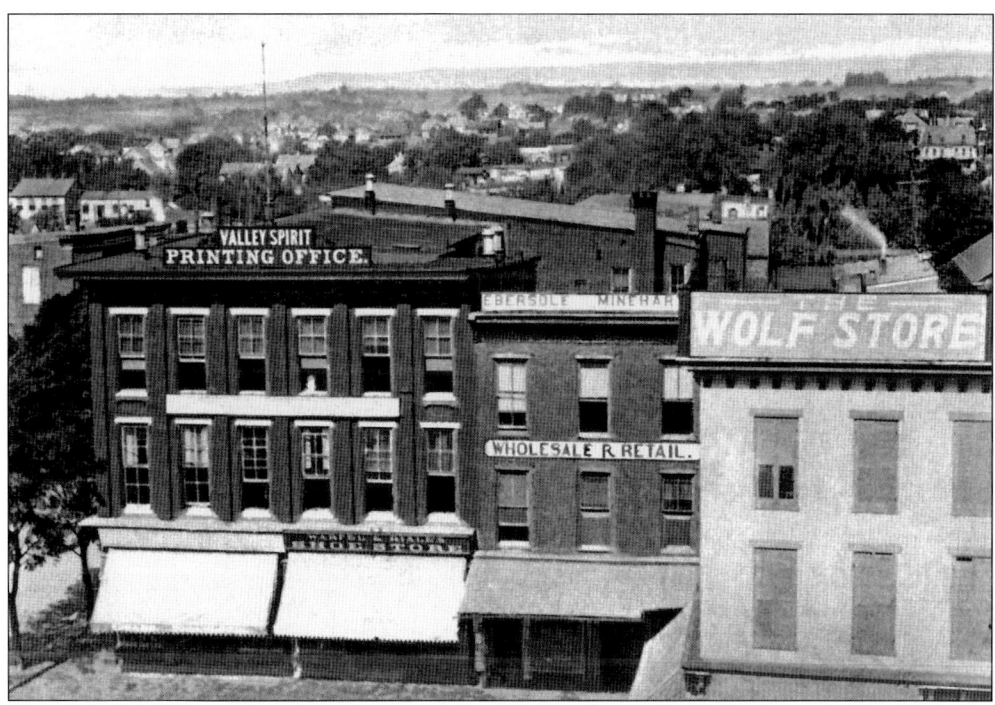

Businesses in 1910 are, from left to right, the Valley Spirit Printing Office, Ebersole and Minheart, and the Wolf Store. The view is looking west from the Chambersburg Trust Company building.

121

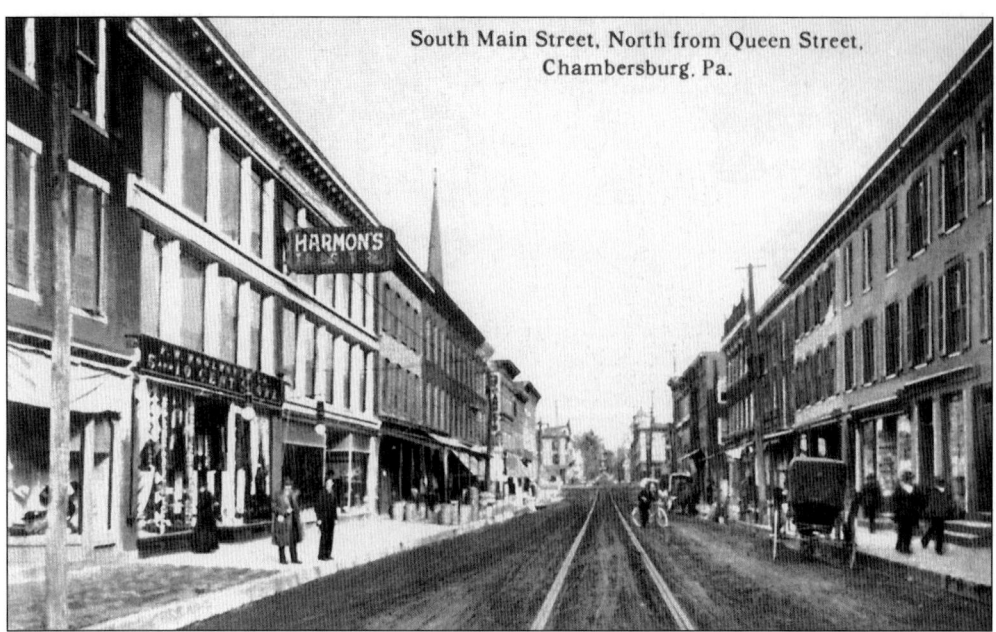

Looking north toward the square, this view shows the intersection of East Queen and South Main Streets in 1909.

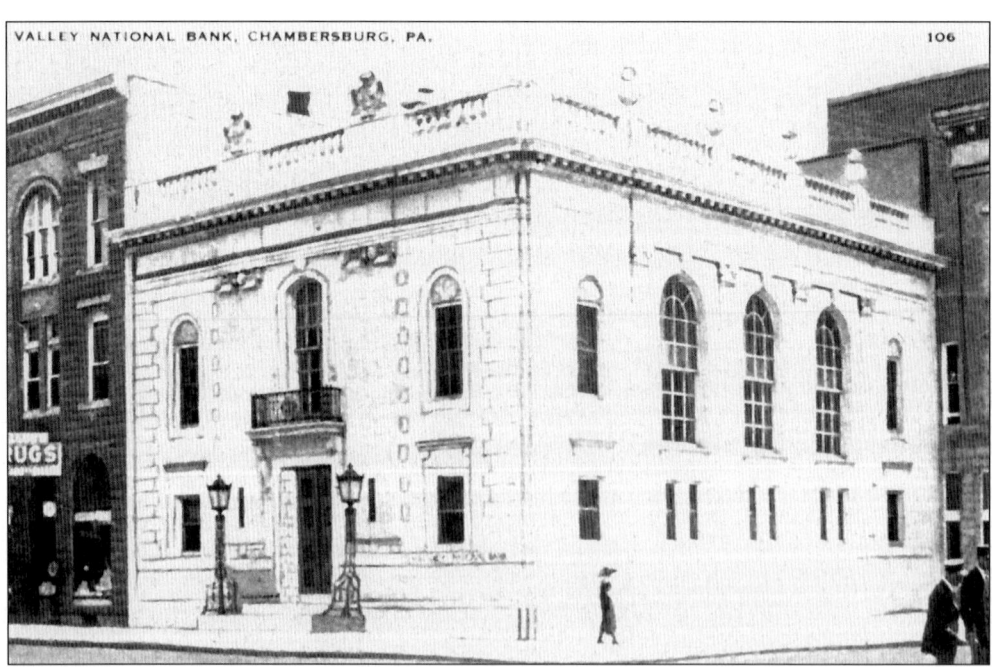

Illustrated here is the newly completed marble Valley National Bank building on Memorial Square in 1915. The bank used Georgian marble.

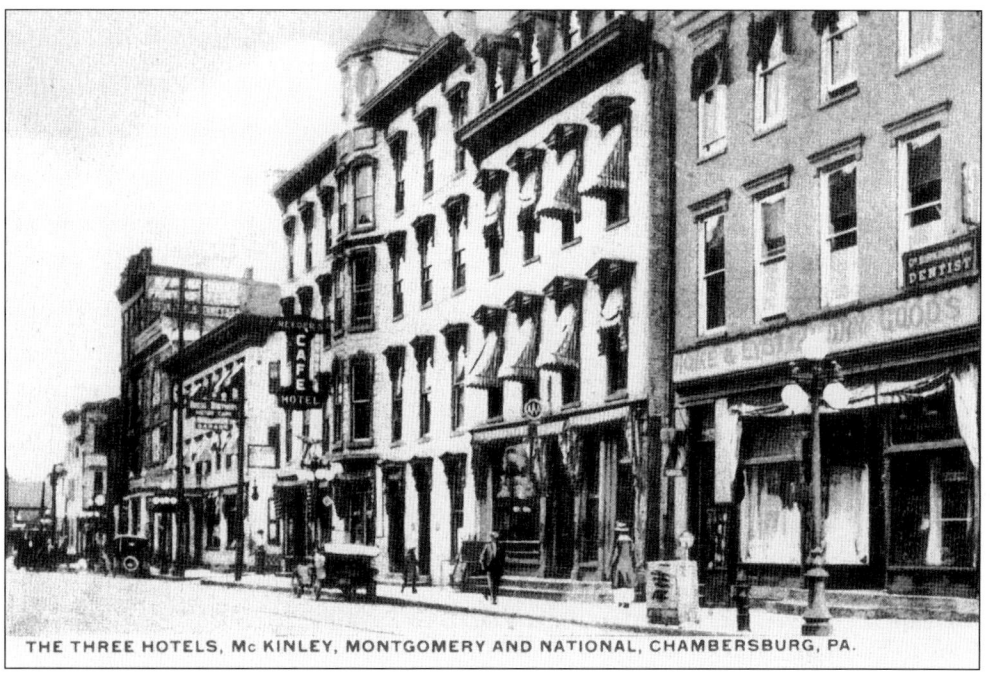

A 1915 lineup of accommodations—McKinley, Montgomery, and National Hotels—gives visitors ample choices.

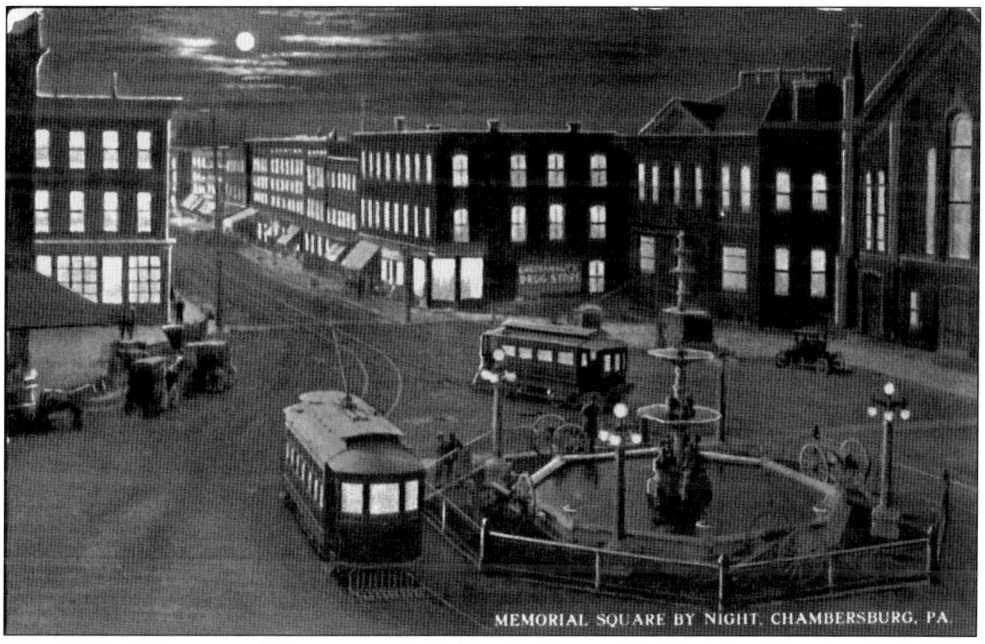

This 1915 night view of the square was taken looking south from the Chambersburg Trust Company, as two trolley cars round the fountain.

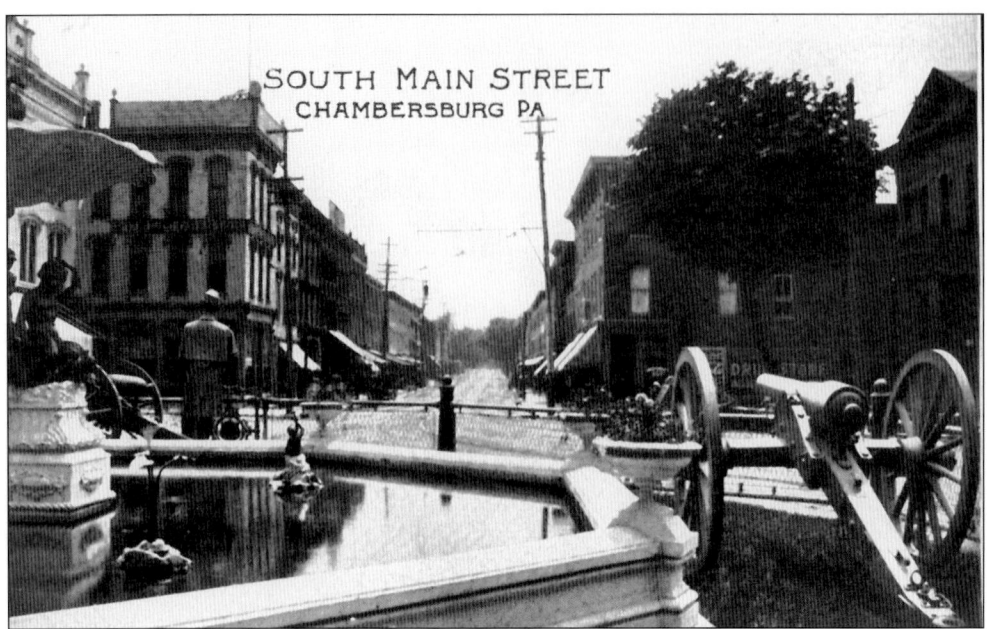

This 1908 view looks across the waters of Memorial Fountain to South Main Street.

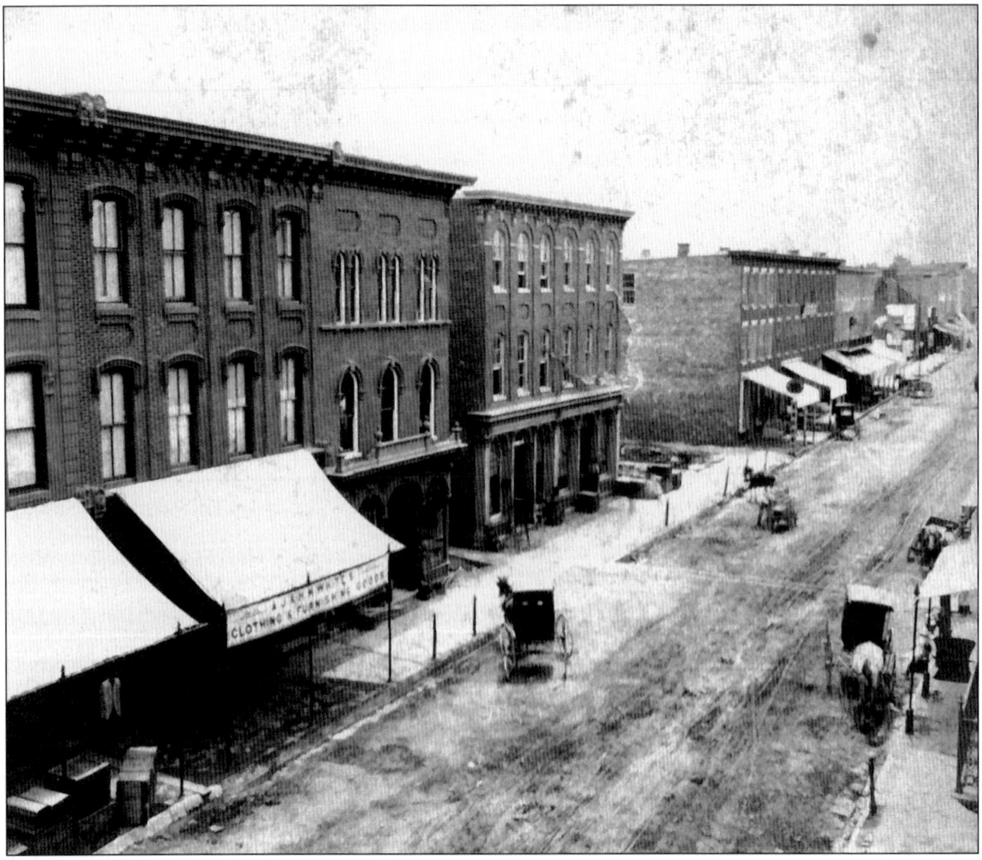

New growth and prosperity are evident in this 1870s photograph of South Main Street.

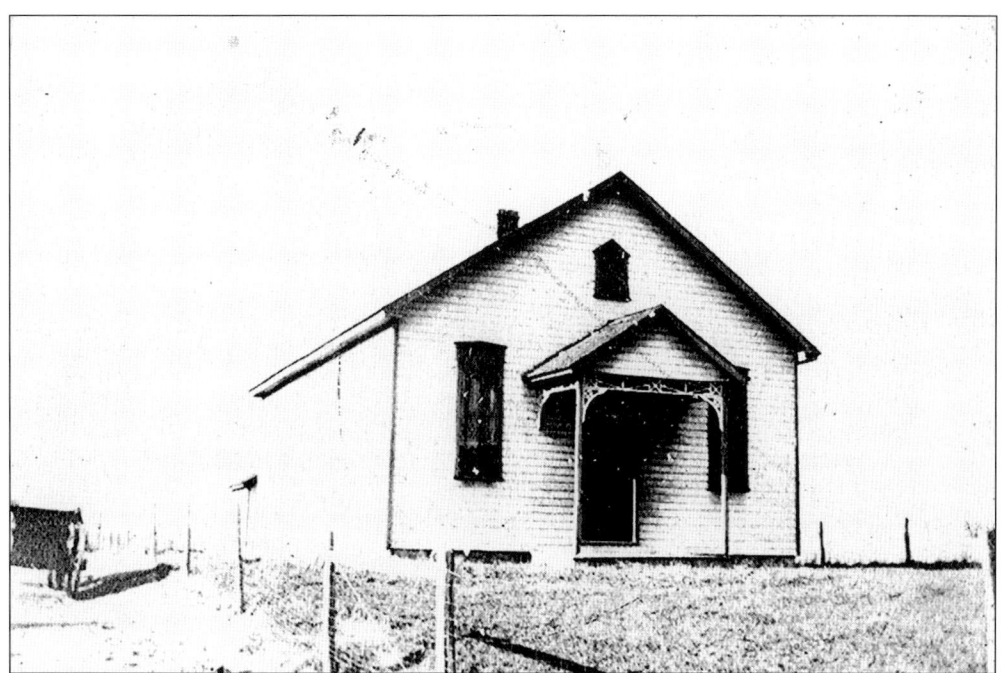

The small white schoolhouse on North Franklin Street was used for classes until 1898. Then, the schoolhouse was sold to Solomon Sleighter for use as a family home.

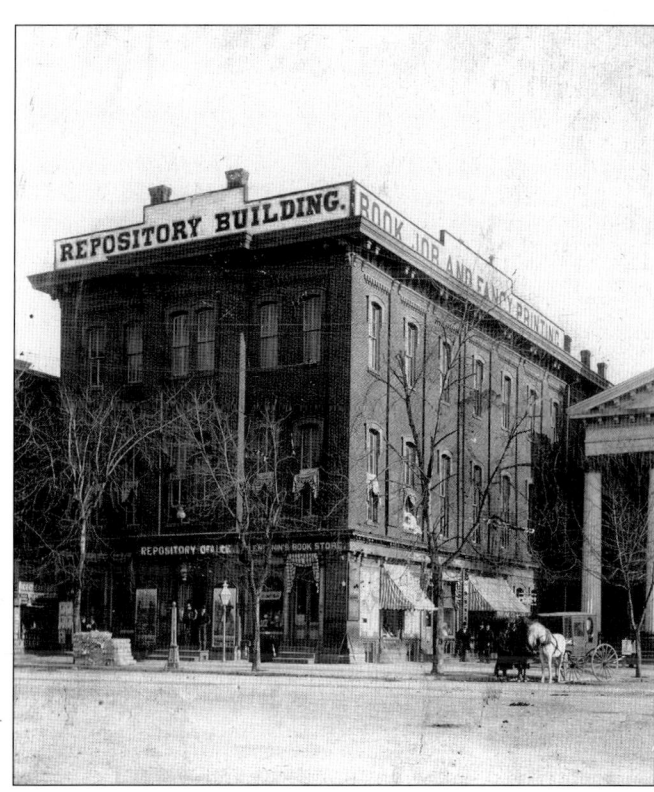

In 1900, the Repository Building was a fixture of Memorial Square. In 1905, the Chambersburg Trust Company replaced it on the northeast quadrant of the Diamond.

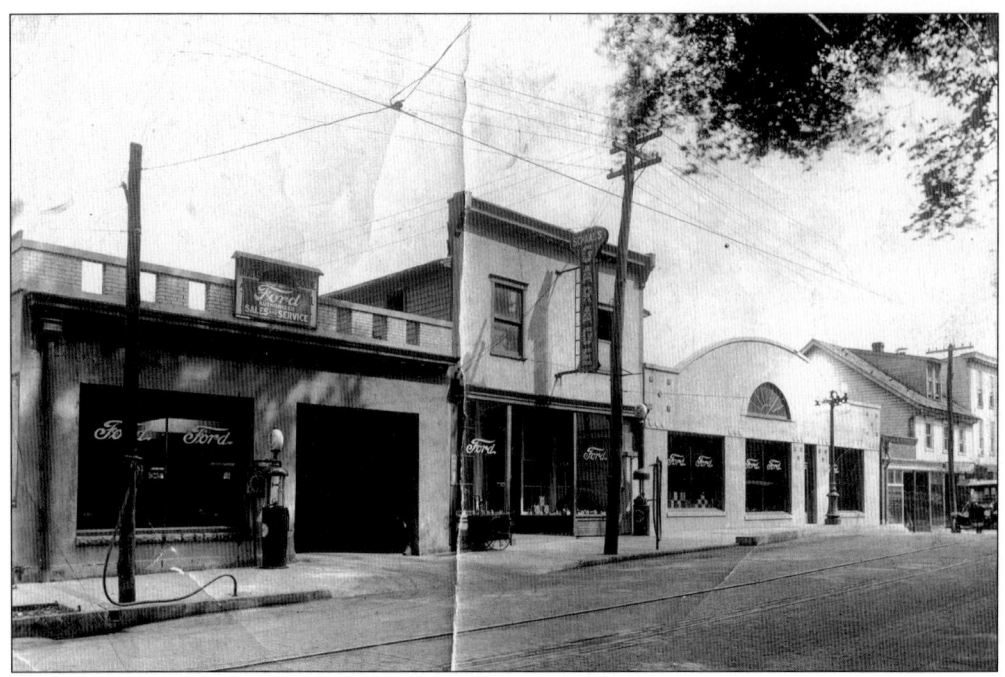

This 1910 photograph shows Schaals Garage on North Main Street at the Falling Spring.

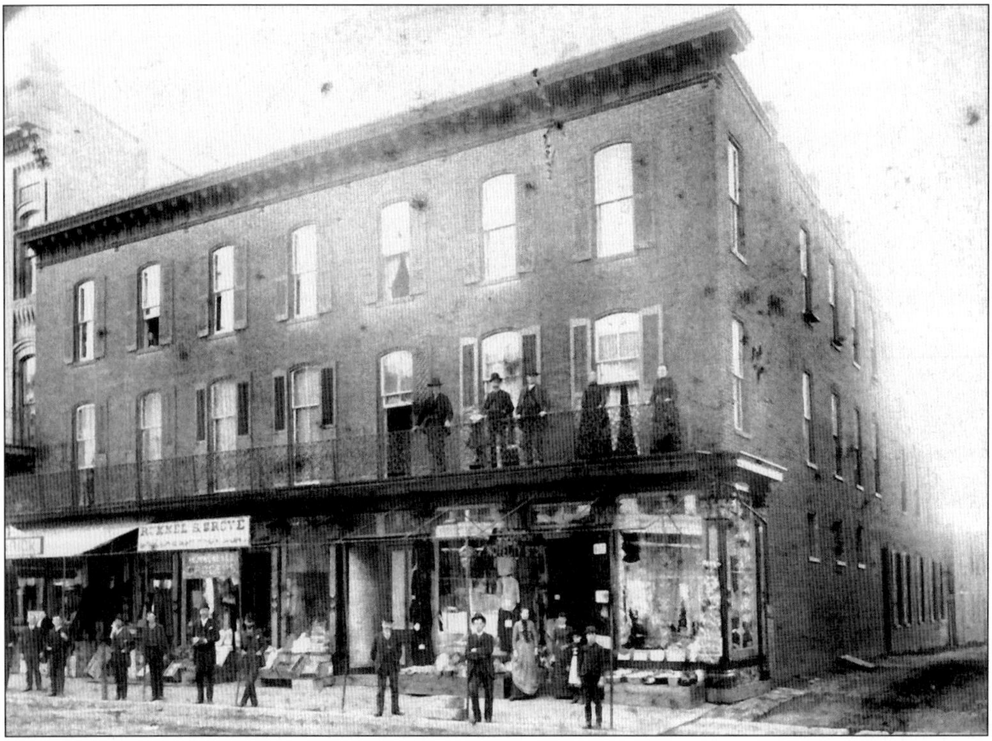

An 1885 scene of North Main and Spring Streets captures businesses and townspeople.

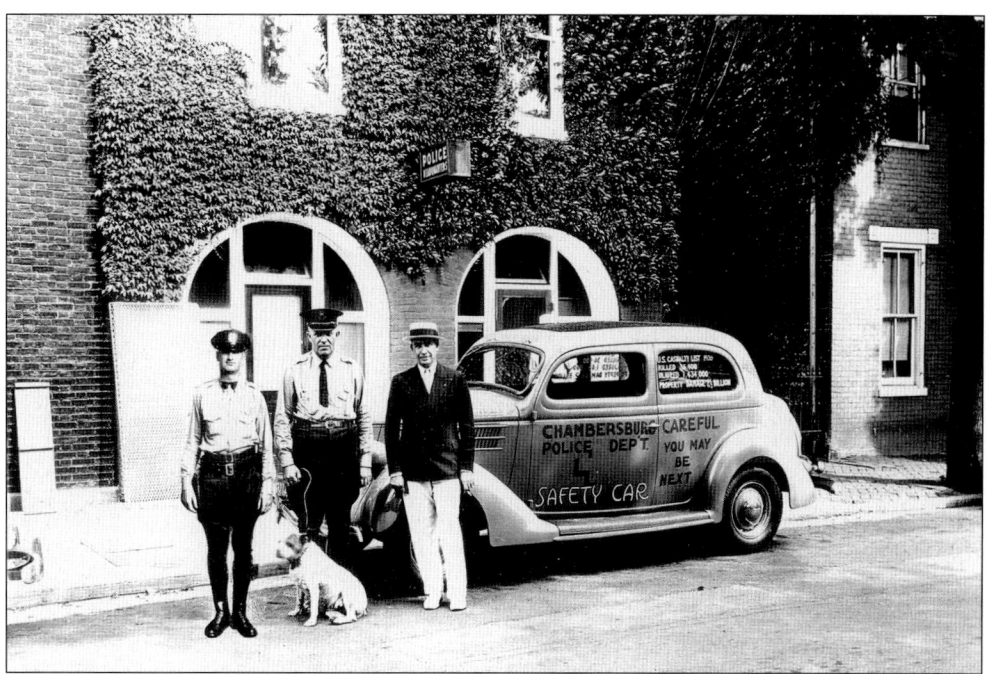

The Chambersburg Police Department and the new safety car are ready for action. In the 1930s, the police department had its headquarters in the former Friendship Fire Company Station next to borough hall on South Second Street. This police station has since been torn down.

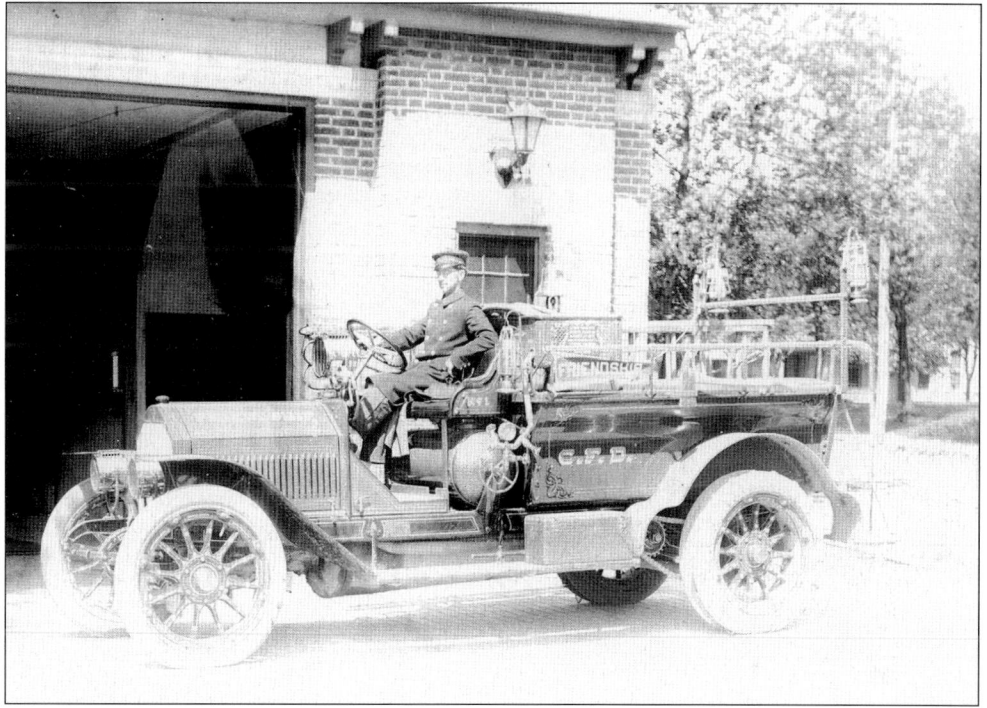

Chet Weagley drives the new 1911 American LaFrance chemical engine of the Friendship Fire Company at the East Point Station.

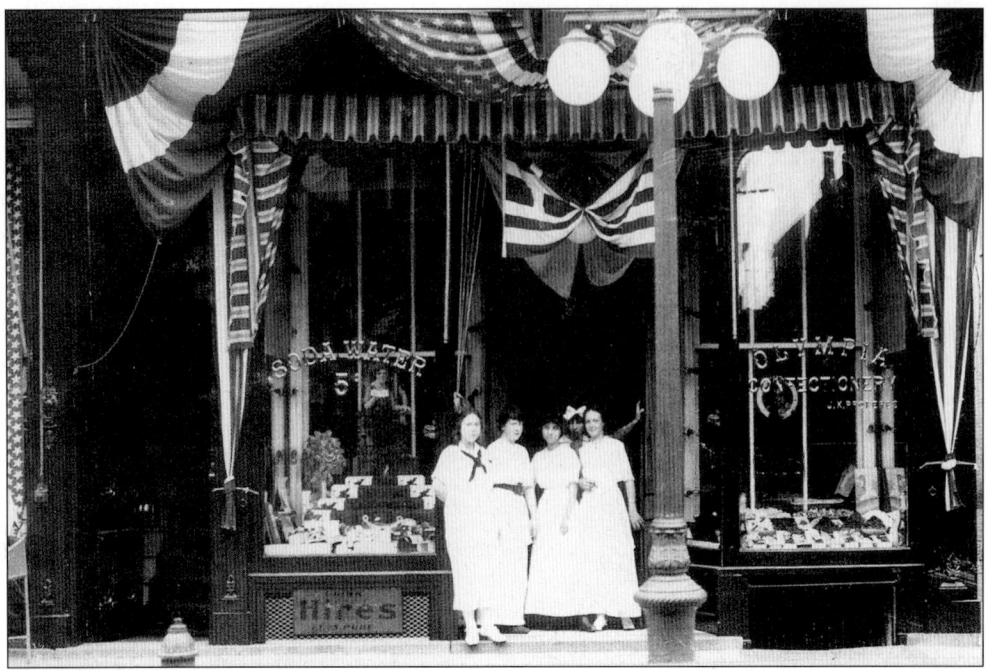

Employees of Olympia Candy Kitchen stand outside the business festooned for Old Home Week of 1914. Notice the Greek flag displayed beneath the bunting.

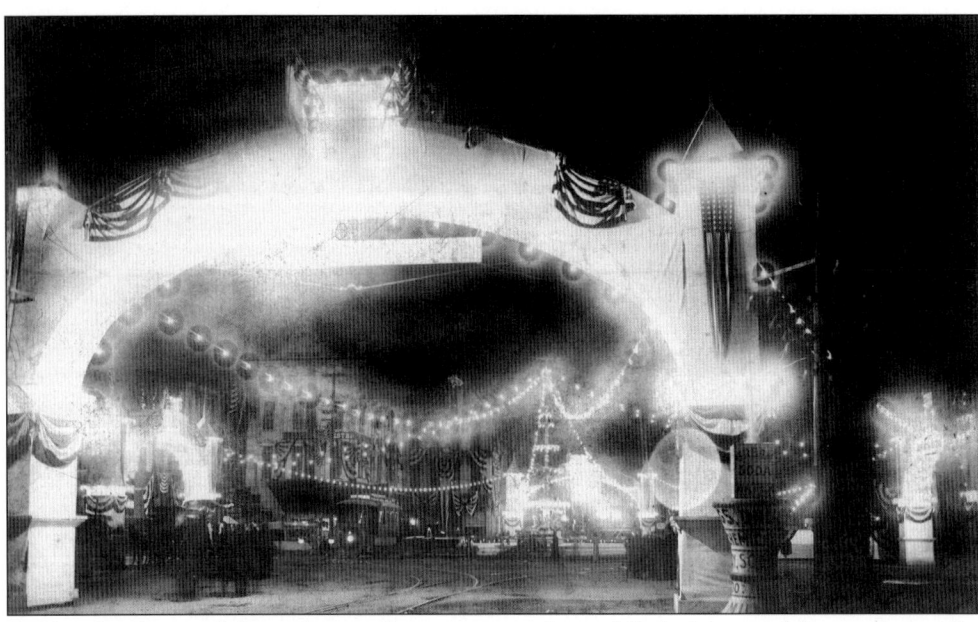

A Chambersburg and Gettysburg trolley navigates a beautifully lit Memorial Square during the Old Home Week celebration of 1906.